NEW

Total English

INTERMEDIATE

Students' Book

B1–B1+

Rachael Roberts, Antonia Clare
and JJ Wilson

Contents

Contents

Contents

Contents

Do you know...?

1 **a** Do you know these tenses? Match the sentences (1–7) with the tenses (a–g).

1 I've lived here since I was a child.
2 She's studying French at the Sorbonne.
3 We left the office at about 7:00 p.m.
4 I'd already eaten lunch so I wasn't hungry.
5 He was playing his guitar when the string broke.
6 I'm leaving the company in July.
7 I write about fifteen emails a day.

a Present Simple
b Present Continuous (for ongoing actions)
c Present Continuous (for future actions)
d Present Perfect
e Past Simple
f Past Continuous
g Past Perfect

b Complete the sentences with the tenses (a–g) from exercise 1a.

1 We use the _____ to describe something that started and finished in the past.
2 We use the _____ to describe a future plan.
3 We use the _____ to describe something that started in the past and continues in the present.
4 We use the _____ to describe something that is a state, habit or general truth.
5 We use the _____ to describe a temporary situation that is happening around now.
6 We use the _____ to describe something that happened before another event in the past.
7 We use the _____ to describe something temporary that was in progress at a time in the past.

2 Can you recognise the <u>underlined</u> parts of the sentences? Label them with the headings in the box.

> idiom (x2)   phrasal verb (x2)   prefix (x2)
> suffix (x2)

1 The story was <u>un</u>believable!
2 Can you <u>give me a hand</u> with this?
3 She <u>grew up</u> in Ecuador.
4 I've <u>given up</u> eating chocolate!
5 This meat is <u>over</u>cooked.
6 Happi<u>ness</u> is the most important thing.
7 This is the poem that I <u>learned by heart</u>.
8 I was always use<u>less</u> at Maths.

3 **a** Complete the mind maps with words from the box.

> beach   coffee   colleague   daughter
> doorbell   hall   husband   island   potato
> roof   sightseeing   stepmother   tourist
> vacuum cleaner   vegetable   yoghurt

b <u>Underline</u> any /ə/ sounds in the words in exercise 3a.

c Add some more words to each mind map.

4 **a** Complete the table with the correct verbs, nouns and adjectives.

verb	noun	adjective
educate	(1) _____	educated
(2) _____	improvement	improved
televise	(3) _____	xxx
govern	(4) _____	xxx
xxx	expense	(5) _____
xxx	beauty	(6) _____
attract	attraction	(7) _____
(8) _____	application	xxx

b Mark the main stress in the words in the table in exercise 4a. How many syllables are there in each word?

5 Put the words in the correct order to make useful phrases for the classroom.

1 could/a/little,/speak/you/please/up ?
2 dictionary,/I/could/your/borrow ?
3 you/paper,/give/some/could/please/me ?
4 these/down/words/write .
5 in/do/English/say/you/how/'X' ?
6 mean/does/'X'/what ?
7 and/the/between/what's/'X'/'Y'/difference ?
8 you/again/say/can/that ?
9 are/page/on/we/what ?

Friends

Lead-in

1 Work in pairs and look at the photos. What relationship do you think the people in each photo might have?

2 Put the words in the box under these headings:
(a) work/school, (b) family, (c) friends, (d) other. Can you add any more words under each heading?

> acquaintance   best friend   boss   classmate   close friend   colleague
> ex-girlfriend   father-in-law   friend of a friend   husband   stepmother
> stranger   old friend   team-mate

3 Match the phrases in **bold** from A with the correct definition from B.

A	B
1 I'm sorry you're leaving. Let's **keep in touch**.	a not stay in contact
2 We **have the same sense of humour** and like the same jokes.	b like to be with him/her
	c know him/her better
3 We're both sporty. In fact, we **have a lot in common**.	d find the same things funny
4 I hope we don't **lose touch** when you move away.	e like/enjoy the same things
5 He's really nice when you **get to know him**.	f stop being friends
6 I really **enjoy her company**.	g understand each other well
7 They **fell out** over money and didn't speak to each other for years.	h stay in contact
8 We're really **on the same wavelength**.	

4 Look at the words from the box in exercise 2 and think of four people you know. Work in pairs and describe your relationship with the people you chose.

1.1 A lot in common?

Grammar auxiliary verbs (*do, be, have*)

Can do encourage further conversation by expressing interest in what is said

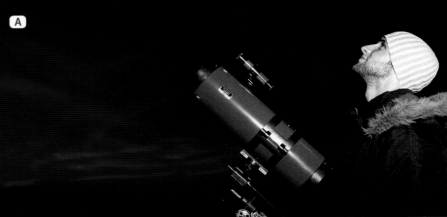

A

B

C

D

E

Speaking and listening

1 Work in pairs. Match the hobbies (1–5) with the photos (A–E).

1 snowkiting   3 juggling   5 sudoku
2 t'ai chi   4 astronomy

2 **a** Complete the phrases in **bold** with the prepositions from the box.

> about (x3)   at   for   on (x2)   in (x2)   to

1 What subjects do you like **reading** _____ ?
2 What do you **use** the Internet _____ ?
3 What activities and hobbies are you **good** _____ ?
4 What do you **spend** too much time _____ ?
5 What do you **worry** _____ ?
6 What types of exercise are you **keen** _____ ?
7 What do you usually **talk** _____ with friends?
8 What cultures are you **interested** _____ ?
9 What clubs do you **belong** _____ ?
10 How many languages are you **fluent** _____ ?

b Work in pairs. Choose five questions from exercise 2a and write down what you think your partner's answers will be.

c Ask your partner your questions. Were your ideas correct?

3 **a** 🔊 1.2 Listen to five dialogues about the hobbies in the photos. Which questions from exercise 2a do the speakers answer?

b What were their answers? Write one key word for each speaker.

c Listen again and make notes about the different hobbies. Then work in pairs and compare your notes.

4 Work in pairs. Do you do any of the activities in the photos? Do you have any other unusual hobbies?

Grammar | auxiliary verbs (*do, be, have*)

5 **a** Look at the Active grammar box. Complete the example sentences with an auxiliary verb. Make sure you use the correct tense.

b 🔵 1.3 Listen and check your answers.

Active grammar

A *Wh-* questions

1 A: *How _____ you learn to do that?*
B: *Well, I started off ...*

B *Yes/No* questions

2 *_____ she have a telescope then?*

3 *_____ you been there?*

C Echo questions (to check understanding or show interest)

4 A: *I'm quite good at juggling.*
B: *_____ you?*

D Negatives

5 A: *Can you juggle with plates?*
B: *No, I _____ think I could do that!*

6 *I _____ even been skiing!*

E Short answers

7 A: *Do you do it regularly?*
B: *No, I _____ .*

8 A: *Have you been there?*
B: *Yes, I _____ .*

9 A: *Isn't it terrifying?*
B: *Yes, it _____ . That's the whole point!*

---

see Reference page 19

6 Find and correct two mistakes in each dialogue.

1 A: What subjects do you likes reading about?
B: Oh, I'm quite interested in sport.
A: Are you? What sports you like?
B: Tennis and football, mainly.

2 A: What do you worry about?
B: I not worry much. I guess sometimes I worry about money.
A: Does you? I do too.

3 A: Use you the Internet a lot?
B: No, not really. I not have time. Do you?
A: Yes, all the time.

4 A: Have you seen that film yet?
B: No, I didn't. What about you?
A: Yes. I saw it last week.
B: Was it any good?
A: Yes, it were.

Pronunciation | intonation in echo questions

7 **a** Write echo questions for these sentences.

I grew up in Peru.
Did you?

1 I live in a seven-bedroom house.
2 My boyfriend has travelled round South America.
3 Next year I'm going to university.
4 Last year I won a medal for swimming.
5 I'm learning to drive at the moment.
6 We both hate spaghetti.
7 They've just moved to Egypt.
8 He eats six eggs a day.

b 🔵 1.4 Listen and check your answers.

c Listen again, and notice if the person asking the echo questions sounds interested or not. What happens to the intonation when he sounds interested?

d Work in pairs. Practise the dialogues in exercise 7a. Try to show that you are interested and encourage your partner to say more.

A: *I grew up in Peru.*
B: *Did you?*
A: *Yes, my father was the ambassador to Peru.*

see Pronunciation bank page 164

Speaking

8 **a** You are going to try to find something in common with someone in the class you don't know very well. First, complete the following sentence in different ways.

I'd like to find someone who ...

• *writes poetry.*
• *is a really good cook.*

b Ask your classmates questions to try and find someone for each of your sentences. Show your interest through echo questions.

A: *Do you write poetry?*
B: *No, I don't, but I do write novels.*
A: *Do you? Have you had anything published?*

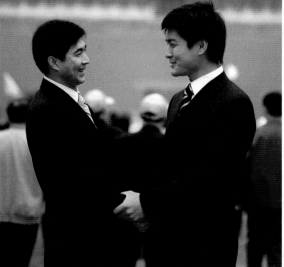

Reading and speaking

9 Work in pairs and discuss the questions.

1 Look at the photos. What aspects of culture do they represent?

2 What are some typical features of your culture?

3 How is your culture different from other cultures you know about? How is it similar?

10 a Work in pairs. You are each going to read about a cultural misunderstanding.

Student A: read the text on this page and answer the questions below.

1 What did Kyle's father-in-law keep doing?

2 How did she usually react?

3 What happened when she got angry?

4 What did her husband explain?

Student B: read the text and answer the questions on page 147.

b Tell your partner about the story you read and listen to your partner's story. Ask questions about anything you don't understand.

c Have you ever had a cultural misunderstanding? Tell your partner what happened.

Not in my culture...

'Ah, Kyle, gordita, como estas?' (translation: 'Ah, Kyle, fatty, how are you?').'

This is how my father-in-law would greet me every time we went over to his house. At first, I thought I needed to be on my best behaviour for my husband's parents, so I would just smile and nod, when really I felt furious as he insulted me about my weight over and over again.

Finally, one day I'd had enough. When my father-in-law mentioned my weight at the dinner table once again, in front of everybody, telling me I looked 'even fatter than normal', I lost my temper, 'Well, you look older and more wrinkly than normal.' Silence. I turned bright red as I realised I'd just said something truly offensive. Eventually someone coughed politely and changed the subject. But, after dinner my husband took me aside. 'Why in the world would you insult my dad like that?!' he asked. I told him, 'I've had enough of the weight comments, tell him to stop insulting me.' And then my husband told me that in Chile, 'gordita' is a term of endearment and is only used lovingly. He also explained that it's not at all impolite to bring up other people's weight loss/weight gain and that if people do, that just means they care about you enough to notice.

So I explained to my husband that telling someone they look fat/fatter is one of the rudest things you can possibly do in my culture. Well, my husband had a little chat with my father-in-law and my size was never mentioned again.

1.2 How many friends?

Listening

1 **a** Work in pairs and discuss the questions.

1 Who do you consider to be your best friend?
2 Where and when did you meet them?
3 What do you like about them?
4 How are they different from you?

b 🔵 1.5 Listen to Pete answering the same questions about his best friend, and note down his answers.

Vocabulary | personality

2 **a** Work in pairs. Complete the definitions (1–10) with the adjectives from the box.

> dependable   encouraging   generous
> jealous   kind-hearted   mean
> pleasant   selfish   sulky   upbeat

A/An _____ person ...

1 is friendly and well-behaved.
2 cares about you and wants to help you.
3 always does what you need them to.
4 is unhappy if you have something they'd like themselves.
5 happily gives you whatever you need.
6 has a positive, optimistic attitude.
7 tries to give you the confidence to succeed.
8 is angry and unhappy for long periods.
9 thinks of themselves first.
10 doesn't like giving anything away.

b Choose three adjectives in exercise 2a which you think are most important in a good friend. Explain why.

c Work in pairs. Tell your partner about a friend who one of the adjectives in exercise 2 describes. Explain why.

When I lost my job last year, my friend Lucia was really encouraging. She kept telling me I would get a better job soon, and I have!

Pronunciation | sounds and spelling: ea

3 **a** 🔵 1.6 Listen to the four ways in which 'ea' can be pronounced. Then put the adjectives from the box in the correct column.

> fearful   jealous   kind-hearted   mean   pleasant   upbeat

/iː/	/e/	/ɪə/	/aː/

b 🔵 1.7 Listen and check your answers.

c Put more words that you know with 'ea' into the correct column.

see Pronunciation bank page 163

Speaking

4 **a** Work in pairs and discuss the questions.

1 When was the last time you made a new friend?
2 How did you meet?

b Complete the How to... box with the headings below.

• at a bus stop   • at a party   • on public transport

> ### How to... start a conversation with a stranger
>
> | A _____ | *Cold today, isn't it?* |
> | | *Excuse me, could you tell me the time?* |
> | B _____ | *Excuse me, is anyone sitting here?* |
> | | *Is it always this crowded?* |
> | C _____ | *So how do you know Jason?* (the host) |
> | | *Have you tried this chicken? It's delicious!* |

c Respond to each conversation starter in the table in exercise 4b.

d Work in pairs. Choose a conversation starter and write a short conversation.

A: *Have you tried this chicken? It's delicious!*

B: *No, it looks good though. You should try some of the fish. I think Mary made it herself.*

How many friends should you have?

People often say that while money may bring wealth, friends bring riches. New research, however, shows that friends may bring both kinds of riches. An American study asked eighteen-year-olds to list their three best friends. Years later, it was discovered that those named most often tended to be earning the most. In fact, every extra friend added two percent to their salary. The researchers believed that this is because people with better social skills do better in the workplace. So, the more friends the better?

One theory states that we all have about 150 friends. This may sound like a lot, but only about five of those are really close friends, the kind you can ring at 4:00 a.m. About another ten are part of an inner group, and these can include family members. Then there are about thirty-five not so close friends, and the other 100 are really just acquaintances. Susie, a market researcher, agrees: 'I have loads of friends, but I'm studying as well as working at the moment, so I only see a few friends once a week or so.'

Have social networking websites changed this? Facebook™, one of the most popular social networking sites, has more than 300 million active users worldwide, all making new friends online. The average number of Facebook friends is 130, but many people have hundreds or even thousands of online friends. Paulo, a graphic designer, thinks he is fairly typical of his generation: 'I have more than 700 Facebook friends, many of them from other countries. It is as easy nowadays to have a friend on the other side of the world as one round the corner.' However, research indicates that while some people may have more than 150 friends, the number of close friends remains exactly the same – about five.

It appears that whatever technology may make possible, human beings can only manage a small number of 'true' friends.

Reading

5 **a** Work in pairs. Do you think that the following statements are true (T) or false (F)?

1 People who have more friends usually earn more money.

2 Most people have about 150 friends.

3 The average number of online friends on Facebook is 700.

4 Most people only have one or two close friends.

b Read the article above and check your answers.

6 Read the article again and answer the questions.

1 According to the American study, how much was each friend 'worth'?

2 Why did the researchers believe that more popular children earned more as adults?

3 How many of the 150 friends mentioned are really acquaintances?

4 How many people use Facebook worldwide?

5 What is the writer's opinion about the effect of technology on how many close friends we have?

7 Read the comments below from a website. Then work in pairs and discuss which opinions you agree or disagree with.

> I would never accept an online 'friend' who I didn't already know. How can you be friends with someone you've never met?
> *Sylwia, UK*

> I'm reading this at work – it's my lunchbreak – and I wanted to comment about the fact that most companies won't let you go on Facebook while you're at work, even in your own time. I don't think it's fair because this is the main way I communicate with my friends.
> *Jon, UK*

> I think people who have hundreds of friends online must just be really self-obsessed and looking for attention.
> *Rui, Portugal*

8 Work in pairs. How many friends do you think is the 'right' number to have? Why?

Grammar | Present Simple and Present Continuous

9 **a** Look at the Active grammar box. Match the example sentences (1–5) with the rules (A–E).

b Complete the table in the Active grammar box with the verbs in the box.

Active grammar

1 *People with better social skills **do** better in the workplace.*
2 *I **have** more than 700 Facebook friends.*
3 *I**'m studying** as well as working.*
4 *I **see** them once a week.*
5 *I**'m reading** this at work.*

We use the Present Simple for …

A habits/routines, e.g. sentence _____ .

B things that are always true/permanent, e.g. sentence _____ .

C describing a state, e.g. sentence _____ .

We use the Present Continuous for …

D things that are happening now at this precise moment, e.g. sentence _____ .

E temporary situations that are happening around now, e.g. sentence _____ .

> ~~believe~~ do eat ~~go~~ have like ~~live~~ need
> play think understand want

Action verbs	State verbs	Both
go, ...	*believe, ...*	*live, ...*

We do not usually use state verbs in continuous tenses.

---

10 Put the verbs in brackets into the correct form of the Present Simple or Present Continuous.

1 _____ (you/read) that book? Can I see it?
2 Sasha _____ (not/work) on Tuesdays, so she's at home now.
3 I'm so tired. I _____ (need) a holiday!
4 That looks hard. _____ (you/want) any help?
5 I'm afraid we _____ (not/have) any tea because I always drink coffee.
6 Where _____ (you/live) at the moment?
7 _____ (you/understand) this computer manual?
8 You look very happy! Who _____ (you/think) about?
9 I _____ (not/want) to leave too late because I _____ (hate) driving in the dark.
10 What horrible weather! I _____ (stay) inside until the rain stops.

11 Make questions from the prompts using the Present Simple or Present Continuous.

1 What/you/do? (job/occupation)
2 What/you/do/at work (or school)/at the moment?
3 How often/you/go out with friends?
4 What/you/like/do?
5 What films/you/like/watch?
6 What/you/usually/do/at the weekends?
7 You/read/a good book/at the moment?
8 You/play (or watch)/any sports/ these days?
9 Why/you/study/English/this year?
10 You/do/any other courses/at the moment?

12 Work in pairs. Ask your partner the questions in exercise 11. Tell the class anything interesting you learned.

see Reference page 19

1.3 Brotherly love?

Listening and speaking

1 **a** 🔘 1.8 Listen to three people talking about someone who they fell out with. Match the speakers (1–3) with the photos (A–C).

b Listen again and complete the notes in the table.

	Speaker 1	Speaker 2	Speaker 3
Who do they talk about?		*Romina – best friend*	
How long have they known/did they know each other?			*one year*
Why/When did they fall out?			
How is their relationship now?			

c Work in pairs and check your answers.

Vocabulary | arguing

2 Listen to the three people in exercise 1a again and complete the table with phrases which have a similar meaning.

get angry	have an argument
lose your _____	have a _____
see _____	_____ over something

3 Work in pairs and discuss the questions.
1 Do you ever have arguments with your friends?
2 Have you ever fallen out with a close friend? What happened?
3 What do friends/family usually argue about?

Reading

4 **a** You are going to read a true story about two brothers. Work in pairs and look at the photos on page 15. How could the items in the box be significant?

> an argument   a business
> a nickname   a shoemaker   a wild cat
> the 1932 Olympic games

b Now read the article on page 15 and check your ideas.

5 Read the article again. Write true (T) or false (F).
1 The Dasslers' father was a sportsman. ☐
2 The brothers first made sports shoes at home. ☐
3 They argued about the shoes. ☐
4 They decided to start their own companies. ☐
5 Puma sells more shoes than Adidas. ☐
6 People in the town have now forgotten the argument. ☐

6 Read the Lifelong learning box. Then practise the skill by finding words in the story which mean the following:
1 provided a product (paragraph 1)
2 created (an institution/company, etc.) (paragraph 4)
3 moved permanently to a different place (paragraph 5)
4 one or more of the most successful companies (paragraph 6)

> ### Guessing from context
> ❗ When you are reading, it is often better to try to guess the meaning of a new word rather than stopping to use a dictionary. It will help you to read more fluently.
>
> *Lifelong learning*

7 Work in pairs. Take it in turns to retell the story using the words/phrases from exercise 2 and the verbs from exercise 6.

Brotherly Love?

Adidas® and Puma® have been two of the biggest names in sports shoe manufacturing for over half a century.

Since 1928 they have supplied shoes for Olympic athletes, World Cup-winning football heroes, Muhammad Ali, hip hop stars and rock musicians famous all over the world. But the story of these two companies begins in one house in the town of Herzogenaurach, Germany.

Adolph and Rudolph Dassler were the sons of a shoemaker. They loved sport but complained that they could never find comfortable shoes to play in. Rudolph always said, 'You cannot play sports wearing shoes that you'd walk around town with.' So they started making their own. In 1920 Adolph made the first pair of athletics shoes with spikes, produced on the Dasslers' kitchen table.

On 1st July 1924 they formed a shoe company, Dassler Brothers Ltd and they worked together for many years. The company became successful and it provided the shoes for Germany's athletes at the 1928 and 1932 Olympic Games.

But in 1948 the brothers argued. No one knows exactly what happened, but family members have suggested that the argument was about money or women. The result was that Adolph left the company. His nickname was Adi, and using this and the first three letters of the family name, Dassler, he founded Adidas.

Rudolph relocated across the River Aurach and founded his own company too. At first he wanted to call it Ruda, but eventually he called it Puma, after the wild cat. The famous Puma logo of the jumping cat has hardly changed since.

After the big split of 1948 Adolph and Rudolph never spoke to each other again and their companies have now been in competition for over sixty years. Both companies were for many years the market leaders, though Adidas has always been more successful than Puma. A hip hop group, Run DMC, has even written a song called *My Adidas* and in 2005 Adidas bought Reebok®, another big sports shoe company.

The terrible family argument should really be forgotten, but ever since it happened, over sixty years ago, the town has been split into two. Even now, some Adidas employees and Puma employees don't talk to each other.

Grammar | Present Perfect Simple and Past Simple

8 **a** Work in pairs. Look at the extracts (1-8) from the story on page 15. Does each one use the Present Perfect Simple or the Past Simple?

1 Since 1928 they have supplied shoes for Olympic athletes.

2 Adidas has always been more successful than Puma.

3 On 1st July 1924 they formed a shoe company, Dassler Brothers Ltd.

4 Run DMC has even written a song called *My Adidas*.

5 They worked together for many years.

6 The family argument happened ... over sixty years ago.

7 The companies have now been in competition for over sixty years.

8 Ever since it happened ... the town has been split into two.

b Read the Active grammar box and choose the correct <u>underlined</u> words to complete the rules. Use the sentences from exercise 8a and the examples to help you.

Active grammar

1 We use the *Past Simple*/*Present Perfect Simple* to talk about actions or states which happened in a finished period of time in the past. There is no connection to now.

2 We use *ago*/*for* with the Past Simple to say when something happened and *ago*/*for* to talk about the period when something happened.

3 We use the *Past Simple*/*Present Perfect Simple* to talk about actions or states which happened in a period of time that is connected to now.

4 We often use *for* and *since* with the Present Perfect. We use *for* + a <u>point</u>/<u>period</u> of time and *since* + a <u>point</u>/<u>period</u> of time.

5 We use *just* with the *Present Perfect Simple*/*Past Simple* to show that an action is very recent.
   *I've **just** bought some new shoes.*

6 We use *not yet*/*already* with the Present Perfect Simple to emphasise that a situation has not started. We use *not yet*/*already* to emphasise that a situation has started or an action has finished.
   *I haven't done the shopping **yet**.*
   *I've **already** finished cooking.*

see Reference page 19

9 Read the texts below about other famous brothers and sisters and choose the correct words in *italics*.

Venus and Serena Williams are both famous tennis stars. They (1) *have played*/*played* each other professionally more than twenty times.

In 2001, the actors Jake and Maggie Gyllenhaal (2) *starred*/*have starred* together in the film *Donnie Darko*, where they (3) *played*/*have played* brother and sister.

Penelope Cruz is a world famous actor, but her siblings, Eduardo and Monica are also quite famous. Eduardo (4) *had*/*has had* several international hits and Monica is a well-known Spanish actor. She would like to star internationally but she (5) *didn't learn*/*hasn't learnt* English yet.

10 Complete the sentences with the time expressions from the box.

> ago   already   for   just   since   yet

1 Kylie and Dannii Minogue have been professional performers _____ they were children.

2 Kylie's first performance on television took place over thirty years _____ .

3 Kylie has _____ achieved a lot in her career, but she still seems to have plenty more to offer.

4 Kylie hasn't _____ had as much success in America.

5 Dannii has been a judge on a TV talent show _____ a few years now.

6 Dannii has _____ started a family. She had her first baby last year.

Speaking

11 Work in pairs. Do you think it's a good idea to go into business with your friends and family? Why/Why not?

1 Vocabulary | phrasal verbs

1 a Read the text below and answer the questions.

1 What languages did the author speak? Why?
2 What language did her father tell her off for using? Why?
3 Why did the author want to become a painter? Why was she not successful?

b *Brought up* is a phrasal verb. Which other phrasal verbs can you find in the text?

I was brought up in a small town near Paris. My parents are English, so I grew up speaking English and French. A young English student lived with us during the school holidays, and she looked after me when my parents were away on business. I remember my father always told us off if he heard us speaking in English, because she was studying French. Usually we changed to French for a few minutes, and then carried on in English when he couldn't hear us, because it was easier for both of us. She was an artist, and we got on very well. I looked up to her, and later tried to become a painter myself. Unfortunately, I took after my father, who wasn't artistic, and so I was never successful.

2 Use the text in exercise 1 to help you match the phrasal verbs from A with the definitions from B.

A	B
1 grow up	a admire and respect someone
2 bring up	b continue (doing something)
3 tell (someone) off	c develop from being a child to being an adult
4 take after (someone)	d take care of (someone or something)
5 look after (someone or something)	e talk angrily to someone because they have done something wrong
6 get on (with) (someone)	f have a friendly relationship with someone
7 look up to (someone)	g look or behave like another member of your family
8 carry on (doing something)	h care for children until they are adults

3 Complete the sentences with a phrasal verb from exercise 2 in the correct form. Use each verb once.

1 You really _____ your father. You look just like him!
2 I don't _____ very well with my mother; we argue a lot.
3 I _____ in Brazil. It was a happy childhood.
4 We _____ arguing, even though Dad had told us to stop.
5 My brother always _____ for borrowing his records because I always scratched them!
6 After their mother died, the children were _____ by their aunt.
7 I still _____ my older brother, and ask him for advice.
8 My sister _____ me when I was ill.

4 Work in groups and answer the questions.

1 Where did you grow up?
2 When you bring up a child, what do you think is the most important thing to teach him/her?
3 As a child, did anyone tell you off? Why? Did this make you stop or did you carry on anyway?
4 Which member of your family do you get on with best?
5 Who in your family do you take after?
6 Who looks after you when you are ill?
7 As a child, who did you look up to?

5 Read the Lifelong learning box and follow the instructions.

Personalising vocabulary

! One of the best ways to remember vocabulary is to make it mean something to *you*.

Using the ideas from exercise 4, write one sentence for each phrasal verb that is true for you.

I grew up in a small country town.

Lifelong learning

1 | Communication

1 **a** Which of the following are the best ways to meet a new partner? Why?

- through friends
- at a party
- at the gym
- on holiday
- while studying
- on an Internet dating site

b ⊕ 1.9 Listen to a short talk about Internet dating and answer the questions.

1 How many people used an Internet dating site in the UK last year?
2 What specialist dating websites does the speaker mention?
3 How is the website *CanIintroduceyou.com* different from the others?

2 Read the profiles of Nadia and Sam, which were written by their friends. Answer the questions below for each profile.

1 How did they meet?
2 What does each friend say about their friend's personality?
3 What does each friend say about their friend's interests?

3 Work in pairs and look at the qualities below. Which five qualities do you think are most attractive in a partner?

- gets on with everyone
- has a great sense of humour
- has an opinion on everything
- is a really good listener
- is genuine, loyal and honest
- is great fun to be around
- is one of the funniest people I know
- is really thoughtful and caring
- is the life and soul of the party
- would do anything for his/her friends
- you will never have a dull moment in his/her company

4 Write a similar profile about a friend of yours. Include the following paragraphs:

1 How you met
2 Personality
3 Interests
4 Conclusion

Key facts:

Name: Nadia Rees
Age: 25
Occupation: Teacher
Location: Bath

I've known Nadia for years. In fact we went to school together and we're still best friends.

Nadia is genuine, loyal and honest. She would do anything for her friends, and is really thoughtful and caring. She is also one of the funniest people I know, and always the life and soul of the party!

She is a fabulous cook and her dinner parties are famous! She enjoys socialising and has lots of friends – she just hasn't met that special person yet.

So what are you waiting for? Get in touch with her!

Richard

Key facts:

Name: Sam Walker
Age: 26
Occupation: Engineer
Location: Liverpool

Sam and I have been friends since we shared a house together at university. We have kept in touch ever since as we were always on the same wavelength.

He has a great sense of humour and you will never have a dull moment in his company. He has an opinion on everything, but is also a very good listener. He's kind, gets on with everyone and is great fun to be around.

He's quite a sporty person, and often spends his weekends mountain climbing or surfing. I think you'd need to be pretty active too – just to keep up with him.

Sam is well worth getting to know, so why not send him an email?

Jenna

Auxiliary verbs: *do, be, have*

Questions

Invert the subject and the auxiliary verb. If there is no auxiliary verb, use *do/does* or *did*.

Yes/No questions
***Are you** Polish?*

Wh- questions
*Where **are you** going? How **did you** learn to do that?*

Echo questions
*'He **lives** in the country.' '**Does he?**'*

Negatives

We use *not* or add *n't* to the auxiliary. If there is no auxiliary verb use *doesn't, don't, didn't*.
***I'm not** afraid.*

Short answers

Repeat the auxiliary verb used in the question.
*'**Have** you finished yet?' 'Yes, I **have**.'*

Present Simple and Present Continuous

We use the Present Simple for habits/routines, things that are always true/permanent and describing a state.
*Seung-Ah **starts** work at eight o'clock.*
*Spain **is** a hot country.*
*Dimitri **is** really happy about his new job.*

We use the Present Continuous for things that are happening now, at this moment and temporary situations that are happening around now (but not at this exact moment).
*Jade**'s having** a shower. **I'm learning** Spanish for my job.*

Main verbs can describe actions or states.

Some verbs have an action meaning as well as a state meaning, so can be used in continuous tenses.
*We**'re having** a wonderful holiday.* (have = action/experience – **can** be used in the continuous)
*We **have** a lovely room by the sea.* (have = possess – **can't** be used in the continuous)

Present Perfect Simple and Past Simple

We use the Past Simple to talk about completed actions or states which happened in a **finished** period of time in the past. There is no connection to now.
*I **went** to Disneyland last year.*

We use *ago* with the Past Simple to say when something happened and *for* to talk about the period of time.
*They met ten years **ago** and worked together **for** two years.*

We use the Present Perfect Simple to talk about completed actions which happened in an unfinished period of time that is connected to now.

*I**'ve eaten** out twice this week.* (this week is not yet finished)
*I**'ve been** to Disneyland.* (some time in my life up to now)

We often use *for* and *since* with the Present Perfect.

We use *for* + a period of time and *since* + a point in time.
*I**'ve known** her for two months/since April.*

We use *just* with the Present Perfect Simple to show that an action is very recent.
*I**'ve just** bought some new trainers.*

We use *not yet* with the Present Perfect Simple to emphasise that a situation has not started, and *already* to emphasise that a situation has started or an action has finished.
*I have**n't** done the shopping **yet**.*
*I've **already** finished cooking.*

Phrasal verbs

Form: verb + one or two prepositions (or adverb)
*He **grew up** in France. I **got on** well **with** her.*

One phrasal verb can have more than one meaning.
Take off: *The plane **took off** at 6:00. I **took off** my coat.*

The meaning often has no connection with the verb.
*We **ran out** of money.* (= there is none left)

Phrasal verbs are often informal/spoken English. Often there is a more formal word which means the same.
*She **looks up** to him.* (= she respects him)

> ### Key vocabulary
>
> **Relationships and arguing**
> acquaintance   be on the same wavelength   boss
> classmate   close/old/best friend   colleague
> enjoy his/her company   ex-girlfriend
> fall out (about/over sthg)   father-in-law
> friend of a friend   get angry   get on well
> get to know him/her   have a lot in common
> have an argument/row   have the same sense of humour
> husband   keep in touch   lose touch   lose your temper
> see red   stepmother   stranger   team-mate
>
> **Verbs/Adjectives + prepositions**
> belong to   fluent in   good at   keen on   read about
> spend money on   talk about   interested in
> use (something) for   worry about
>
> **Personality**
> dependable   encouraging   generous   kind-hearted
> jealous   mean   pleasant   selfish   sulky   upbeat
>
> **Phrasal verbs**
> bring up   carry on   get on with   grow up   look after
> look up to   take after   tell off

 Listen to the explanations and vocabulary.
ACTIVEBOOK

 see Writing bank page 153

1 | Review and practice

1 Choose the correct words in *italics*.

1 Mary *is/has* taking a shower.
2 *Does/Has* the postman delivered the post yet?
3 They *are/do* writing in their journals now.
4 *Had/Have* your friends spoken to you today?
5 I *don't/haven't* understand this question.
6 *Do/Are* we going to the theatre tonight?
7 She *has/is* never been to Hawaii before.
8 *Doesn't/Don't* his mother live here?
9 *Haven't/Didn't* we seen this film already?

2 Complete the dialogues with auxiliary verbs.

1 A: Hi. _____ you know many people here?
   B: Yes, a few. Some of us _____ doing an English course together.
2 A: _____ you live near here?
   B: No, we _____ . We live in Italy.
3 A: _____ you staying in a nice hotel?
   B: Actually, we _____ like it very much.
4 A: _____ you know this area well?
   B: No, we _____ . We _____ never been here before.
5 A: _____ you like the city?
   B: Yes, we _____ enjoying our stay here.
6 A: _____ you worked here long?
   B: No, I _____ . Only one year.
7 A: Liz! What _____ you doing here in Rio?!
   B: I _____ travelling around South America!
8 A: _____ we met before?
   B: Yes, we _____ . We met in Jakarta.

3 Complete the telephone conversation with the Present Simple or Present Continuous form of the verbs in brackets.

Sara: Hi, It's me. I'm just ringing for a chat. How are you?
Lucy: Oh, fine, you know. How are things?
Sara: Well, I (1) _____ (not/feel) very well, actually.
Lucy: Oh no, what's the matter?
Sara: I (2) _____ (not/know) exactly. Probably just a cold. What about you?
Lucy: Well, I (3) _____ (work) in a different office this week.
Sara: Why's that?
Lucy: I (4) _____ (help out) at another branch because there are a lot of people away. Actually, I (5) _____ (enjoy) the change this week. I (6) _____ (like) meeting new people.
Sara: (7) _____ (do) the same job?
Lucy: More or less, but I (8) _____ (deal) with clients more here. I (9) _____ (think) I might try and do more of that when I go back to my own office.
Sara: Well, it sounds great.
Lucy: Yes, mmm. I'm a bit tired though. I usually (10) _____ (get up) at about 7:30, but this week I (11) _____ (get up) at about six! You know I (12) _____ (hate) getting up that early.

4 Complete the email with the Past Simple or Present Perfect Simple form of the verbs in brackets.

Hi Mateus,

It's amazing to get in touch with you again on Facebook. You asked for my news. Well, since I (1) _____ (leave) university three years ago, I (2) _____ (do) a Master's degree in Portuguese literature. I'm now teaching at London University – I (3) _____ (be) here for nearly a year now. It's hard work, but the students are great! Last year I (4) _____ (get) married – to Sheila, remember her? She (5) _____ (work) in Portugal for a year, but (6) _____ (come) back to the UK last year so we could be together. What else? We (7) _____ (buy) a house and we (8) _____ (be) very busy re-decorating it. It's nearly finished now. Why don't you come and stay?

Hope to hear from you again soon,

Chris

5 Complete the sentences with a word or phrase which means the same as the words or phrases in brackets.

Let me introduce you to my _colleague_ Gustav. (someone you work with)

1 He was a complete _____ . (someone you don't know)
2 We get on well because we have a lot _____ . (share similar interests)
3 Barbara is _____ Spanish. (speaks very well)
4 When she told me what she'd done, I really _____ . (lost my temper)
5 Are you sure? That's very _____ of you! (happily give you whatever you need)
6 I told my boss I was having problems at work, but he wasn't very _____ . (positive towards me)
7 Sophie really _____ her big brother. (admires and tries to be like)
8 Mike _____ smoking even when he felt ill. (continue)
9 I'm not very _____ watching TV. (like/ interested in)
10 When we left school, I _____ with him. (stopped being in contact)

Lead-in

1 Work in pairs and discuss the questions.

1 Which of the different forms of media shown in the photos do you use most?

2 Has this changed in recent years? Why?

2 Read the article. Are your habits similar to those described? Work in pairs and compare your habits with your partner's.

Recent research has shown that young people now spend more time on the Internet than watching TV. This is partly explained by the fact that the average person surveyed does five other things at the same time as watching TV, including going online to look at websites or to IM (instant message) their friends.

Television remains popular, however, particularly reality shows and soaps. Young people are less likely to watch documentaries or chat shows and tend to get their news online. If they do read a newspaper, their favourite sections are the sports pages, gossip and human interest stories, rather than current affairs or the business section.

Film is also still very popular, particularly comedies and horror films. In recent years, the docu-drama, such as Morgan Spurlock's *Super-size Me*, about McDonald's, has also become fashionable.

3 **a** What vocabulary can you find in the article in exercise 2 connected with different media? Complete the table.

Computers	Television	Film	Newspapers
Internet			

b Add any other words you know to each category in exercise 3a. Then work in pairs and compare your ideas.

2.1 Silver screen
| Grammar | defining relative clauses |
| Can do | give opinions and agree/disagree |

Speaking and reading

1 Work in pairs. Look at the photos from the film *Man on Wire*. What do you think the film is about?

2 a Read the film review and answer the questions.

1 What type of film is it?
2 What is the film about?
3 Did the critic like the film? Why/Why not?
4 Do you think you would enjoy it? Why/Why not?

b Read the review again and write true (T) or false (F).

1 The World Trade Center had just been completed when Petit decided to do his high wire walk. ☐
2 He finally made his walk between the twin towers six years later. ☐
3 He was already an experienced high wire walker when he made the crossing at the twin towers. ☐
4 Petit and his team managed to get permission to walk between the towers. ☐
5 They used a bow and arrow to get the wire across from one tower to the other. ☐
6 Petit's team filmed him as he crossed the wire. ☐
7 As soon as he saw the policemen waiting he came off the wire and let them arrest him. ☐

MAN ON WIRE

A film to make you feel alive ...

In 1968 a young Frenchman, Philippe Petit, saw a picture in a newspaper which would change his life. He was sitting in a dentist's waiting room when he saw an artist's impression of the soon-to-be-built World Trade Center and decided that one day he would walk on a high wire between the twin towers.

Man on Wire is the gripping story of a man who made his dream happen. The film starts on Tuesday August 7th, 1974, the day when Petit finally achieved his goal. We see him heading for the twin towers and then, through interviews and flashbacks, we see everything that led up to that day.

▪ The film first shows us how Petit made his earlier high wire walks at Notre Dame and Sydney Harbour Bridge, using film and photos taken from the time.

▪ Then the film almost becomes a crime thriller as we see how Petit and his team forged documents, got past security guards and somehow managed to set up the wire between the towers without anyone seeing them or hearing anything.

▪ There were hundreds of unforeseen difficulties; not least how to get the wire from the tower where they stood across to the other tower. They finally solved this by shooting it across with a bow and arrow!

▪ Finally Petit makes his great walk between the towers. There is no film of the original walk, so the whole thing is shown using photos that were taken at the time, a poignant reminder of how the towers used to look. He stayed 1,350 feet above the ground, apparently quite relaxed, for 45 minutes. The policemen whose job it was to arrest Petit, could only stand and watch while he smiled and laughed at them.

▪ What Petit did was, of course, actually a crime, but that doesn't seem as important as the fact that it was a fascinating and inspiring adventure. A film to make you feel alive.

Grammar | defining relative clauses

3 **a** Complete the extracts from the review with the words in the box.

> that   when   where   which   who   whose

1 In 1968 a young Frenchman, Philippe Petit, saw a picture in a newspaper _____ would change his life.
2 *Man on Wire* is the gripping story of a man _____ made his dream happen.
3 The film starts on Tuesday August 7th 1974, the day _____ Petit finally achieved his goal.
4 There were hundreds of unforeseen difficulties; not least how to get the wire from the tower _____ they stood, across to the other tower.
5 The whole thing is shown using photos _____ were taken at the time.
6 The policemen _____ job it was to arrest Petit, could only stand and watch while he smiled and laughed.

b Complete the Active grammar box with the relative pronouns in the box in exercise 3a.

Active grammar

*Man on Wire is the gripping story of a man **who made his dream happen**.*

'who made his dream happen' is an example of a defining relative clause; it defines exactly who or what we are talking about. This is essential information about a person, a place or a thing.

We use *that* or _____ for people.

We use _____ or _____ for things or animals.

We use _____ for places.

We use _____ for possessions.

We use _____ for time.

In spoken English we often use *that* instead of *who* or *which*.
*The actress **that** stars in that film has beautiful eyes ...*

We can leave out the pronouns *who*, *which* or *that* if they are the object of the relative clause.
The director was able to use film (which) Petit took in the 70s.

see Reference page 33

4 Add *who*, *which* or *where* to each sentence.
1 That's the studio the last Bond film was made.
2 Goldeneye is the name of the house Ian Fleming wrote the original stories.
3 *Dr No* is the first Bond book was made into a film.
4 George Lazenby is the man only played Bond once.
5 Daniel Craig is another actor took the role.
6 Derby County is the football team Bond actor Timothy Dalton supports.

5 Rewrite the sentences using a relative pronoun. Make any necessary changes.

Daniel Radcliffe stars in the Harry Potter films.
Daniel Radcliffe is the actor who stars in the Harry Potter films.

1 The first Harry Potter film was made in 2001.
   2001 is the year ...
2 Joanne Rowling's books were turned into the Harry Potter films.
   Joanne Rowling is the author ...
3 Most of the outdoor scenes were filmed in Scotland.
   Scotland is the country ...
4 Warner Brothers produced the films.
   Warner Brothers is the company ...
5 Richard Harris and Michael Gambon have taken the role of Dumbledore.
   Richard Harris and Michael Gambon are the actors ...
6 The first three films made $1.3 billion.
   $1.3 billion is the amount of money ...

Speaking

6 Work in pairs. Tell your partner about a film you have seen. Describe ...
- the type of film.
- the main characters.
- what happens in the film.
- some scenes you remember.

Speaking and listening

7 Work in pairs. Look at the posters and discuss the questions.

1 Do you ever watch foreign language films? Why/ Why not?

2 What kind of foreign language films do you like/ dislike?

8 **a** Work in pairs. When you watch a foreign language film, do you prefer dubbing or subtitling? Why?

b 🔵 1.10 Listen to three people discussing the same question and compare their ideas to yours.

c Listen again and answer the questions. Write *Sue*, *Ekaterina* or *Ben*.

1 Who doesn't like the original actors' voices being replaced?

2 Who thinks subtitles are too short to carry all the meaning of the original?

3 Who thinks that subtitles can be quite inaccurately translated?

4 Who thinks it's difficult to concentrate on watching and reading subtitles?

5 Who thinks it may be confusing to have one voice translating the lines of every character?

6 Who thinks that it depends on what you're used to?

9 Complete the How to... box by putting the headings in the box in the correct places (A–E).

> Agreeing   Asking for an opinion
> Disagreeing   Giving an opinion
> Saying it may change (according to what happens)

How to... give opinions and agree/disagree

A _____	I think ...
	I guess ...
B _____	What do you think?
	What's your opinion?
C _____	I agree actually.
	That makes sense.
D _____	That's true, but ...
	I'm not sure about that.
E _____	Well, maybe it just depends (on/ who/when) ...

10 **a** 🔵 1.11 Listen to five statements. Decide if you agree or disagree with them.

b Listen again and write a response using a phrase from the How to... box in exercise 9.

c Work in pairs and discuss your opinions.

11 Read the Lifelong learning box and follow the instructions.

Using the media!

❗ 1 A great way to improve your English is to interact with the language outside the classroom. Make a list of ...

- the magazines that you read in English.
- the books that you have read and enjoyed in English.
- the websites that you read in English.
- the TV programmes that you watch in English.

2 Work in pairs and exchange lists. Ask your partner about their list.

A: *What's Australianetwork.com?*
B: *It's a website where you can download short videos in English.*
A: *What's this book about?*
B: *It's about a man who ...*

Lifelong learning

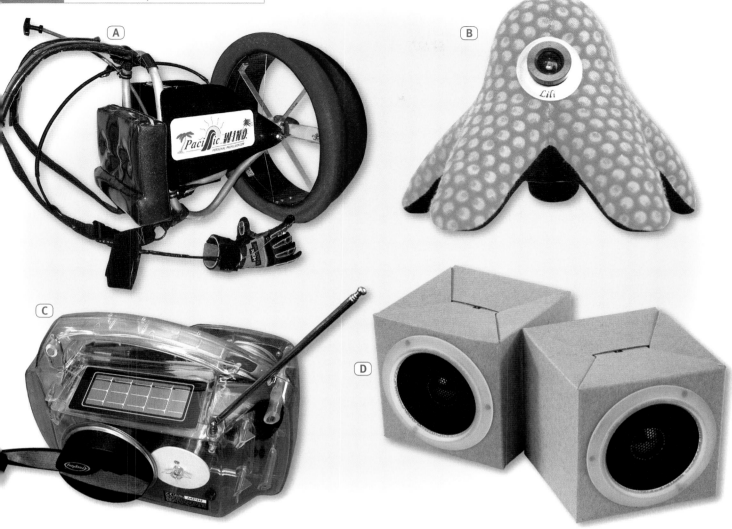

Listening

1 **a** Look at the gadgets (A–D). They all have something in common. What do you think it might be?

b 🔊 1.12 Listen to a radio programme about the gadgets (A–D). Match a gadget to each speaker (1–4).

1 Julian
2 Anna
3 Chris
4 Joe

c What do all the gadgets have in common?

2 Listen again and make a list of the good and bad points of each gadget (A–D). Work in pairs and compare your lists.

3 Work in pairs. Decide which gadget you would most like/least like to have. Explain why.

Speaking

4 Complete the How to... box with the prepositions *of*, *for*, *by* and *to*.

How to... describe an object

Comparing it to something else	It's a kind _____ music player. It's similar _____ an mp3. It looks like an mp3 player.
Describing its function	It's used _____ playing music. It's used _____ joggers. It's a thing _____ playing music.
Describing its features	It's made _____ plastic. It's rectangular/square/circular etc.

5 **a** Think of a gadget you or someone you know owns. Think about how to describe it using the language in the How to... box in exercise 4.

b Work in pairs and tell your partner about the gadget.

Vocabulary | television

6 **a** Work in pairs. The words in the box collocate with *television*. Does each word go before or after *television*?

> channel commercials digital live on (the) presenter producer programme satellite screen set viewers

b Put the word in brackets in the correct place. Then complete the sentences with your own ideas.

1 The best _____ television _____ (channel) is ...

2 My favourite _____ television _____ (presenter) is ...

3 ... is the worst thing _____ television _____ (on).

4 _____ television _____ (digital) is better because ...

5 ... is the most exciting _____ television _____ (programme) I've ever seen.

c Divide the adjectives in the box below into *positive* and *negative*.

> annoying boring entertaining exciting gripping incredible inspiring moving nauseating nonsense unrealistic unwatchable

Pronunciation | /n/ and /ŋ/

7 **a** 🔊 1.13 Look at the word *entertaining*. How many letter 'n's are there? Listen to the word being pronounced. How is the last 'n' pronounced?

b Underline the 'n's in all the words in exercise 6c. Which ones are pronounced /n/ and which /ŋ/?

c 🔊 1.14 Listen and check your answers. Repeat the words.

d Work in pairs. Think of programmes you have seen which you could describe using the adjectives in exercise 6c.

I thought it was ...

I found it ...

the Marconiphone 702

Completely reliable ...
and built to last

It was made over seven decades ago – and unlike modern gadgets it is completely reliable: it was built to last.

A television that was around for King George VI's 1937 Coronation and survived the Second World War is now thought to be Britain's oldest working set.

The black-and-white Marconiphone 702 dates back to 1936 and is still in its original condition. It has a 12-inch screen and was manufactured around November 1936, the same month as the BBC television service from Alexandra Palace was first broadcast.

The set is likely to have screened landmark occasions including George VI's Coronation Procession, the 1948 London Olympic Games and the Queen's Coronation in 1953. When new, it cost 60 Guineas – the equivalent of around £11,000 today.

The set has been converted from analogue to digital, bringing it firmly into the twenty-first century. Jeffrey Borinsky, a consultant engineer from North London, entered a competition to find the country's oldest TV. He has owned the set for ten years. He said: 'I still enjoy watching my Marconiphone occasionally, especially cartoons from the 1930s, which the original owner might also have seen on the set. Now it is digital, it can be used for many years to come.'

The competition was set up in May by Iain Logie Baird, television curator at the National Media Museum in Bradford and grandson of the inventor of TV, John Logie Baird. He said: 'A small fraction of pre-War televisions still exist – many stopped working or were simply thrown out when a newer set arrived, and we know about 3,000 were lost in the London bombings.'

The set will join a display of televisions from across the ages at the National Media Museum.

Reading

8 Work in pairs. Look at the photos of televisions and discuss the questions.

1 When do you think they were made?

2 How are they similar or different from televisions today?

9 Read the article. What do the numbers in the box refer to?

> 1948   3,000   1936   11,000   12

10 Read the article again and write true (T), false (F) or not given (NG).

1   The television is in excellent working order. ☐
2   It was removed from London during the Second World War. ☐
3   It is possible to use the television to watch digital TV. ☐
4   Jeffrey Borinsky has owned the television since it was made. ☐
5   Jeffrey particularly likes watching old programmes on the set. ☐
6   Iain Logie Baird is an inventor. ☐
7   The majority of pre-War TVs were destroyed during the War. ☐
8   The television will now go to a museum. ☐

Grammar | the passive

11 Look at the Active grammar box. Complete the example sentences using the article on page 26 to help you. Then match the rules (A–C) with the sentences (1–3).

Active grammar

Present Simple	*It _____ thought to be Britain's oldest working set.*
Past Simple	*It _____ made over seven decades ago.*
Present Perfect Simple	*The set _____ converted from analogue to digital.*
Modal verbs	*It can _____ used for many years to come.*

A   We use the active to describe what someone/something does.

B   We use the passive to describe what happens to someone or something.

We often use the passive to describe processes:
*Then the glass **is heated** …*
and in more formal or written contexts:
*It **is thought** to be …*
and to avoid saying who is responsible:
*The washing-up **hasn't been done** yet!*

C   If we want to say who or what does the action in a passive sentence we often use *by*.

1   *The competition was set up in May **by Iain Logie Baird**.*
2   *Iain Logie Baird **set up** the competition in May.*
3   *The competition **was set up** in May.*

---

12 Complete the second sentence so it means the same as the first.

1   In 1939 people could only receive one channel – the BBC.
    In 1939 only one channel _____ – the BBC.
2   In the 1930s a television was owned for ten to fifteen years.
    In the 1930s people _____ a television for ten to fifteen years.
3   Nowadays people replace their television every two to three years.
    Nowadays a television _____ every two to three years.
4   All pre-War televisions were made in Britain.
    The British _____ all pre-War televisions.
5   The Chinese make ninety percent of televisions now.
    Ninety percent of televisions _____ the Chinese now.
6   In 1936 people could watch the BBC for just two hours a day.
    In 1936 the BBC _____ for just two hours a day.

13 a   Add one missing word to each sentence.

1   A father and son who made millions of pounds from fake DVDs have jailed for six years.
2   Hundreds of thousands of DVDs were produced workers hired by the gang.
3   The DVDs sold cheaply in pubs and markets.
4   It is estimated the police that the criminals made around £43,000 a day from the operation.
5   The gang members lived a life of luxury until they caught.
6   However, police believe that most of the money the gang made been taken out of the country.
7   Is estimated that criminal gangs in the UK make about £300 million a year from fake DVDs.
8   Police dogs have now trained to find hidden DVDs.

b   🔵 1.15 Listen and check your answers to exercise 13a.

see Reference page 33

2.3 Stories in the news

Grammar Past Simple and Past Continuous

Can do describe an important event from your life

Speaking and listening

1 **a** Work in pairs and discuss the questions.

1 Do you believe everything you read in the news? Why/Why not?

2 Read the opinions below. Do you agree with them?

Different newspapers report the same story in different ways.

Newspapers sometimes try to make news stories sound worse than they are.

Newspapers have to make stories sound exciting in order to sell.

b 🔵 1.16 Listen to Eben and Rachel discussing question 1 in exercise 1a. Look at the opinions in exercise 1a and note down who agrees with them – *Eben*, *Rachel* or *both*.

2 **a** Complete the newspaper headlines (1–6) with the words in the box.

> delivers   escapes   inherits   saves
> survives   takes

1 Traffic police officer in Bangkok _____ baby in car

2 Lost driver _____ a wrong turn for 5,000 miles

3 Circus monkey _____ and destroys a restaurant

4 Top chef _____ giant lobster from cooking pot

5 Sailor _____ four months at sea

6 Cat _____ £350,000 house and £100,000 from owner

b Match the headlines (1–6) in exercise 2a with the pictures (A–F). Then work in pairs and describe what you think happened in each situation.

Reading

3 **a** Read the news stories (A–F) quickly. Match the headlines (1–6) from exercise 2a with the stories.

b Write the letter(s) of the news story/stories next to the topics (1–7) below.

1 restaurants: *B, D*

2 travel

3 animals

4 people getting lost

5 food or drink

6 babies or pets

7 survival

c Work in pairs and compare your answers.

A

B

C

D

E

F

A

A nervous driver who went on a day-trip to Calais ended up in Gibraltar after a five-day mystery tour. Mrs Bright, a recent divorcee, was planning to go to France to buy some wine for a party to celebrate her divorce. However, as she was driving around Calais looking for the supermarket, she took a wrong turn and lost her way. Without a map, and unable to speak French, she was too embarrassed to ask for directions and eventually she found herself in Gibraltar.

B

A giant lobster, saved from the cooking pot by a top chef, has been returned to the sea. Chef Anton Gretzky said he was planning to serve the lobster at his expensive restaurant, but decided he couldn't boil such a fine creature. An employee from the Aquarium Restaurant in Victoria, Australia, took the lobster, named Billy, to the coast to free him. Gretzky said: 'He has been on this Earth much longer than I have.'

C

Pooker, a grey and white cat, has become Britain's most famous pet. The eight-year-old cat inherited a £350,000 house and £100,000 after its owner, Mrs Rafaella Barese, died. Mrs Barese's neighbours will use the £100,000 to buy food for the lucky cat. The rich and famous always seem to make new friends easily. After just one day, two local cats were trying to move in with Pooker.

D

A monkey, who escaped from a local circus, caused €10,000 of damage to a pizzeria after the owner of the restaurant tried to feed it bread and salad. The monkey, named Lala, was sitting in the restaurant bathroom when the owner found her. The escapee dropped a vase, then started throwing paper towels around, and finally turned on the water taps and flooded the restaurant in Lehre, Germany.

E

'He was eating a seagull when we found him,' said a member of the South African navy team that rescued Vietnamese refugee, Parn Hung Kuk from the Atlantic Ocean. Kuk took a day-trip from Cape Town in his boat. After getting lost in a storm, he was rescued four months later. 'He was living on seagulls, a turtle and rain water. It's a miracle he's still alive,' said the rescue ship's captain.

F

Bangkok traffic police helped to deliver another baby yesterday. Sergeant Sakchai Kodayan is one of 130 members of the city traffic police whose special skills include giving first aid to motorists and helping mothers as they give birth. 'I was drinking a coffee and having a cigarette in a café by the road when a taxi driver shouted for help,' said Sakchai. 'His passenger was having a baby. It was a boy. The woman said she would call it Sakchai as a way to say thank you.' Sakchai has so far assisted with the birth of twenty-eight babies in his career.

4 Read the news stories again. Answer the questions.

1 a Where did Mrs Bright want to go?
   b Why didn't she ask for directions?
2 a Why didn't the chef cook the lobster?
   b What did the chef do with the lobster?
3 Who will look after Pooker the cat now?
4 What damage did Lala the monkey do?
5 What did Parn Hung Kuk eat for four months?
6 a What special skills does Sergeant Sakchai Kodayan have?
   b Why did the taxi driver ask for help?

5 a Look at the table. Complete the collocations (1–7) from the news stories with the words in the box. Then match them to the correct definitions (a–g).

cause   get   give   return   move   take (x2)

Collocation	Definition
1 _____ a wrong turn (story A)	a stop working for a short time
2 _____ lost (story E)	b go to live in the same house
3 _____ in with someone (story C)	c go/give back to
4 _____ damage (story D)	d help someone when they have an injury
5 _____ to the sea (story B)	e not know where you are
6 _____ first aid (story F)	f drive in the wrong direction
7 _____ a break (story F)	g break something by physically attacking it

b Work in pairs. Use the phrases (1–7) in the table in exercise 5a to retell the stories.

c Work in pairs and discuss the questions.

1 Which stories did you find most interesting/unbelievable/funny?
2 What interesting stories have you heard/seen/read about recently?

Pronunciation | word stress on word endings

6 a Look back at the news stories and complete the table with words ending with the following letters.

-ee	-eer	-ese	-ette
divorcee			

b 🔊 1.17 Listen to the words from exercise 6a. What do you notice about the stress pattern? There is one exception – what is it?

c Can you add any other words to the columns in exercise 6a?

see Pronunciation bank page 163

Grammar | Past Simple and Past Continuous

7 **a** Read the Active grammar box and answer question 1.

b Read rules A and B and find more examples of the Past Continuous in the news stories on pages 28–29. Then answer question 2.

Active grammar

Mrs Bright <u>was planning</u> to go to France …
She <u>was driving</u> around Calais …

1 Do the <u>underlined</u> verbs describe something complete or something temporary and in progress?

A We use the Past Continuous and Past Simple together to say that something happened in the middle of a longer action.

*I **was taking a break** in a café by the road when a taxi driver **shouted** for help.*

B The Past Continuous is often used to set the scene at the beginning of an article or story.

*This happened about eight years ago when I **was studying** for my degree. I **was feeling** a bit tired and …*

2 Which verbs are not normally used in the continuous form?

---

see Reference page 33

8 Complete the sentences with the Past Simple or Past Continuous form of the verbs in brackets.

They *were watching* (watch) a film in the cinema so they *didn't realise* (not/realise) it *was snowing* (snow) outside.

1 I _____ (work) in a school in Prague when I _____ (meet) my boyfriend.
2 When I _____ (be) a child, I _____ (like) swimming.
3 My sister _____ (arrive) just as I _____ (cook) some lunch.
4 I _____ (know) I wanted to marry him the first time I _____ (meet) him.
5 He _____ (not/break) his arm while he _____ (play) rugby. He _____ (fall) down the stairs.
6 I _____ (check) on the children and both of them _____ (sleep).
7 The phone rang while I _____ (listen) to my mp3 player and I _____ (not/hear) it.
8 I think I _____ (see) you yesterday in the station. _____ (wear) a blue shirt?

9 Complete the story by putting the verbs/verb phrases from the box in the correct place.

> didn't know   fell   hoping   visited   was
> was expecting   was having   ~~was staying~~

I remember when my little sister was born. I was ten years old, and I **was staying** in London with my parents. I knew my mother a baby, but I how soon it would arrive. I was really for a girl. It happened when I at a friend's house. It was her birthday and so she a party. My grandmother came to collect me, but when she told me the news I was so excited that I ran down the stairs, and I and broke my arm. I my mother and sister in hospital, and I had to spend the night there with my arm in plaster too.

Speaking and writing

10 Look at the stages for organising a story below. Then identify the four stages in the story in exercise 9.

1 Setting the scene: who? when? what? where?
2 The main sequence of events: what happened?
3 The big event: usually something unexpected.
4 Result: what happened in the end.

11 **a** Choose one of the events below. Make notes on what you were doing, where you were living and what you were hoping for at the time.

- someone was born
- you received some good news
- you received your exam results
- something important happened in your country
- an important/interesting event in your life

b Plan the sequence of your story using the four stages in exercise 10.

c Work in groups. Take it in turns to talk about your events.

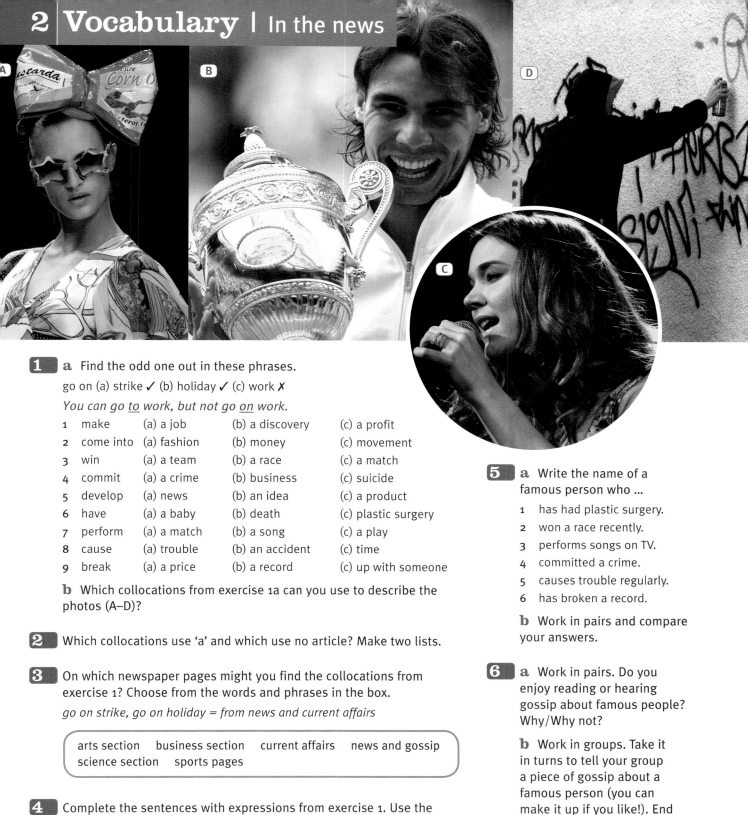

2 Vocabulary | In the news

1 **a** Find the odd one out in these phrases.

go on (a) strike ✓ (b) holiday ✓ (c) work ✗

You can go <u>to</u> work, but not go <u>on</u> work.

1	make	(a) a job	(b) a discovery	(c) a profit
2	come into	(a) fashion	(b) money	(c) movement
3	win	(a) a team	(b) a race	(c) a match
4	commit	(a) a crime	(b) business	(c) suicide
5	develop	(a) news	(b) an idea	(c) a product
6	have	(a) a baby	(b) death	(c) plastic surgery
7	perform	(a) a match	(b) a song	(c) a play
8	cause	(a) trouble	(b) an accident	(c) time
9	break	(a) a price	(b) a record	(c) up with someone

b Which collocations from exercise 1a can you use to describe the photos (A–D)?

2 Which collocations use 'a' and which use no article? Make two lists.

3 On which newspaper pages might you find the collocations from exercise 1? Choose from the words and phrases in the box.

go on strike, go on holiday = from news and current affairs

> arts section   business section   current affairs   news and gossip
> science section   sports pages

4 Complete the sentences with expressions from exercise 1. Use the correct tense.

1 Yesterday The Rolling Stones _____ that did the most to make them famous: *I Can't Get No Satisfaction*.
2 When his father died, Paul Getty _____ billions of dollars.
3 Marie Curie _____ that changed the world: she found radium.
4 When a food or drinks company _____ for the international market, it takes years to test it.
5 Many ageing celebrities _____ in order to look young, but it doesn't guarantee everlasting beauty!
6 In the UK there is a 45 percent possibility that criminals will _____ after their release from prison.
7 Ice on the roads _____ yesterday, but luckily no one was hurt.

5 **a** Write the name of a famous person who ...

1 has had plastic surgery.
2 won a race recently.
3 performs songs on TV.
4 committed a crime.
5 causes trouble regularly.
6 has broken a record.

b Work in pairs and compare your answers.

6 **a** Work in pairs. Do you enjoy reading or hearing gossip about famous people? Why/Why not?

b Work in groups. Take it in turns to tell your group a piece of gossip about a famous person (you can make it up if you like!). End by giving your opinion on their behaviour.

I can't believe anyone could do that!

That's a terrible way to behave, don't you think?

I feel quite sorry for her...

c Take it in turns to give your opinion about each piece of gossip. Look at the How to... box on page 24 to help you.

1 Work in pairs and discuss the questions.

1 Which of the following makes you want to go and see a film?

- advertising
- what your friends say about it
- who is starring in it
- who directed it
- reviews

2 Look at the film posters (A–C). Which film would you prefer to see? Why?

2 **a** 🔵 1.18 Listen to a description of a film. Which film (A–C) is it about?

b Listen again and complete the notes.

Type of film	It's a _____ film.
Summary of plot	It's about _____ who buys the house where _____ as a child. Her son starts to see _____ in the house and then he suddenly _____ .
Characters	The main characters are _____ . There is also a rather spooky _____ .

3 🔵 1.19 Listen to more information about the film in exercise 2 and make notes. Work in pairs and compare.

4 **a** Work in pairs. Choose a well-known film you have both seen and prepare to describe it. Make notes using the headings in exercise 2b.

b Work with another pair and tell them about your film. Can they guess which film you are describing?

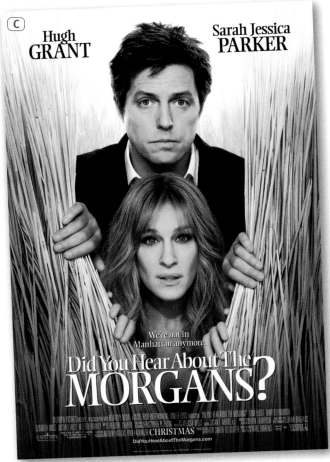

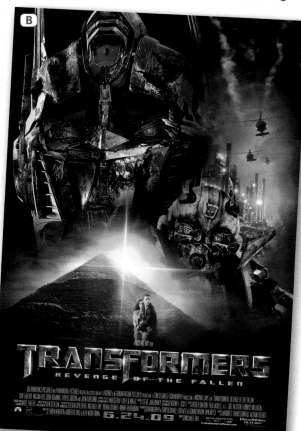

Defining relative clauses

A 'clause' is part of a sentence. A defining relative clause makes it clear who or what we are talking about in a sentence. It gives essential information.

*The man **who lives next door** had an accident.*

Relative clauses begin with relative pronouns:

who for people; *which* for things and animals, and *whose* for possessions.

After place, area, room, etc. we use *where*.

After time, day, year, etc. we use *when*.

We don't use *what* as a relative pronoun.

*The vase **that** I broke was very expensive.* (NOT: ~~The vase what I broke was very expensive.~~)

In less formal and spoken English we often use *that* instead of *who* or *which*.

*The police caught the man **that** robbed the bank.*

We can leave out the pronouns *who*, *which* or *that* if they are the object of the relative clause.

The film which I saw was called Heroes.

The film I saw was called Heroes.

The boy who she met was nice.

The boy she met was nice.

The passive

We make the passive with the verb *to be* + past participle.

*James **is paid** a lot of money.*

***Are** you **being followed**?*

*We **were given** a new car to drive.*

*She **has been told** this before.*

In **active sentences**, the person (or thing) who does the action comes first.

The man kissed the baby.

In **passive sentences**, the person (or thing) affected by the action comes first and is the main focus.

The baby was kissed by the man.

The person (or thing) who did the action is often not known or not the main focus.

The programme has been shown since 1959. (The focus is on the programme, not who has shown it.)

We use *by* to include the person (or thing) who did the action in a passive sentence.

*The book was written **by** Faulks.*

The passive often sounds 'impersonal'. It is used in formal English and often in the news.

*The President **was asked** to resign.* (It isn't important who asked him to resign.)

Past Simple and Past Continuous

The Past Continuous form: *was/were + -ing*

We use the **Past Continuous** to talk about what was happening at a particular moment in the past.

*What **were** you **doing** at 10 o'clock last night?*

We use the **Past Simple** for complete, finished actions in the past.

When the Past Simple and Past Continuous are used together, the Past Continuous refers to the longer, background action or situation. The Past Simple refers to the shorter action or main event that happened to interrupt it.

*I **was walking** through the park when the storm **began**.*

We use the **Past Continuous** for temporary actions and situations.

*I **was living** in Barcelona last summer.*

We use the **Past Simple** for longer or permanent situations.

*I **lived** in Berlin for ten years when I was a child.*

We do not usually use the continuous form with 'state' verbs such as *like*, *want*, *know* and *understand*.

Key vocabulary

Internet
IM (instant messaging)   online   website

Film
comedy   docu-drama   horror film   romantic film thriller

Television
channel   commercial   digital   documentary reality/chat show   live   presenter   producer programme   satellite   screen   soap   (television) set viewers

Describing films and TV
annoying   boring   entertaining   exciting   gripping incredible   inspiring   moving   nauseating   nonsense unrealistic   unwatchable

Newspapers
arts/business section   current affairs   gossip human interest story   sports pages

News collocations
go on strike/on holiday   make a discovery/a profit come into fashion/into money   win a race/a competition commit a crime/suicide   develop an idea/a product have a duty/plastic surgery   cause trouble/an accident perform a song/a play   break a record/a promise

---

Listen to the explanations and vocabulary.

ACTIVEBOOK

 see Writing bank page 154

2 | Review and practice

1 Complete the news stories with the active or passive form of the verbs from the box. Change the tense as necessary. You may use some verbs more than once.

> announce   call   discover   find   kill   sell
> start

A new service which will _find_ anyone's mobile phone number _has been announced_.

One thousand people (1) _____ by a freak storm in South Africa. The storm (2) _____ in the early hours of the morning.

Zac Efron (3) _____ as the star of a new film, the most expensive ever made.

A cure for cancer (4) _____. Scientists (5) _____ the breakthrough at a conference yesterday.

The film director Richard Attenborough (6) _____ much of his art collection after claiming that there was no more room on his walls.

Yesterday a three-year-old boy successfully (7) _____ an ambulance after he (8)_____ that his mother had fallen down the stairs.

A ring which once belonged to the opera singer Maria Callas (9) _____ in an attic. The new owner (10) _____ it online, with a reserve price of nearly £100,000.

2 Complete the television guide with the relative pronouns from the box. In which sentences can you use *that*?

> when   where   which   who   whose

7.30 **Brothers in Arms:** Marlon is a lawyer (1) _____ brother works with ex-criminals. Now he wants Marlon to help him. Has Marlon reached a time in his career (2) _____ he can take a risk?

8.00 **Home Questions:** the quiz show (3) _____ asks contestants questions about the place (4) _____ they were born.

8.30 **The Year** (5) _____ **I Made History:** Roy Johns speaks to the people (6) _____ have been in the news this year. Guests include Milly Cheiz, a doctor (7) _____ anti-cancer treatment is being tested in Australia, and Moses Kenui, an athlete (8) _____ shocked the world when he broke four athletics records in one year.

9.30 **News**

10.00 **Restaurant:** follows the progress of two restaurants (9) _____ famous chefs have visited. They both opened last year – one in Clydehead, a town (10) _____ there is 60 percent unemployment, and one in Tindell, a city (11) _____ the rich are happy to pay €350 for dinner.

11.00 **Fright Kids:** comedy horror film about a woman (12) _____ has twins.

3 Choose the correct words in *italics*.

1 I *was/was being* at school when I *started/ was starting* learning French.

2 We *watched/were watching* TV when we *heard/were hearing* about the accident.

3 **A:** What *did you do/were you doing* this time yesterday?
  B: I *read/was reading* a novel.

4 When I last *saw/was seeing* my sister, she *looked/was looking* for a flat in Madrid.

5 I *crashed/was crashing* into the car because I wasn't looking where I *went/was going*.

6 **A:** *Did they win/Were they winning* when you left the match?
  B: No. They *lost/were losing* 2 – 1, but there were still twenty minutes left.

7 While I *studied/was studying* yesterday I *found/was finding* this great website.

8 **A:** *Did you see/Were you seeing* our new boss at the conference?
  B: Yes. He *wore/was wearing* a white suit. *Didn't you notice/Weren't you noticing* him?

9 **A:** What *did you do/were you doing* under the table?
  B: I *just looked/was just looking* for something I dropped.

10 I'm quite good at acting because I *studied/ was studying* drama at university.

4 Complete the sentences with suitable words or phrases from the unit.

1 Did you read about the play? It was in the _____ section of the paper.

2 I saw an interesting _____ about Ancient Egypt on TV yesterday.

3 I'm sure that actor's had _____ . He looks twenty years younger!

4 Which _____ of the paper do you read? I like the sports pages.

5 The company made a _____ of €50,000 this year.

6 Speeding drivers cause a lot of _____ .

7 Asafa Powell broke the _____ for the 100 metres. He ran it in 9.77 seconds.

8 There's an _____ about immigration in the newspaper today.

9 Platform shoes are back! The shoes from the 70s have _____ fashion once again.

10 American actor Anne Hathaway is going to _____ on the London stage in a new play by John Miller.

11 My husband threw his shoe at the television and broke the _____ into a thousand pieces.

12 The _____ announced the winner of the game show.

Lifestyle

3

Lead-in

1 **a** What does *home* mean to you? Write notes about your favourite rooms, smells, views, special objects and your feelings about home.

b Work in groups and compare your answers.

2 **a** Decide in which section of the table (A, B, C or D) the words and phrases in the box belong.

> an apartment   a cellar   a commercial district   a fireplace   a garden
> a garage   a gate   a park and a playground   a studio flat   the suburbs

House	Area/neighbourhood
A I live in ... a (semi) detached/terraced house a block of flats a cottage	**C I live in ...** a residential area the centre/outskirts of town
B It's got ... a lift an attic a balcony a good view high ceilings a drive wooden floors stairs	**D It's got ...** lots of green spaces shops and restaurants cinemas and theatres

b Make a list of any other words you know for each section of the table.

3 **a** Work in pairs. Take it in turns to describe the houses in the photos using the expressions from exercise 2a.

b Describe the place where you live.

I live in a block of flats. It's quite modern. It has a ...

3.1 Your place or mine?

Reading and speaking

1 Look at the photos. Try to match the outside of the properties (A–B) to the insides (1–2). How are they similar to, or different from where you live?

2 Read the texts below and match the property descriptions with the photos. Were your answers to exercise 1 correct?

Your home – My home

We help families to exchange homes with other families, so both can experience a fantastic break in another country without it costing a fortune!

Property 1

Bright and comfortable apartment in the centre of Seville, in a quiet street with no heavy traffic around; in fact, the only noise you can hear during the day is the bells of the cathedral nearby.

The apartment is decorated in a very traditional Sevillian style, with plenty of plants and sunlight. The property is on the third floor (there is a lift) and covers an area of 60 square meters. There are two bedrooms, one with a single bed and one with a double bed.

The apartment has recently been completely refurbished and opens onto the balcony with a beautiful view of the cathedral.

The area

The apartment is in the historical centre of Seville. It is a very beautiful area, with narrow bustling streets and little gardens behind iron gates. There are plenty of local bars and restaurants serving 'tapas' (typical Spanish dishes).

Your home – My home

Property 2

Ideal for a family holiday, this is a beautiful four-bedroomed Victorian house, situated on a quiet residential road. This charming property has a large living area and a separate dining room and well-equipped kitchen. Upstairs there are four bedrooms, all doubles, and two ensuite bathrooms, one with a shower and one with a bath. There is a large garden, with a patio area where you may enjoy a typical English afternoon tea!

The area

The property is located close to Wimbledon Park, with a children's playground. The nearest tube station, just five minutes walk away, will take you straight into central London, where you will find all the museums, shops, theatres and restaurants you could wish for!

3 **a** Read the property descriptions again and write *property 1* or *property 2* next to each question.

Which property ...

1 is near the centre of the city?
2 has outside space?
3 has more than one bathroom?
4 is near public transport?
5 is near places where children can play?
6 has a balcony?
7 has been redecorated?

b Work in pairs. Which of the two properties would you prefer to live in for a month? Why?

Listening

The Armitage family

The Dos Santos family

4 **a** 🔊 1.20 Listen to two couples talk about their plans for a home exchange. Write *D* (Dos Santos) or *A* (Armitage) next to the activities they mention.

1 visit museums
2 see cathedrals
3 enjoy the local cuisine
4 go shopping
5 visit friends
6 go to the beach

b Look at the extracts from the listening. Then listen again and choose the correct words in *italics*.

Miriam: ... we (1) *'ll spend/'re spending* more than one month in London. We've never been there before.

Miriam: And I'm (2) *going to do/doing* lots and lots of shopping.

Interviewer: Great. There are some wonderful shops in London. I (3) *'ll give/'m giving* you the address of a great shoe shop.

Jeremy: Spain has such a rich culture ... We (4) *'ll go/'re going* to see the cathedrals.

Jeremy: We're (5) *going to try/trying* all the local dishes.

Jeremy: We (6) *won't/aren't going to* go to McDonald's. Forget it!

Grammar | future plans

5 Match the sentences (1–6) in exercise 4b with the rules (A–C) in the Active grammar box.

> ### Active grammar
>
> We can use the Present Continuous, *be going to* or *will* to talk about future plans.
>
> A We use *be going to* to talk about something you've decided to do.
>   e.g. sentences _____
>
> B We use *will* for a decision made at the time of speaking, or an offer.
>   e.g. sentences _____
>
> C We use the Present Continuous to talk about arrangements (plans that you have already organised, i.e. you have arranged the dates).
>   e.g. sentence _____

see Reference page 47

6 Complete the texts with words and phrases from the box.

> is going to (x2)   're going to (x2)   'll (x2)
> 's moving   'm starting

Sarah and Jeremy

I (1) _____ a new job in June and it's in Oxford, so we (2) _____ need to move house. We'd like to buy somewhere in the countryside, so we (3) _____ to look at some of the small villages outside the city. Jeremy says he (4) _____ take a day off next week to go and look.

Miriam and Carlos

My mother (5) _____ in with us next year, because she's old and doesn't want to stay on her own. She (6) _____ to sell her house. Carlos isn't too happy about this plan, but he says he (7) _____ put up with it to please me. It (8) _____ be great because I'll have some help looking after the baby.

Speaking

7 **a** Imagine you are going to live abroad for a month. Decide on ten things you will need to do before you go.

get a passport, buy some suntan lotion

b Work in pairs. Try to guess what is on your partner's list by asking questions.

A: *Are you going to get a passport?*

B: *No, I've already got one.*

c When you have guessed all you can, look at your partner's list and offer to help them.

I'll get you some suntan lotion, I'm going into town later.

8 **a** Write three or four questions to ask other students about their plans for …

- their education/career.
- their next holiday.
- their (family's) future.
- this evening.
- their home.
- this weekend.

b In groups, ask and answer the questions about your future plans.

A: *Katia, what are you planning for the weekend?*

B: *I'm going to visit my aunt. She's having a party to celebrate her …*

Listening

9 Work in pairs. Look at the pictures of the Armitage and Dos Santos families during their home exchange. What do you think the problems were?

10 **a** 🔊 1.21 Listen to interviews with Miriam and Jeremy and check your ideas for exercise 9.

b Listen again and make notes. List four problems Miriam and Jeremy each had.

c 🔊 1.22 Listen to Miriam phoning the company to complain. Answer the questions.

1 How long did it take to get to the centre?
2 What was wrong with the bathroom?
3 Why was the house in such a mess?
4 What did Miriam have to buy and why?
5 What was the problem with the heating and hot water?
6 What compensation did the representative offer Miriam?

11 Look at the How to… box. Listen again and write *M* next to the phrases Miriam says and *R* next to those the company representative says.

How to… complain politely

Stating a complaint	*I don't like to complain, but …* *I'm sorry, but …* *I'm sorry but it just isn't good enough.*
Disagreeing politely	*Well, …* *Actually, …*
Asking for what you want	*I'd like you to …* *I think you should …*
Apologising/ sympathising	*I'm sorry to hear that.* *We must apologise about/for that.* *I do apologise for the inconvenience.*

Speaking

12 **a** Look at your notes from exercise 10b. What four problems did Jeremy's family have? What compensation do you think he should ask for?

b Work in pairs.

Student A: You are Jeremy. Ring the company to complain and say what you would like them to do about the problems.

Student B: You are the company representative. Talk to Jeremy, try to explain and apologise.

Reading

1 **a** 🌐 1.23 Listen to some sounds. Are you in the city or the country? Tick (✓) the sounds in the box you hear.

> bees buzzing   birdsong
> car horns   engines
> people talking   sirens
> waves crashing

b Think about where you live. What sounds can you hear ...

- in the morning?
- in the evening?
- in the afternoon?
- at night?

c Do you enjoy these sounds? Work in pairs and compare your answers.

2 **a** 🌐 1.24 Listen and read the poem. Match the photos (A–D) with the verses (1–4).

b What can the poet hear and see in each verse? Does he enjoy the sounds and sights of the city?

3 **a** What examples can you find in the poem of words which rhyme?

sputters – gutters

b Some words, such as *bang*, *crash*, *pop*, *click* sound like the sound they describe. What examples of words like this can you find in the poem?

swish

c What examples can you find of words close together which begin with the same sound?

swish – swash
pulse – people

4 Work in pairs. Do you enjoy city life, or do you prefer a smaller town or the country? Why?

City I love

1 In the city
I live in
city I love
mornings wake
to
swishes, swashes,
sputters
of sweepers
swooshing litter
from gutters

2 In the city
I live in
city I love –
afternoons pulse
with
people hurrying,
scurrying
races of faces
pacing to
must-get-there
places.

3 In the city
I live in –
city I love –
nights shimmer
with lights
competing
with stars
above unknown heights.

4 In the city
I live in –
city I love –
as dreams
start to creep
my city
of senses
lulls me to sleep.

Glossary

swish	(*noun*)	– the sound of something moving quickly and quietly through the air
swash	(*noun*)	– the sound of water hitting a surface
sputter	(*noun*)	– a noise like a small explosion
swoosh	(*verb*)	– making the sound of air or water moving quickly
scurrying	(*verb*)	– moving quickly with short steps
pacing	(*verb*)	– walking with regular steps
shimmer	(*verb*)	– to shine with a soft light
lull	(*verb*)	– to make someone feel calm and ready to sleep

39

Vocabulary | adjectives describing places

5 a Look at the adjectives in the box. Find pairs of words that mean the opposite.

> bustling   clean   dull   enormous
> friendly   lively   modern   picturesque
> polluted   quiet   tiny   ~~touristy~~
> traditional   ugly   ~~unspoilt~~   unwelcoming

unspoilt – touristy

b Think of a town or city for each adjective.

Tokyo is enormous.

Listening

6 a 🔊 1.25 Listen to Heather talking about Kyoto in Japan. Which of the adjectives in exercise 5a does she use?

b Listen again. Which of these things did she like or not like about Kyoto?

- old buildings
- shops
- temples
- people
- restaurants
- nightlife
- climate

7 a Write a list of what you think makes a city good or bad to live in.

Good: beautiful views Bad: dirty

b Work in pairs and compare your lists. Which cities do you think are good to live in?

Reading

8 Read the article on page 41. Does it mention any of the cities you thought of in exercise 7?

9 Read the article again and find which city or cities ...

1 has/have a very old university.
2 is/are good for skiing.
3 has/have a very good subway system.
4 has/have thirty-seven beaches.
5 is/are quite polluted.
6 has/have a series of gardens round the old city.
7 has/have beaches within easy reach.

10 Work in pairs. Would you ever move to these cities? Why/Why not?

WHY NOT MOVE TO...?

Fed up with where you're living, or just fancy a change? We take a look at some of the best cities in the world to live in. So, why not move to ...

Santiago, Chile?

Santiago has one of the most attractive settings of any city in the world, circled by snow-topped mountains. Unfortunately, the mountains hold in the pollution, so it isn't one of the world's cleanest cities. Despite that, life expectancy is higher than the global average and the quality of life is very good.

The city is fast becoming a major economic centre, with one of the most efficient subway systems in the world. It also has a lively arts scene and leafy urban parks. Outside the city, an hour will take you to the mountains, for skiing, hiking or snowboarding, or to the coast for surfing or scuba diving.

Sydney, Australia?

If you're an outdoors type, you won't find anywhere better to live than Sydney. Hot summers and mild winters mean that you can be outside most of the time, swimming or surfing at the city's thirty-seven beaches, walking in the bush ... the list is endless. Sydney was also recently voted the friendliest city in the world. It is the world's fifteenth most expensive city, though, so you'd better be prepared to work hard as well as play hard!

Vancouver, Canada?

Vancouver has been named the world's most liveable city on several occasions over the last decade. Although the weather is not as good as in some cities, it's at least very mild. The city is clean and, perhaps most importantly, it's very beautiful. The city lies with the Strait of Georgia on one side and the Coast Mountains on the other, providing some of the finest skiing in the world. Vancouver has a reputation for being more relaxed than other cities and, certainly, the Vancouverites have the longest lifespans of any city in Canada, with an average life expectancy of 81.1 years.

Krakow, Poland?

With more than forty public parks, Krakow is one of Europe's leafiest cities. Perhaps the most famous park, the Planty, is a collection of about thirty gardens which go all the way around the Old Town. Krakow also has one of the best preserved medieval city centres in Europe, with churches around every corner and the second oldest university in Central Europe. It also offers hundreds of restaurants and bars, hidden away in narrow streets and cellars. It is also sunnier than you might imagine, with average temperatures of 24 degrees in summer.

Grammar | comparatives and superlatives

11 Match the rules (A–I) in the Active grammar box with the underlined examples in the article.

Active grammar

	Comparatives	Superlatives
One-syllable adjectives	A + -er than	F + the -est
Two (or more) syllable adjectives	B more + adjective + than	G the most + adjective
Two-syllable adjectives ending in -y	C remove -y and add -ier than	H the -iest
Irregular adjectives: e.g. bad	D worse than	I the worst
For negative comparatives	E not as + adjective + as	

see Reference page 47

12 Complete the text with the comparative or superlative forms of the adjectives in brackets. Add *than* where necessary.

Just finished my tour of Russia, which is (1) _____ (big) country in the world and one of (2) _____ (interesting) too. My flight was much (3) _____ (comfortable) this time – big seats! Also, the service was (4) _____ (good) last time – free food and drink! When I arrived in Warsaw, the people at Customs were (5) _____ (friendly) before (on my first trip I waited an hour while they checked my passport!). Fortunately, Poland isn't (6) _____ (cold) Moscow, which was freezing! This afternoon I had (7) _____ (delicious) lunch of my trip so far: a Polish speciality called *bigos* in a great restaurant in (8) _____ (old) part of the city.

13 a Complete the comparative sentences about cities that you know.

1 You won't find anywhere _____ than _____ .
2 The _____ is/are not as _____ in some cities.
3 _____ has a reputation for being _____ than other cities.

b Now use the phrases in the box to write five superlative sentences about cities that you know.

> probably the ... in ...
> ... of any city in ...
> one of the most ...
> one of the world's ...
> some of the best ... the ...

Speaking

14 a Work in groups. Decide together on the three best places to live in your country (or the country where you are studying).

b Tell the other groups which places you chose and explain why.

3.3 Eco-homes

Grammar	future possibility
Can do	take notes while listening

Reading

eco-friendly /ˈiːkəʊˌfrendli/ *adj* not harmful to the environment

1 Work in pairs. Look at the definition above and discuss the questions.

1 Have you made any changes to the way you live in order to be more eco-friendly?

2 If so, explain what you have done and why.

2 a Read the title and introduction to the article below and look at the words in the box. How do you think each word is significant in the article?

> adaptable   climate   flooding   fuel   household waste
> insulated   recycling   self-sufficient   sound waves

b Read the article and check your predictions.

3 a Read the article again and answer the questions.

1 How is a 'passive house' mainly heated?

2 What is the advantage of moveable walls?

3 How will the plants in the fish tank help the fish?

4 What can the energy created by the fish tanks be used for?

5 Why will there be no more private swimming pools?

6 What two things will 'clever' fridges be able to do?

b Work in pairs. Which of the predictions in the article do you think are likely to happen? Why?

What does the future hold?

We spoke to Professor John Williams, futurologist, for his expert predictions on life in the next few decades.

❝Well, the first thing to say is that I don't believe we're all going to be living in treehouses and walking or cycling everywhere. We are going to have to make changes though.

Unfortunately, it looks quite likely that the climate <u>may</u> change significantly, with hotter summers, colder winters and more flooding. At the same time, fuel for heating or air conditioning <u>will probably</u> become much more expensive. For these reasons, our houses <u>will definitely</u> have to become much better insulated. People are already building so-called 'passive houses', which have little or no central heating at all, relying on the bodyheat of the people who live there.

Homes <u>probably won't</u> be as big, and so we will need more adaptable furniture, such as sofa-beds, and when we are not using our furniture we will be able to fold it away into wall cabinets. Houses could have moveable walls so that the same space can be arranged in different ways. Tabletops may double as computer screens or DVD players.

New technology will make us more self-sufficient. Kitchens may have fish tanks which, as well as providing fish to eat, also produce fresh vegetables (see photo). The plants will provide oxygen for the fish. These tanks will be powered by household

Listening

4 🔊 1.26 Listen to Tracy and Stig discussing the predictions in the article. Tick (✓) the predictions they think are likely and cross (✗) those they think are unlikely.

		Tracy	Stig
1	Homes will be smaller.		
2	People will stop using cars.		
3	People will keep fish to eat.		
4	Fridges will be intelligent.		
5	Robots will be more common.		

waste and create energy, which can then be used to run the family car – though we <u>might not</u> all have cars!

Water will definitely be more expensive and the home of the future will probably be designed to use much less. Washing machines and dishwashers might use sound waves to shake dirt off. We may even take showers using sound waves. What water we do use will be recycled and used again round the house and private swimming pools will become a thing of the past.

We will also certainly have more robots in our houses, though they won't look like the ones in films. There will probably be small robots designed to clean the fridge or open the curtains. Clever fridges will tell us when food is about to go out of date and even suggest recipes, and we will be able to communicate with our homes by mobile phone wherever we are. 🙰

Grammar | future possibility

5 Complete the Active grammar box using the <u>underlined</u> words and phrases from the article. Then answer the questions.

> ### Active grammar
>
> **Certain**
> ➕ *Our houses _____/**certainly** have to become much better insulated.*
> *We **definitely** won't waste so much.*
>
> **Probable**
> ➕ *Fuel _____ become much more expensive.*
> *Homes _____ be as big.*
>
> **Possible**
> ➕ *The climate _____/**might**/**could** change significantly.*
> *We **may**/_____ all have cars.*
>
> 1 How does the position of the adverb (*probably*, *definitely*, *certainly*) change in positive and negative sentences?
> 2 Which modal verb can't be used in the negative to talk about possibility?

see Reference page 47

6 Choose the correct words in *italics*.

1 Technology *probably will/will probably* become less expensive.
2 We *definitely will/will definitely* be able to do more and more online.
3 We *probably won't/won't probably* use so much water.
4 We *might not/couldn't* all have our own cars.

7 Look at the sentences about twenty-five years ago and change them to make predictions about the next twenty-five years.

Twenty-five years ago ...

most people had cars.

In the next twenty-five years there will probably be fewer cars because of the price of fuel.

1 People wrote more letters.
2 Most people didn't have the Internet.
3 People watched videos rather than DVDs.
4 People didn't worry about wasting water.
5 Most people didn't have mobile phones.
6 People didn't buy organic food.

8 **a** Write seven predictions for people in your class. Don't write their names.

She'll probably move to the USA.

He might become a famous musician.

b Exchange your predictions with other students. Guess who the predictions are about.

A

B

C

D

Vocabulary | compound nouns

9 Read the descriptions (1–4) of different types of home and match them to the photos (A–D). What would it be like to live in each of them?

1 This treehouse has two floors, with a beautiful wooden staircase, a full kitchen, bedroom, bathroom and even a fireplace.

2 A motorhome with a difference – instead of being pulled by a car, it's powered by a bike. Inside there is a bed, shelves and even pictures on the walls.

3 Dug into the hillside, a skylight in the roof provides natural light and solar panels provide electricity.

4 This yurt, a kind of tent, is compact but well-equipped. To save space there are bunk-beds on the left and a sofabed on the right.

10 a *Motorhome* is a compound noun (a noun made from two smaller words put together). Can you find other compound nouns in the descriptions in exercise 9?

b Match words in box A with words in box B to make compound nouns.

A

> washing   central   sofa   wall   computer   DVD   mobile   air   fish   swimming   bunk

B

> heating   cabinets   conditioning   phone   machine   pool   player   screen   bed   tank   bed

Pronunciation |
word stress in compound nouns

11 a Look at your answers to exercise 10b. Which are *noun + noun* and which *adjective + noun*?

b 🔊 1.27 Listen to the compound nouns from exercise 10b and mark which word is stressed.

c What type of compound noun has the stress on the second word – noun + noun or adjective + noun?

see Pronunciation bank page 163

Speaking

12 Work in pairs and discuss the questions.

1 Which of the items from exercise 10b have you got?

2 Would life be easier with/ without any of these items? Why?

3 Which are the most important to you? Why?

1 **a** Which parts of the words in the box are prefixes? Which are suffixes? What do you think the prefixes and suffixes mean?

> endless   forgetful   successful   unfair   unspoilt

b Add some more examples to the prefix table below. Use a dictionary or ask your teacher to help you.

Prefixes	Examples	Your examples
un = not	uninteresting unusual	un_____
re = again	rearrange review	re_____
ex = former/ previous	ex-boyfriend ex-Prime Minister	ex-_____
mis = wrong	mispronounced misheard	mis_____
dis = not	dislike disappear	dis_____

2 **a** What are the noun and/or verb forms of the adjectives in the suffix table below?

b Add some more examples to the table.

Suffixes	Example adjectives	Your examples
ive	creative, attractive, ...	_____ ive
(l)y	dirty, friendly, ...	_____ y/ly
ful	careful, helpful, ...	_____ ful
less	useless, careless, ...	_____ less
able/ible	enjoyable, comprehensible, ...	_____ able _____ ible

3 Read the Lifelong learning box. Can you think of any other words you have learned recently which use prefixes or suffixes? Use a dictionary to help you.

> ### Word building
>
> ! When you learn a new word, find out if it uses prefixes and suffixes, and if it has other forms (for example, the noun can change to a verb). This will help you to increase your vocabulary.

Lifelong learning

4 Read the advertisements below. Then complete them with the correct form of the words in **bold**.

5 Write a short advertisement for one of the things below, or use your own ideas. Try to include at least three words with prefixes or suffixes.
- a flat to rent
- a flatmate
- a new person for a team or club

FLAT TO RENT

Airy flat (60 square metres) in _____ area of London. Two bedrooms, sitting room, bathroom. _____ neighbours. _____ rent – £680.

Call **Mr Johnson** on 0207 931674

air
peace
friend
week

Home needed!

_____ cat, Musa soon to be _____ needs _____ owner with large, _____ garden.

Please call Luke on **01823 273305**

love
home
response
sun

Flatmate wanted

Very _____ flatmate is wanted to share home full of _____ , _____ antiques. No _____ people, please.

Call Miss Crabbins – **393 3321**

care
expense
break
mess

3 | Communication

Can do | describe hopes, dreams and ambitions

1 Read the advertisement looking for people to be on a TV programme. What happens in the programme? How can you apply to appear on it?

Country or City?

Ian Brown and Chiara Woods help people find their dream home, whether they want to move from the city to the country, or vice versa.

In each programme we find out where the person lives, why they want to move and what exactly they're looking for. Then we take them to the area they've chosen and show them round some dream properties. We also let them try out their new lifestyle, be it raising animals or clubbing all night!

If you want to change your lifestyle for the one you've always dreamed of, then please apply.

Prepare a short speech explaining ...
• why you dream of moving to the country or city.
• what you plan to do when you move.

Interviews will be held in London.

2 **a** 🔵 1.28 Listen to two people giving their speeches to the TV production team and complete the notes in the table.

	Speaker 1	Speaker 2
Where do you live now?	In the suburbs of the city.	In a _____ .
What type of lifestyle do you have?	It's very _____ .	It's quite healthy but a bit dull.
Why do you want to move?	I hope to _____ .	My dream is to _____ .
What are your plans for your new home?	I'm going to _____ . I'll probably _____ . I might _____ .	I'm going to _____ . I'll definitely _____ . I could _____ .

b Listen again and check.

c Work in groups. Should Speaker 1 or Speaker 2 be chosen for the programme? Why?

3 Complete the sentences in the How to... box so they are true for you.

How to... talk about hopes, dreams and ambitions

I hope to ...
My hope is to ...
I dream of ...
My dream is to ...
I have a lifelong dream of ...
My ambition is to ...

---

4 **a** You are going to apply to be on *Country or City?* Make notes answering the questions in exercise 2a. Use the Reference page to help you with grammar and vocabulary.

b Work in groups of four: two speakers and two judges.

Speakers: take it in turns to make your speeches.

Judges: ask questions to find out more information.

c Change roles and repeat. Then decide who should be chosen for the programme. Tell the class and explain why.

Future plans

We use **be going to** to talk about plans for the future or intentions (things you have already decided to do).

I'm going to take a holiday in March.

Sue isn't going to buy that car.

With the verbs *go* and *come* we often use the Present Continuous.

We use the Present Continuous to talk about fixed future arrangements (usually involving another person).

I'm meeting Sam at 2p.m. (I called him this morning to arrange it)

Are you coming to the party this evening? (You have been invited)

In many cases you can use either *be going to* or the Present Continuous.

I am playing rugby tomorrow.

I am going to play rugby.

We use *will* for unplanned decisions (made at the time of speaking), offers or promises.

I'll/won't tell her I saw you.

Will you carry this box for me?

For general predictions you can use *will* or *be going to*.

I think Brazil will/are going to win the next World Cup.

Comparatives and superlatives

One-syllable adjectives, or two-syllable adjectives ending in *-y*

Adjective	Comparative	Superlative	Notes
old	old**er** (than)	(the) old**est**	Add *-er, -est*
big	big**ger** (than)	(the) big**gest**	With short vowels (/ɪ/, /e/, /ɒ/,/æ/), double the consonant.
friendly	friendl**ier** (than)	(the) friendl**iest**	If the adjective ends in *-y*, change it to *-i* and add *-er, est*.

Two-syllable, and longer adjectives

Adjective	Comparative	Superlative	Notes
useful	more/less useful (than)	(the) most/least useful	Add *more* (+), or *less* (–),
dangerous	more/less dangerous (than)	(the) most/ least dangerous	(the) most (++), or (the) least (– –)

Irregular adjectives

good – better (than) – (the) best   *bad – worse (than) – (the) worst*

far – further (than) – (the) furthest or *far – farther (than) – (the) farthest*

(not) as + adjective + as

*The train is **as expensive as** flying.* (the same)

*It's **not as warm as** last week.* (different)

Future possibility

We use *will/won't* + adverb to say how likely something is in the future. *Will* comes before the adverb in affirmative sentences and after the adverb in negative sentences.

I'll definitely go. (you are certain)

I certainly won't go. (you are certain)

I'll probably stay. (quite certain)

I probably won't stay. (quite certain)

We use *may/might/could* when you are not certain.

Do not use *could* in the negative to talk about possibility.

Alice may meet us later for a drink.

The shop might not be open.

With modal verbs (*will, may, might, could*) we use the infinitive without *to*.

Key vocabulary

Home

apartment   attic   balcony
block of flats   ceiling   cellar
centre of town   commercial district
cottage   (semi-) detached house
drive   fireplace   floor   gate
green spaces   lift   neighbourhood
outskirts of town   residential area
park   playground   stairs   studio flat
suburbs   terraced house   view

Adjectives describing places

bustling   clean   dull   enormous
friendly   lively   modern   picturesque
polluted   quiet   tiny   touristy
traditional   ugly   unspoilt
unwelcoming

Compound nouns

air conditioning   bunk bed(s)
central heating   computer screen
DVD player   mobile phone   sofa bed
swimming pool   wall cabinets
washing machine

Environment

adaptable   climate   flooding   fuel
household waste   insulated
recycling   self-sufficient   soundwaves

 Listen to the explanations and vocabulary.

ACTIVEBOOK

 see Writing bank page 155

3 Review and practice

1 Choose the correct words in *italics*.

1 I'm *thinking/will think* of moving house soon.
2 *Will you go/Are you going* out tonight?
3 We would love to come and see you at the weekend, but Lorenzo *is working/will work*.
4 **A:** Who is that at the door?
 B: I'll *go/'m going to go* and see.
5 What *will/are* you going to wear to the theatre tonight?
6 I can't see you on Sunday because I'm *playing/will play* football with some friends.
7 I am too tired to finish the washing up now. I think I'll *do/'m doing* it in the morning.
8 What *are you doing/will you do* after class?

2 Rewrite the sentences using the phrases in brackets so that the meaning stays the same.

I don't know if I'll find a flat I like.
(might not) *I might not find a flat I like.*

1 I think I'll go and look at flats tomorrow.
 (probably) _____
2 I don't think I will be able to afford one right in the centre.
 (probably won't) _____
3 But I have a good chance of finding one in the outskirts of town.
 (might) _____
4 I don't have a lot of time, so it's possible that I won't be able to see very many flats tomorrow.
 (might not) _____
5 But I'm almost certain I'll find one if I keep looking.
 (probably) _____
6 Maybe I'll find a flatmate to help with the bills.
 (could) _____

3 Complete the second sentence so it has the same meaning as the first.

The blue sofa and the green sofa both cost €200.
The blue sofa is *as cheap as* the green sofa.

1 The white cabinet is 96 cm tall, the blue one is 78 cm tall.
 The white cabinet is _____ the blue one.
2 No rooms in the house are bigger than the sitting room.
 The sitting room is _____ in the house.
3 I thought the curtains were very beautiful, but not the rug.
 The curtains were _____ the rug.
4 The sofa was more comfortable when it was new.
 The sofa is not _____ it was when it was new.
5 The bedroom and the bathroom are the warmest rooms in the house.
 The bedroom is one _____ rooms in the house.

4 Complete the sentences with comparative forms of the words in the box. Use *than* if necessary.

> cold   crowded   easy   far
> old-fashioned   picturesque   polluted
> ~~quick~~   quiet

It takes such a long time to drive to Scotland. We usually fly because it's *quicker*.

1 Bangkok is such a noisy city. I'd prefer to live somewhere _____ .
2 There were so many people on the train. It was _____ usual.
3 We saw them a lot when they lived in Paris, but now they have moved _____ away.
4 Our old apartment was much _____ our new one, which is really modern.
5 Look at all the snow! It's much _____ today _____ it was yesterday.
6 Cities are so ugly. I prefer living in the countryside where the views are _____ .
7 Some parts of the city are _____ others because of all the traffic.
8 It's _____ to find your way around New York streets _____ in London because in New York the streets have numbers.

5 Rewrite the letter using the opposite of the underlined words.

Dear Juliana,

I'm here in El Paso for six months. I'm staying in a house in the <u>modern</u> (historical) part of town. The part of town where I'm staying is really (1) <u>clean</u>, (2) <u>picturesque</u> and (3) <u>unspoilt</u>. The house is (4) <u>enormous</u>. During the day it's very (5) <u>quiet</u>. The city centre is very (6) <u>lively</u> at night and I go for a walk with friends most evenings. My landlady is quite (7) <u>unwelcoming</u>.

Speak to you soon.

Clara

Lead-in

1 **a** Work in pairs. If you won a lot of money, would you ...
1 spend it on yourself?
2 spend it on family and friends?
3 give it away to a good cause?
4 put it in a bank and not tell anyone about it?

b Is it possible to have too much money? Why/Why not?

2 **a** Complete the table with the verbs and phrases from the box.

> earn   good value for   have got ... to spare   inherit   invest ... in
> it's not worth the   lend   make   not have enough   run out of   save
> spend   steal   use your ... wisely   waste

Money	Money and time
	spend

b Can you add any more words or phrases to the table in exercise 2a?

3 **a** Write down one thing that ...
1 is a waste of money/good value for money.
2 you'd like to do but you don't have enough time to do.
3 you do to use your time wisely.
4 you spend a lot of money on.
5 you would do today if you had lots of money to spare.
6 you'd like to invest money or time in.

b Work in groups and compare your ideas.

Grammar	question tags
Can do	use intonation to check and confirm information

Reading and listening

1 **a** Look at the photos and film poster. How do you think they are connected?

b Work in pairs. Look at the words in the box from the article below. What do you think the article is about?

> charm cheated consultant egotistical
> good-looking illegally mystery pretended
> prison $3 million trickster

c Read the article. Match the headings (1–5) to the paragraphs (A–E).

1   Childhood and tricks
2   Frank today
3   Wanted all over the world
4   The FBI's opinion of Frank
5   Three top jobs and five happy years

dicaprio   hanks

catch me   if you can

The true story of a real fake.

The true story of a real fake

A _____

Frank Abagnale, a good-looking American boy with more dreams than money, pretended to be first a pilot, then a doctor and then a lawyer.

For five years he travelled the world for free, stayed in expensive hotels and had relationships with beautiful women. By the age of twenty-one he had tricked and cheated his way to $2.5 million.

B _____

In the golden age of James Bond, Abagnale really was an international man of mystery. He was wanted by the FBI and Interpol (International Police) in twenty-six countries. His good looks and greying hair helped him, but his charm was his most important tool. He dressed well and everybody believed the stories he made up. Leonardo DiCaprio, who plays Frank Abagnale in the film *Catch me if you can* said, 'Frank Abagnale is one of the greatest actors who has walked the Earth.'

C _____

Abagnale was a lonely child. When his mother, who was French, broke up with his father, a New York shopkeeper, Abagnale had to choose which parent to live with. Instead, aged sixteen, he dropped out of school, ran away from home and began his life as an international trickster. He used magnetic ink to change bank code numbers illegally. He managed to steal $40,000 of other customers' money before the banks worked out what he was doing. He also got a Pan Am pilot's uniform by saying that his was lost at the dry cleaner's and that he had an urgent flight.

This allowed him to stay in any hotel he wanted: Pan Am always paid the bill. He even pretended to be a doctor and worked as a hospital administrator for a year. With no formal training, he picked up the skills by reading medical books and watching other doctors at work.

D _____

Abagnale broke the law repeatedly. He ran out of luck in France, where he spent time in prison, before the FBI finally caught up with him in the US. Despite his crimes, Abagnale never had any enemies. Joseph Shea, the FBI man who arrested him and later became his friend, said, 'I think Frank is close to genius. What he did as a teenager is incredible. His crimes weren't physical. There were no guns, no knives, he just used his brain. He's charming and I admire him. I think he's a good man and a moral character, but, like anybody, he wants to better himself and in this country, money is the way to do it. He makes $3 million a year and that's a lot more than I ever made.'

E _____

These days Abagnale doesn't need to trick anybody: he is a successful consultant. He advises companies on security, and he also lectures – for free – at the FBI Academy. It is ironic that he has ended up working for the people who were trying to catch him for so long! He wrote his autobiography in the 1970s and sold the film rights for $250,000. Abagnale says, 'When I was twenty-eight I thought it would be great to have a movie about my life, but when I was twenty-eight, like when I was sixteen, I was egotistical and self-centred. We all grow up.' That's true. But not many people grow up like Frank Abagnale.

Vocabulary | phrasal verbs

4 Find nine phrasal verbs in the article and put them in the correct place in the mind maps.

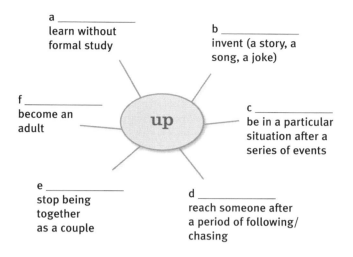

a _____
learn without
formal study

b _____
invent (a story, a
song, a joke)

f _____
become an
adult

up

c _____
be in a particular
situation after a
series of events

e _____
stop being
together
as a couple

d _____
reach someone after
a period of following/
chasing

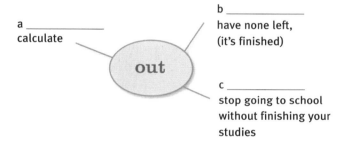

a _____
calculate

b _____
have none left,
(it's finished)

out

c _____
stop going to school
without finishing your
studies

2 a Read the article again and answer the questions.

1 How old was Frank when he left home?

2 What did he look like?

3 How did he get his first $40,000?

4 How did he get a pilot's uniform?

5 Who was Joseph Shea? What type of person do you think he was?

6 What does Frank do now?

7 How does Frank feel about his past?

b ⬤ 1.29 Close your books and listen to a summary of Frank's story. Write down seven mistakes in the summary and correct them.

Frank Abagnale wasn't English. He was American.

3 Work in pairs and discuss the questions.

1 Joseph Shea said, 'I think he's a good man and a moral character.' What do you think of Frank?

2 Frank says, 'I thought it would be great to have a movie about my life.' Would you like a movie about your life? Why/ Why not? Which actor would you choose to act as you?

5 One of the sentence endings is not possible. Which one?

He dropped out of (a) ~~his exams~~ (b) *school* (c) *university*.

You can drop out of school and university but not exams.

1 I broke up with (a) my girlfriend (b) my relationship (c) my husband.

2 They made up (a) stories (b) an excuse (c) acting.

3 We worked out (a) what the problem was (b) the answer (c) wrong.

4 She picked up (a) Spanish very quickly (b) some information (c) a new haircut.

5 We ran out of (a) enough milk (b) money (c) things to do.

6 I caught up with (a) my studies (b) myself (c) you easily.

7 She ended up (a) living with me (b) work as a doctor (c) in Warsaw.

Speaking

6 Work in pairs and retell Abagnale's story using the phrases below.

1 His mother **broke up with** ...

2 He **dropped out of** ...

3 He made $40,000 ... the banks **worked out** what he was doing ...

4 He pretended to be ... he **picked up** the skills by reading medical books ...

5 He **ran out of** luck in France ...

6 The FBI finally **caught up with** him ...

7 He **ended up** working for ...

Listening and speaking

7 **a** Read the text about the Ghosh test below and answer the questions.

1 What is the purpose of the Ghosh test?
2 Who or what was it named after?
3 Does it always work? Why/Why not?

The Ghosh test, named after a famous law case, is a way of judging what are the 'ordinary standards of most reasonable and honest people'. It is used in courts to help the jury decide if the person on trial knew they were being dishonest or not. A recent survey of 15,000 people in Britain, however, has shown that people do not always agree about what is wrong, and, as a result, the Ghosh test may have to be changed.

b Work in small groups. Look at the situations from the Ghosh test survey and try to order them from most (1) to least (6) dishonest.

☐ Taking stationery (pens, paperclips, etc.) home from work.

☐ Buying a dress for a special occasion, wearing it, and then returning it to the shop.

☐ Lying about your age on an Internet dating site.

☐ Switching price labels in a shop so you pay less.

☐ Copying a CD from a friend.

☐ Copying a piece of written work from the Internet.

c ● 1.30 Listen to two friends doing the same task. Do they agree with you?

Grammar | question tags

8 **a** ● 1.31 Look at these extracts from the listening in exercise 7c. Some words have been removed. Listen and add the missing words.

A: OK, so which of these do you think is the most dishonest thing to do?

B: Right, well, I think it would have to be copying work from the Internet.

A: I guess so. What about copying a CD from a friend? I do that a lot.

B: Er, yes, I suppose I shouldn't really. What about taking stationery home from work?

A: I think that depends what it is. I don't think the odd pen is a problem.

b Does the conversation sound more natural with or without the missing words?

c ● 1.32 Now listen to some other extracts (1–7) and decide if the person is really asking a question, or expecting agreement. How do you know?

9 Read the Active grammar box and choose the correct underlined words to complete the rules.

Active grammar

To make question tags, we repeat the *main verb*/*auxiliary verb*. *

If the question is positive, the question tag is *negative*/*positive*.

If the question is negative, the question tag is *negative*/*positive*.

If there is no auxiliary verb, the question tag uses *the main verb*/*do, does or did*.*

*The verb *to be* acts as an auxiliary verb in question tags.

see Reference page 61

10 Complete the questions with the correct question tags.

1 Stealing is wrong, _____ ?
2 You didn't cheat, _____ ?
3 It's illegal, _____ ?
4 You have never stolen anything, _____ ?
5 You don't do that, _____ ?
6 You're copying my answers, _____ ?
7 You will tell me the truth, _____ ?
8 I wouldn't lie to you, _____ ?

Pronunciation | intonation in question tags

11 **a** Listen again to the extracts (1–7) from exercise 8c and choose the correct options.

1 To ask a real question the intonation of the question tag is:

a ⌄ b ⌃

2 When we expect the other person to agree with us, the intonation of the question tag is:

a ⌃ b ⌄

b Work in pairs and practise asking the questions in exercise 10. Decide if your partner is asking a real question, or expecting agreement.

see Pronunciation bank page 164

12 Work in pairs and discuss how you feel about the following things. Use question tags.

• Telling white lies.
• Keeping money you find in the street.
• Copying someone's homework.
• Pretending you haven't got any change when someone asks you for money.
• Telling someone else's secret.

4.2 Getting rich quick

Grammar	modal verbs of obligation and prohibition
Can do	carry out a survey and present results

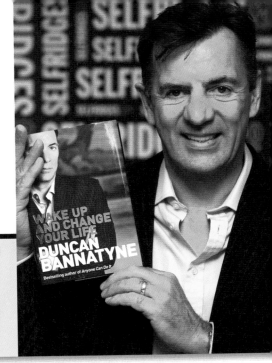

Speaking

1 **a** Work in pairs. Think of as many ways as possible to get rich quickly. Make a list and compare your ideas with another pair.

b Think of some famous multimillionaires. What type of reputation do they have? Do people like and admire them?

Vocabulary | personal qualities (1)

2 **a** Work in pairs. Check you understand the expressions in the box. Check any words you don't know with another pair.

> be ambitious
> be charming
> be confident
> be determined
> be egotistical
> be extravagant
> be flexible
> be generous
> be good with figures
> be good with people
> be mean
> be tolerant
> have a sense of humour
> know your strengths and weaknesses
> work long hours

b Work in pairs and discuss the questions.

1 For which jobs do you need the qualities in the box in exercise 2a?

2 Which qualities do you think you have? Which qualities would you like to have? Why?

3 Look at the definition of *entrepreneur* below. Which qualities and habits do you think are necessary to be a successful entrepreneur?

> **entrepreneur** /ˌɑːntrəprəˈnɜːr/
> someone who starts a company and arranges business deals

Reading

3 **a** Read the article about a British entrepreneur. Which of the qualities in exercise 2a do you think he has?

Duncan Bannatyne is a successful businessman with a chain of health clubs and hotels. He also appears on the BBC series *Dragons' Den*, where he judges new entrepreneurial ideas.

❛ The only thing I enjoyed at school was maths. I had the ability to add up, but my maths teacher didn't have much time for me because I couldn't write down how I got the answers. I hated things like English – I was slightly dyslexic. I was hopeless at sport, too, having no coordination. I could see that the kids who went to high school had better toys than me so I made it my mission to do as well as I could, so that I could pass the exam and get into the best school. I worked hard, and when I passed – I was the only one in the family who did – my parents were so proud of me.

I started delivering newspapers when my mother said I couldn't have an ice cream because we were too poor. When I went to the newsagent's, he told me that there was no need for a delivery boy. I said that my mother would like her paper delivered, but he told me, 'That's one person; I need 100.' I knocked on 150 doors. When the ice cream van came around again, I had enough money to buy ice creams for my whole family.

When I left school, I didn't use my entrepreneurial skills for fifteen years. I was in the Navy and then worked as a garage mechanic. It was always at the back of my mind, though. When I was twenty-nine, I was on a beach in the Channel Islands with my girlfriend and we decided to go back to the mainland and make money. Believe it or not, my first entrepreneurial venture was *Duncan's Super Ices*, which expanded from a single ice cream van to a small fleet. ❜

Adapted from *The Independent*.

b Read the article again and write true (T) or false (F).

1 Bannatyne's favourite school subject was English. ☐

2 He wasn't very good at sports. ☐

3 He wanted to go to high school to make his parents proud. ☐

4 When he left school he worked as a mechanic before joining the navy. ☐

5 He was nearly thirty when he set up his first business. ☐

c Do you think Duncan Bannatyne has the qualities and habits of a typical entrepreneur? Why/Why not?

Listening

4 **a** 🔊 1.33 Listen to the first part of a seminar and answer the questions. Who is it for? What is the topic?

b 🔊 1.34 Listen to the rest of the seminar. What entrepreneurial qualities does the speaker mention?

c Listen again and complete the notes below.

How to be an entrepreneur

Be mean. You **shouldn't** (1) _____ . You **should** start (2) _____ . You **mustn't** (3) _____ your money. Bill Gates doesn't care about looking good because he **doesn't have to** (4) _____ . Be confident. You **must** (5) _____ in yourself. You **have to** work (6) _____ . Be ambitious.

Grammar | modals of obligation and prohibition

5 Match the modal verbs in **bold** in exercise 4c with the correct meaning (A–E) in the Active grammar box. Then answer the question.

Active grammar

A I strongly advise you to do it.
1 _____ 2 _____

C It's the right thing to do, in my opinion.
3 _____

B I strongly advise you not to do it.
4 _____

D It isn't the right thing to do in my opinion.
5 _____

E It is not necessary but you can do it if you want to.
6 _____

Look at these pairs of sentences. In each case do the modal verbs express advice (A) or obligation (O)?

1 *You **mustn't** smoke in here.*
  *You **mustn't** waste your money.*

2 *You **have to** wear a suit to work.*
  *You **have to** see that film!*

3 *You **must** believe in yourself.*
  *You **must** have a passport if you want to enter the country.*

See Reference page 61

6 Complete this advice for people setting up their own business with a suitable modal verb from the Active grammar box in exercise 5. Use each modal verb once.

1 You _____ have a good idea.
2 It _____ be different from anything else on the market.
3 You _____ have financial skills as well as technical skills.
4 You _____ buy expensive equipment – try renting it.
5 You _____ give up easily.
6 You _____ start a business just because you can't find a job.

7 **a** Complete the second sentence so it means the same as the first, using a suitable modal verb. More than one answer may be possible.

1 It is essential not to give up.
  You _____ give up.
2 It is not necessary to work twenty-four hours a day.
  You _____ work twenty-four hours a day.
3 He can't go home until he has switched off all the lights.
  He _____ switch off all the lights before he goes home.
4 Smoking is forbidden here.
  You _____ smoke here.
5 I think it's a good idea to have a plan.
  You _____ have a plan.
6 I strongly suggest you get an accountant.
  You _____ get an accountant.

b Decide whether each sentence in exercise 7a is giving advice (A) or talking about obligation or prohibition (O).

Pronunciation | connected speech

8 **a** 🔊 1.35 Listen to these extracts from the seminar. What happens to the sounds in brackets?

1 You mus(t) believe in yourself.
2 You mus(t)n('t) waste your money.
3 Bill Gates doesn('t) wear a suit.
4 Don('t) spen(d) money on expensive holidays.
5 You shouldn('t) think about the limits of your business.

b Choose the correct rule.

1 /t/ and /d/ are often not sounded after a vowel sound.
2 /t/ and /d/ are often not sounded when they come before a consonant sound.
3 /t/ and /d/ are often not sounded when they are between two other consonants.

c Listen again and repeat.

See Pronunciation bank page 164

Reading

9 **a** Work in pairs. What advice would you give someone who wanted to be rich?

b Read the article. Does it mention any of your ideas?

10 **a** Read the article again and complete the following sentences, according to what the article says.

1 If you see a bargain in the sales you should …
2 You should never go food shopping without …
3 You should only buy high fashion if …
4 If you are buying something expensive, make sure you …

b Do you think the advice in the article is useful? Why/Why not?

Vocabulary | shopping

11 **a** Look at the article again and find words and phrases connected with shopping. Put them in the table below.

Verbs	Nouns	Adjectives
spend	money	cheap(er)

b Check your ideas on page 147.

Speaking

12 **a** You are going to carry out a survey to find out more about people's attitudes to money. Work in small groups. Look at the questions and write four more yes/no questions. Use ideas from the article, or your own ideas.

1 Do you often buy things on impulse?
2 Do you think it is a good idea to write a shopping list before you go food shopping? Why/Why not?

b Now interview other people in your class. Make sure you each interview different people.

c Tell people in your group what you found out and combine your information.

d Tell the class your results. Use the language in the How to… box.

How to… report survey results

Most (of)	: the class	: said …
Three (of)	: the people	: thought …
Quite a few (of)	: we interviewed	: believed …
Hardly any (of)	: people	:

GOOD WITH MONEY

Most people think that being good with money is about saving it rather than spending it. However, what's most important is how and why you spend it. Ask yourself:

Do I need it, can I afford it, can I get it cheaper somewhere else?

Impulse buys

An impulse buy is when we buy something that we hadn't originally planned to. Often this is because we see something reduced in the sales. 'Oh look', we think, 'what a bargain, I can save £50 buying this'. But it isn't saving £50, it's spending £100 on something you don't actually need. If you are about to buy something like this, put it down and wait a day. It gives you time to decide if you really do need it.

Food shopping

Very often we end up throwing away part of what we've bought, or ending up with a lot more at the checkout than we planned. Don't go food shopping when you're hungry – you'll end up with a trolley full of junk food. And make a shopping list and stick to it.

Clothes shopping

Fashion is a way for businesses to make lots of money selling us things we don't need. A high fashion item can only be worn a few times before it's out of fashion. Can you really afford to pay hundreds of pounds for something you'll only wear a few times? If you want to follow high fashion, make sure you buy it really cheaply.

Shop around

Never buy any big ticket item without shopping around to see where you can get it most cheaply. The Internet can really help here, with lots of price comparison websites to make sure you're getting the best deal. Take a look at the reviews as well, to make sure you're not making an expensive mistake. Always keep the receipt in case you need a refund.

4.3 Spend more!

Grammar	Zero and First Conditionals with *if/when/unless/as soon as*
Can do	ask for and give clarification

Reading and speaking

1 Work in pairs. Look at the photos and discuss the questions.

   1 How do supermarkets/salespeople/ advertisements persuade people to spend money?

   2 Have you ever bought something because you saw an advert, or bought something from a supermarket you didn't plan to buy? Why?

2 Decide what information could complete the sentences.

   1 Good salespeople can sell _____ , to _____ , at _____ .

   2 Most salespeople will get to know their client by asking questions about _____ , _____ and _____ .

   3 Salespeople may try to 'mirror' the _____ of a buyer.

   4 People in the UK buy _____ percent of their food in supermarkets.

   5 Supermarkets often _____ to help us relax.

   6 Supermarkets became very successful after introducing _____ in the 1950s.

   7 Advertisements which use _____ are ten percent more effective.

   8 Advertisements are more memorable if they are _____ .

   9 Chocolate adverts should make your _____ .

3 Work in groups of three.

Student A: read about salespeople on this page.
Student B: read about supermarkets on page 147.
Student C: read about advertising on page 151.

Which sentences from exercise 2 are in your article?

4 Work in your groups and check your answers to exercise 2. Does any of the information surprise you?

5 Work in your groups and discuss the questions.

   1 What are your favourite/least favourite advertisements? Why?

   2 Do you prefer shopping at supermarkets or small, specialised shops? Why?

   3 Have you ever bought something that you didn't really want because of a good salesperson? What happened?

How you are persuaded to spend more by ...

salespeople.

If you really believe in a product, this will help you sell it. But the best professional salespeople can sell anything, to anybody, at any time. They do this by using very simple psychological techniques. It is human nature to prefer to speak rather than to listen, and good salespeople use this. They ask buyers what they want before showing how their product is the best.

Most salespeople will get to know their client by asking questions about hobbies, family and lifestyle. If customers think of the salesperson as a friend, they will probably keep coming back to the same man or woman.

Salespeople will try to behave like the buyer. If the buyer makes jokes, the salesperson does too. If the buyer wants detail, the seller provides it. The salesperson may even try to 'mirror' the body language of the buyer. Lastly, salespeople will use careful language. They will not say 'if you buy ...', bu 'when you buy', so that they cannot fail.

Warning signs:

- Body language: when the salesperson moves away from the desk, or towards the door, it gives the impression that the sale is complete.
- Appointment book open: it is hard to say 'no' when the salesperson is already making an appointment.
- Repetition: the salesperson repeats the last phrase you said. It gives the illusion of interest.

Grammar | Zero and First Conditionals with *if/ when/unless/as soon as*

6 **a** Read the example sentences (1–6) in the Active grammar box. Use the rules A and B to decide if they are Zero Conditionals or First Conditionals.

b Look at the sentences (1–6) in the Active Grammar box again. Then complete the rules in C with the words in the box below.

c Underline six more examples of the First Conditional in the three articles on pages 56, 147 and 151.

Active grammar

1 ***If*** *customers think of the salesperson as a friend, they* ***will*** *probably keep coming back to the same man or woman.*

2 ***If*** *I buy lots now, I* ***won't*** *have to come back later.*

3 ***If*** *the advertisement makes us feel good, then we* ***start*** *to associate good feelings with the product.*

4 *Supermarkets usually* ***offer*** *these* ***when*** *a fruit and vegetable is in season.*

5 ***As soon as*** *you walk into the shop, you* ***can*** *smell bread and coffee.*

6 ***Unless*** *you buy this (face cream), you* ***will*** *look old.*

Zero and First Conditionals

A Zero Conditional sentences describe real or possible situations that are always true.

We use *if* + present tense + present tense or a modal verb.

B First Conditional sentences describe situations in the future which we see as a real possibility.

We use *if* + present tense + *will* or a modal verb.

The order of the clauses can be reversed.

C (when   unless   as soon as)

For Zero Conditionals, *if* and (1) _____ have the same meaning.

For First Conditionals, we use (2) _____ rather than *if* to show that something is 100 percent certain to happen.

We use (3) _____ instead of *if* to emphasise that an event happens immediately.

(4) _____ + positive verb means the same as *if ... not*.

---

see Reference page 61

7 Match the beginnings of the sentences in A with the endings in B.

A	B
1 I will miss everyone	a we might make fewer mistakes.
2 I will be home by six	b unless it rains.
3 If we study hard,	c when I leave my job.
4 I will show my friends around the city	d when they arrive.
5 I will buy a new suit	e as soon as I get paid.
6 I am going to have a barbecue	f unless the train is delayed.

8 **a** Rewrite the sentences below three times using the words a–c. How does the meaning change?

1 If they offer me the job, I will take it.
   a when
   b might
   c as soon as

2 When I see Tom, I'll tell him.
   a as soon as
   b If
   c can

b Rewrite the sentences below using *unless*. Make any other necessary changes.

1 If you don't pay the bill on time, you'll get a fine.

2 If there isn't something urgent to discuss, he won't phone us.

3 I will help you if you help me.

4 If Sandro doesn't find an apartment soon, he'll have to stay at home.

5 If you work hard, you'll do well in your exams.

6 It will be a great day out if it doesn't rain.

Speaking

9 **a** Complete the sentences so they are true for you.

I'll study tonight if I have time.

1 I'll buy a new ... as soon as ...

2 I'll ... next weekend if ...

3 If there is enough time ... , I'll ...

4 I'll go on holiday ... unless ...

5 I'll change my ... when ...

b Work in pairs and discuss your sentences.

Listening and speaking

10 Work in pairs. Look at the advertisements and discuss the questions.

1 What are these advertisements for? Do you think they work? Why/Why not?
2 Do you like watching advertisements on TV? Why/Why not?
3 Are there any advertisements which you particularly like/dislike? Describe them to your partner and explain why.

11 a ⊕ 1.36 What do you think 'behavioural advertising' might be? Listen to a radio programme and check your ideas.

b Look at the statements below. Then listen again and write true (T) or false (F) according to the speakers.

1 It is easier to avoid watching ads on TV nowadays. ☐
2 Companies who use behavioural advertising know what websites you have visited. ☐
3 Companies who use behavioural advertising know where you live and work. ☐
4 Ninety-five percent of people in a recent poll liked the idea of behavioural advertising. ☐
5 Sixty percent of people in the same poll would rather have adverts than pay for online content. ☐

c Work in pairs and discuss the questions.

1 How do you feel about behavioural advertising?
2 Would you rather have adverts or pay for online content? Why?

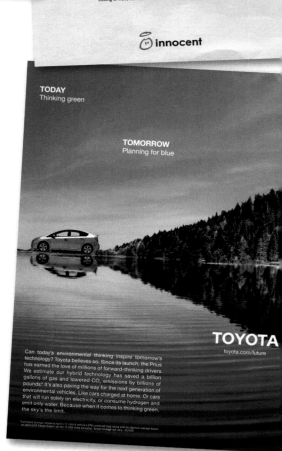

12 a Read the How to... box. Then listen again and tick (✓) the phrases you hear.

How to... ask for clarification

Asking for clarification	*I'm sorry, I didn't quite get that ...*
	Could you explain that again?
	Sorry, I'm not with you.
Checking that you have understood	*Are you saying that ... ?*
	So what you're saying is that ... ?
	Do you mean ... ?

b Choose a topic from the list below and make notes about an object or activity you know about.

- how to make something (e.g. a cake)
- how something works (e.g. a mobile phone)
- how to do something (e.g. play a sport)

c Work in pairs. Take it in turns to explain your object or activity. Ask your partner for clarification.

1 Work in pairs. Discuss the difference in meaning between each pair of words.

1 debit card/credit card
2 receipt/bill
3 coin/note
4 fare/fine
5 price/fee
6 reduction/refund
7 change/cash

2 Choose the correct word in *italics*.

1 a Hurry up. We're going to *lose/miss* the bus.
  b I have *lost/missed* my wallet. I can't find it anywhere.
2 a Did you have a good *travel/trip*?
  b My job involves a lot of *travel/trip*.
3 a Yes, I enjoyed the picnic. It was good *fun/funny*.
  b Charlie Chaplin films are so *fun/funny* that I laugh out loud.
4 a He *said/told* me to come at 11:00.
  b He *said/told* the train was late.
5 a She found a good *work/job* in a bank.
  b She is lazy and doesn't like *work/job*.
6 a She is going to *lend/borrow* me another book.
  b Can I *borrow/lend* your pen?
7 a Can you *remember/remind* me to call Giovanni tomorrow?
  b I can never *remember/remind* his name!
8 a The National Bank was *robbed/stolen* last week.
  b $200 million was *robbed/stolen*.

3 Read the Lifelong learning box. Then write similar notes for the other words in *italics* in exercise 2.

Lifelong learning

Personalising vocabulary

❗ Write notes to help you remember how to **use** new vocabulary. A good dictionary will help you. For example:

rob/steal
You *steal* something from someone/somewhere but you *rob* a place, e.g. a bank.

travel/trip
Travel is a general word for talking about moving from one place to another. *Trip* refers to a specific journey and the time you spend there, e.g. business trip.

fun/funny
Use *fun* to talk about activities you enjoy doing. *Funny* describes something that makes you laugh.

say/tell
You *say* something (to someone) but you *tell* someone something, or *tell* someone to do something.

4 Complete the sentences with words from exercises 1 and 2.

1 Am I too early? You _____ me the shop opens at 8:00 a.m.
2 I can _____ you €10. Can you pay me back soon?
3 'Waiter! Could we have the _____ , please?'
4 I have come to report a crime. My bag was _____ last night.
5 Do you have any _____ for the bus? I only have a £5 note and I need the exact money.
6 On my last holiday I went on a _____ to India.
7 I parked my car in a no-parking area and had to pay a _____ .
8 That's great! Jenny got the new _____ she applied for.
9 Do you think the Mr Bean films are _____ ? I always laugh when I watch them.
10 I'm sorry I'm late. I _____ the train.
11 I prefer to use a _____ card so I can pay later.
12 I'm sorry but this jumper doesn't fit. Can I have a _____ , please?
13 The museum charges an entrance _____ .

5 Choose ten words on this page you find particularly difficult to remember. Write sentences which are true for you using these words.

When I buy something I always put the receipt in my bag.

4 Communication

Can do give reasons for opinions

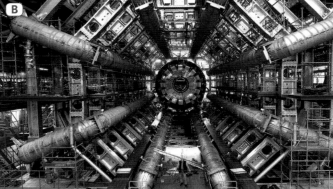

1 **a** Work in pairs and look at the photos. What does each one show? How much money do you think was spent on each thing? Match the numbers (1–3) to the photos (A–C).

1 $4.6 billion   2 $140 million   3 $85.00

b Read the article to check your answers.

2 **a** 🔵 1.37 Listen to Polly and Jonathon discussing the article. Which thing(s) ...

1 does only Jonathon think is a waste of money?

2 do they both think is a good use of money?

3 do they both think is a waste of money?

b Listen again. What reasons do they give for their opinions?

3 **a** Work in two groups.

Group A: choose three facts from the article. Think of reasons why they are/were a waste of money. Use *as*, *if* and *because*.

Spending $13.4 million on an advert is a complete waste of money because/as most people don't watch them anyway.

If you've got money to spare, why spend it on a sandwich? You could have a great meal for that!

Group B: choose three facts from the article. Think of reasons why they are/were a good use of money. Use *as*, *if* and *because*.

The Large Hadron Collider is worth the money if it tells us how the Universe started.

I think Superman 3 was good value for money as/because it was such a popular film.

b Work with a student from the other group. Discuss your facts and why you think they were a waste of money/worth spending money on.

4 **a** Work in pairs and choose one of the statements below that you both agree or disagree with. Think of three good reasons for your opinions.

1 Taxes should be quite high to make society a better place.

2 All money should be lent interest-free.

3 Lottery prizes should be no higher than $1 million.

4 People should not be allowed to leave their money to their children.

5 No one should be starving when there is enough money in the world to go round.

b Find new partners and discuss your statements, giving reasons for your opinions.

Film: *Superman 3* cost $258 million, the most ever spent on making a film. However, if you take inflation into account, *Cleopatra* (1963), which cost $44 million, beats it, at $295 million in today's money. The film, starring Elizabeth Taylor, nearly bankrupted the film company. However, the Soviet-produced *War and Peace* cost $100 million in 1968, which is over $500 million in today's money.

Man on the moon: it cost the US approximately $2.2 billion (which around $40–50 billion in today's money) to send a man to the moon.

Painting: Jackson Pollock's painting, *Number 5, 1948*, sold for $140 million in 2006.

Science: the Large Hadron Collider in Geneva, Switzerland has been created to try and discover how the Universe began. The cost so far – $4.6 billion.

Advertising: a British insurance company spent $13.4 million in 200 on an ad starring Bruce Willis and Elle McPherson. The point of the a To let the public know the company had changed its name.

Sandwich: the most expensive sandwich in the world was created in 2006 for $85. The cost was due to the beef used, which came fro Japanese Wagyu cows, raised on a special diet and regularly massag

Phone number: The phone number 8888 8888 was bought by Sichuan Airlines Co. Ltd (China) for $280, 723. Why? The number eight is a lucky number in China.

Question tags

Affirmative statements use a negative tag.
*They **are** French, **aren't** they?*

We use this structure when you think the answer is *yes*.

Negative statements use an affirmative tag.
*I **won't** be needed, **will** I?*

We use this structure when we think the answer is *no*.

If there is no auxiliary verb, use *do*, *does* or *did*, or their negatives.
*She **went** home, **didn't** she?*

For short answers, we also use the auxiliary verb.
*She **doesn't** eat meat, **does** she?*
*No, she **doesn't**.*

To ask a 'real' question, where we want to check information, the intonation of the question tag goes down, then up.

When we expect the other person to agree with us, the intonation of the question tag goes up, then down.

Modals of obligation and prohibition

Obligation

Have to is often used for rules/ regulations.
*You **have to** show your passport at Customs.* (It's a law.)

Must is often used when the obligation comes from the speaker. *Must* is never followed by *to*.
*I **must** stop smoking.* (I think this.)

Both *have to* and *must* can also be used to advise someone strongly to do something.
*You **must** start looking after yourself better!*

Prohibition

Mustn't means *it is prohibited/not allowed*.
*You **mustn't** eat in the classroom.*

No obligation

Don't have to means you have a choice.
*You **don't have to** wear a suit to work.* (It's not necessary but you can if you want to.)

Recommendation

*You **should** go.* (It's a good idea.)
*You **shouldn't** smoke.* (It isn't a good idea.)

Zero and First Conditional with *if/when/unless/as soon as*

Zero Conditional

To talk about real or possible situations which are always true we can use *if* + present tense + present tense (or a modal verb).
*If it **rains** (generally), I **stay** at home.*

First Conditional

To talk about real possibilities in the future we can use *if* + Present Simple + *will/can/should/may* (and other modal verbs).
*If it **rains** (on a specific future occasion), I'**ll** stay at home.*

when/as soon as/unless

Unless means *if not*.
Unless it rains, I'll go out.

We use *when* to show the situation is certain.
When you visit, I'll cook dinner. (It's certain that you will visit)

We use *as soon as* to emphasise that an event happens immediately.
As soon as I see him, I'll tell him.

! We don't usually use *if* + *will* in conditional sentences.

We can reverse the clauses and remove the comma.
If it rains, I stay at home.   I stay at home if it rains.

Key vocabulary

Time and money verbs
earn   good value for   have got ... to spare   inherit   invest in   it's not worth the   lend   make   not have enough   run out of   steal   use your ... wisely   waste

Phrasal verbs
break up with   catch up with   drop out of   end up   grow up   make up   pick up   run out of   work out

Personal qualities (1)
ambitious   charming   confident   determined   egotistical   extravagant   flexible   generous   good with figures   good with people   have a sense of humour   know your strengths and weaknesses   mean   tolerant   work long hours

Shopping
afford   bargain   big ticket item   cash   cheap   checkout   credit card   debit card   expensive   impulse buy   price comparison websites   purchase   receipt   reduced   refund   save   spend   shop around   the sales

Easily confused words
coin/note   fare/fine   fun/funny   lend/borrow   miss/lose   receipt/bill   change/cash   remember/remind   rob/steal   say/tell   travel/trip   work/job

 Listen to the explanations and vocabulary.
ACTIVEBOOK

 see Writing bank page 156

1 Complete the questions with the correct question tags.

1 I can't park here, _____ ?
2 I need to phone him, _____ ?
3 The guests will be here soon, _____ ?
4 She had a headache, _____ ?
5 This match is boring, _____ ?
6 I'm a genius, _____ ?
7 We're going out later, _____ ?
8 They haven't called yet, _____ ?
9 I shouldn't give her the money, _____ ?
10 You woke up early this morning, _____ ?

2 Match the questions (1–10) in exercise 1 with the answers (a–j).

a No, they haven't.
b Yes, we are.
c No, you can't.
d No, you shouldn't.
e Yes, it is.
f No, you're not.
g Yes, you do.
h Yes, I did.
i Yes, they will.
j Yes, she did.

3 Read the text. Some lines have one extra, incorrect word. Write the extra word in the space or tick (✓) if there is no extra word.

Memo to: all staff **From:** management	
At the meeting we agreed on some rules.	✓
All staff should look smart to	to
at all times but workers don't never have	___
to wear a suit unless requested. Staff	___
must to go outside to smoke and should	___
try not to blow smoke in through the	___
windows. Workers mustn't not leave dirty	___
cups in the workspaces and food must not	___
to be consumed in the office. Staff do	___
not have to be eat in the canteen, but	___
lunch breaks must not have exceed one hour.	___

4 Choose the correct words in *italics*.

1 People under eighteen *don't have to/mustn't* smoke in England. It's illegal.
2 You *don't have to/mustn't* eat if you don't want to. It's your choice.
3 You *don't have to/mustn't* be late for work.
4 Ken's so rich he *doesn't have to/mustn't* work.
5 We *don't have to/mustn't* miss the last bus.
6 Markus *doesn't have to/mustn't* work on Sundays, but he often goes into the office.

5 Complete the sentences with *if*, *when* or *unless*.

1 _____ you want to make a lot of money, you'll have to work hard.
2 You won't be successful _____ you're very determined.
3 _____ you are good with figures, don't do your own business accounts.
4 You should leave your desk tidy _____ you finish work each day.
5 No one else will believe in you _____ you don't believe in yourself.
6 _____ you have a good business idea you could make a lot of money.

6 Correct the mistake in each sentence.

1 If I will see you tomorrow, I will give you the book.
2 She won't act in the film unless that she receives her normal salary.
3 We'll go as soon the taxi arrives.
4 If I drink another cup of coffee, I will be not able to sleep tonight.
5 I can't hear you unless you don't shout.
6 When I next go shopping, I'll to buy some milk.
7 Unless you drive carefully, you won't crash.
8 As soon as you will see him, call me.

7 Complete the sentences with the words in the box.

> advert   around   figures   lend   picked
> refund   run   trip   up   value

1 I can't even buy you a coffee because I've _____ out of money.
2 This computer only cost me $400. Do you think that is good _____ for money?
3 **A:** What's wrong with Joe?
   B: He's just broken _____ with his girlfriend.
4 **A:** I didn't know you could speak Russian.
   B: Yes, I _____ it up when I was living there.
5 My wife deals with the money for the business, because I'm not very good with _____ .
6 Before I buy anything big, I always shop _____ to try and get the best price.
7 We need to find a new flatmate, so we're putting an _____ in the local paper.
8 **A:** I'm flying to Paris in the morning.
   B: Have a good _____ !
9 The MP3 player I bought didn't work, so I took it back for a _____ .
10 Can you _____ me some money until the end of the month?

Lead-in

1 Work in pairs and look at the photos. Do you do any of the activities in your free time? What kind of person likes these activities?

2 a Put the activities/equipment in the box into the correct columns.

> ~~aerobics~~   a musical instrument   athletics   cards   climbing
> computer games   cooking   cycling   dancing   drawing   exercise
> football   horse riding   jogging   karate   painting   photography
> reading   sailing   skiing   snowboarding   socialising   squash
> surfing   swimming   volleyball

Play	Go	Do	No verb
		aerobics	

b 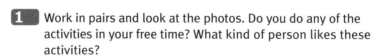 1.38 Listen and check your answers. Mark the word stress.

3 Think of three activities you enjoy. What equipment do you need for them? Use the words in the box to help you.

> belt   board   boots   brush   canvas   costume   goggles   helmet
> net   poles   racquet   rope   saddle   trainers

4 Work in pairs and discuss the questions.
1   Which activities do you do now/did you do when you were younger?
2   Which activities are/were you good at/hopeless at?
3   When/Why did you start (or stop) doing these activities?

Grammar	Present Perfect Continuous and Present Perfect Simple
Can do	describe your response to a picture

Speaking and listening

1 Work in pairs and look at the paintings. Which do you like/dislike? Why?

2 **a** 🔵 1.39 Listen to three people talking about the paintings at an exhibition. Number the pictures in the order they talk about them.

b Look at the How to... box. Then listen again and tick (✓) the phrases you hear.

> ### How to... describe your response to a picture
>
> *It makes me feel ...*
> *It reminds me of ...*
> *I think it's meant to show ...*
> *I like the way ...*
> *It looks (as if) ...*

c Look at the adjectives in the box. Which adjectives do the speakers use to describe each poster? Listen again and check.

> colourful   depressing   disturbing
> intriguing   odd   sad   striking
> unusual   vivid

3 Work in pairs. Choose one of the paintings on this page or another painting you know and describe it using the phrases in the How to... box.

4 **a** Work in pairs. Which of these activities do you think is creative? Why/Why not?

- painting
- learning a language
- writing poems or stories
- housework
- discovering a new scientific theory
- cooking
- solving a problem at work

b Which of these definitions of creativity do you agree with?

Being creative is about creating works of art: painting; music; poems and so on.

Being creative is about using your imagination to do anything. Everyone is creative in different ways.

To be truly creative you have to be original; to do something in a completely new way.

5 **a** 🌐 1.40 Listen to Mike, Tom and Ruth talking about creativity and answer the questions.

1 Which definition in exercise 4b does each speaker agree with?

2 What does each speaker do that is creative?

b Listen again. Who says these phrases? Write *Mike*, *Tom* or *Ruth*.

1 I've been trying to open my own restaurant for ages ...

2 I've given some away as birthday presents ...

3 I've been playing with my three children this morning and the room is a complete mess ...

4 I've made up lots of my own recipes.

5 I've been taking classes ... for three months.

c Work in pairs. What do you do that is creative? Tell your partner.

Grammar | Present Perfect Continuous and Present Perfect Simple

6 **a** Look at the sentences in exercise 5b. Which use the Present Perfect Simple and which use the Present Perfect Continuous?

b Read the Active grammar box. Then match the example sentences (1–3) with the rules (A–C).

1 I've been trying to phone you.

2 I've been studying Chinese since last year.

3 I've been trying to lose weight for the summer.

Active grammar

We use both the Present Perfect Simple and Continuous to talk about actions/states or activities which have some connection to now.

We use the Present Perfect Continuous (*have*/*has* + *been* + *ing*) ...

A to emphasise how long something has taken.
I've been trying to start my own business for ages.
e.g. sentence _____

B to indicate that an activity or a situation is temporary or incomplete.
I've been staying here while I try to buy a flat.
e.g. sentence _____

C to emphasise the repetition of an activity.
I've been going jogging every night.
e.g. sentence _____

7 The sentences below use the wrong verb tenses. Work in pairs and say why the underlined tenses are wrong.

1 A: How long <u>have you waited</u>?
B: Hours!

2 <u>I've cleaned</u> this morning. I've almost finished.

3 A: <u>I've been giving up</u> smoking!
B: That's great. Do you feel healthier?

4 A: How long <u>have you been knowing</u> Jim?
B: About two months.

5 Sorry I haven't seen much of you lately, <u>I've played tennis</u> every weekend.

Pronunciation | weak forms

8 **a** 🌐 1.41 Listen to the following sentences. What happens to the pronunciation of *have* and *been*?

1 I've been swimming.

2 I've been learning Chinese.

3 We've been living abroad.

4 They've been looking after me.

b Listen again and repeat.

see Pronunciation bank page 164

9 **a** Read the blog and complete it with the Present Perfect Simple or Present Perfect Continuous form of the verb in brackets. Sometimes both may be possible.

What I've been doing lately ...

This morning is the first time for a while I *have been able to* (be able to) to write my blog. The last few weeks (1) _____ (be) very busy. I (2) _____ (work) hard on a new painting. When it's finished, it's going to be part of an exhibition at Newport Gallery. I (3) _____ (never/exhibit) there before but it is a lovely space.

Jon (4) _____ (start) his new job. He seems to be enjoying it and he (5) _____ (make) a lot of new friends.

And we (6) _____ (look) at houses. We (7) _____ (stay) with my parents while we try to find the perfect place. It isn't that easy. I (8) _____ (see) one I liked but Jon wasn't very keen.

b Write your own blog about what you have been doing lately.

c Work in pairs. Show your partner your blog and answer their questions about it.

see Reference page 75

Reading

10 Work in pairs and discuss the questions.

1 Is everyone imaginative?
2 Which is more important for artists: hard work or inspiration?
3 Are there any techniques which can help us to develop our imagination?
4 Are children more creative than adults?

11 **a** Read the first paragraph of the article. Which of the questions in exercise 10 does it discuss?

b Read the rest of the article and put the paragraph headings (a–c) in the correct places 1–3.

a No limits!
b Be someone else!
c Making connections

12 Read the article again and answer the questions.

1 Which statement is true?
  a Most people aren't imaginative.
  b Only children are imaginative.
  c We are all imaginative.
2 How does the first technique work?
  a You link your problem with an image or word.
  b You link your problem with the word 'match'.
  c You have to think of a present for a friend.
3 In the second technique, what must you imagine?
  a That you are rich.
  b That you aren't limited in any way.
  c That you can ski.
4 What do you do in the third technique?
  a Imagine you are a negotiator.
  b Imagine you are a different person.
  c Imagine you are a fiction writer.
5 In the third technique, what type of questions should you ask?
  a Questions about other people's shoes.
  b Questions about business techniques.
  c Questions about motivation and making changes.

Speaking

13 **a** Work in groups. Look at the problems on page 147 and discuss how to solve them.

b Tell another group what you discussed, what creativity techniques you used, and what solutions you found.

c Read the solutions to the problems on page 148. Are they similar to your ideas?

---

3 ways to become more creative

Most people believe they don't have much imagination. They are wrong. Everyone has imagination, but most of us, once we become adults, forget how to access it. Creativity isn't always connected with great works of art or ideas. People at work and in their free time routinely think of creative ways to solve problems. Maybe you have a goal to achieve, a tricky question to answer or you just want to expand your mind! Here are three techniques to help you.

1 ____

This technique involves taking unrelated ideas and trying to find links between them. First, think about the problem you have to solve or the job you need to do. Then find an image, word, idea or object, for example, a candle. Write down all the ideas/words associated with candles: light, fire, matches, wax, night, silence, etc. Think of as many as you can. The next stage is to relate the ideas to the job you have to do. So imagine you want to buy a friend an original present; you could buy him tickets to a match or take him out for the night.

2 ____

Imagine that normal limitations don't exist. You have as much time/space/money, etc. as you want. Think about your goal and the new possibilities. If, for example, your goal is to learn to ski, you can now practise skiing every day of your life (because you have the time and the money). Now adapt this to reality. Maybe you can practise skiing every day in December, or every Monday in January.

3 ____

Look at the situation from a different point of view. Good negotiators use this technique in business, and so do writers. Fiction writers often imagine they are the characters in their books. They ask questions: what does this character want? Why can't she get it? What changes must she make to get what she wants? What does she dream about? If your goal involves other people, put yourself 'in their shoes'. The best fishermen think like fish!

5.2 Time well spent?

Listening

1 a Look at the activities in the box. How much time do you think you spend doing these things each day?

> playing computer games   reading
> sport and exercise   watching TV and DVDs
> working or studying   shopping   housework
> sleeping   eating   anything else

b Work in pairs and compare your answers.

2 🔘 1.42 Read the information about Hannah Cheung. Then listen to an interview with Hannah and complete the information in the diagram below.

Hannah Cheung is a film-maker. Recently she timed everything she did for one month for a film she is planning to make. The diagram below shows how she spends her free time.

8%	(1) _____
20%	HOUSEWORK
(2) ___	WATCHING TV
9%	GOING OUT WITH FRIENDS
(3) ___	READING
7%	(4) _____
15%	CINEMA AND DVDS
16%	OTHER

3 a Listen again and complete the notes.

Hannah says:
I didn't **expect** to see these results …
I **can't stand** (1) _____ .
I **don't mind** (2) _____ the housework but it's not very interesting …
I'd **prefer** (3) _____ less of that kind of thing.
I **enjoy** reading …
I always **look forward to** (4) _____ a new book.
I **love** cooking …
I **try** (5) _____ a proper meal at least four nights a week.
I often **invite** (6) _____ over to have dinner …
I never **manage** (7) _____ much exercise.
I never **seem** to find the time.
That's one thing I'd **like** (8) _____ .

b Look at the audioscript for track 1.42 on page 170 to check your answers.

Grammar | *-ing* and infinitive

4 a Read the Active grammar box and put the words in **bold** from exercise 3a under the correct headings (A–D).

b Now put the verbs in the box under the headings (A–D).

> adore   advise   agree   allow   decide   hate
> refuse   remember   remind   stop

Active grammar

When one verb follows another, the second verb is either an *-ing* form (e.g. *going*) or an infinitive (e.g. *to go*).

A Verbs followed by an *-ing* form
can't stand, mind, …

B Verbs followed by the infinitive
expect, prefer, …

C Verbs followed by object + infinitive
told, tell, invite, …

D Verbs followed by *-ing* or infinitive (usually with a change in meaning)
*I tried **to call** him but he was out.*
(make an attempt)
*Have you tried **calling** him?*
(do something to see what will happen)
try, …

see Reference page 75

5 Choose the correct words in *italics*.

1 What hobbies do you enjoy *doing/to do* in a big group/alone?
2 What do you expect *doing/to do* in your free time when you are old?
3 Is there any housework that you can't stand *doing/to do*?
4 What should you stop *to do/doing* if you want to be healthier?
5 Is there anything you stop *to do/doing* on your way home from class?
6 Who would you most like to invite *to go/going* out for dinner?

Speaking

6 Work in groups. Ask and answer the questions in exercise 5. Tell other students what you found out.

Reading

 7 **a** Work in pairs and discuss the questions.

1 Do you prefer books, films or plays? Why?

2 Do you usually read reviews before going to see a film or play, or buying a book? Why/ Why not?

3 Have you ever liked something that had a lot of bad reviews, or not liked something that everyone else loved?

b If a book has been made into a film, which do you usually prefer, the book or the film? Which of the following opinions do you agree or disagree with? Why?

The book is always better than the film because the film always cuts bits out and changes too much.

The film has to be seen as a separate thing – why should it be just like the book?

You should always see the film first, then read the book.

I prefer books because you can imagine the characters in your mind. The film just spoils that.

8 **a** Read the reviews. Which appeals to you the most? Why?

b Read the reviews again. Are the sentences true (T) or false (F)?

1 The reviewer thinks that the puppets in *War Horse* are better than the actors. ☐

2 The reviewer preferred the film of *War Horse* to the play. ☐

3 The reviewer thinks the play is realistic. ☐

4 The audience were very enthusiastic about *War Horse*. ☐

5 *The Shadow of the Wind* has sold a lot of copies. ☐

6 The reviewer thinks the story in *The Shadow of the Wind* moves slowly. ☐

7 The book Daniel chooses is very rare. ☐

8 The reviewer liked everything about the book. ☐

9 *New Moon* is the second in a series of films. ☐

10 The reviewer thinks that the acting in the film is very good. ☐

11 The reviewer doesn't say anything positive about the film. ☐

12 There are some similarities between the film and a Shakespeare play. ☐

Theatre
War Horse

War Horse, **adapted from** the book by Michael Morpurgo, **tells the story of** a horse in the First World War. Before seeing the play I couldn't imagine how this story could work **on stage** – but it does. Joey and the other horses in the play are astonishingly life-like **puppets** and they **steal the show**. Very quickly, you come to completely believe in them and the unfolding story. In fact they are so good that the human characters seem less **well-rounded** in comparison. The **sound effects** are also incredible and with the **dramatic lighting** create the terrifying sensation of being right in the middle of battle. Although *War Horse* is not a musical, the **musical score** is a highlight, with simple but beautiful **melodies** and **lyrics**. The play is altogether **an amazing spectacle** and I was unsurprised when the **applause** from the **audience** lasted for more than five minutes at the end. Now I can't wait to see Spielberg's film version!

Books
The Shadow of the Wind

A worldwide **best-seller** from the Spanish **author**, Carlos Ruiz Zafón, *The Shadow of the Wind* is an unusual and moving book which will undoubtedly become **a modern classic**. **The book is set in** Barcelona where there is an old bookshop, called the Cemetery of Forgotten Books, right in the centre of the old city. As its name suggests, the bookshop sells only forgotten and **out of print** books. **The main character**, Daniel, visits the bookshop as a child and is allowed to choose a book to keep and look after. The book he chooses is called *The Shadow of the Wind*. As he grows up several people seem very interested in this book, which is the only copy left in the world. Gradually, he discovers that he is in great danger from a mysterious man who has the same name as one of the characters in the book. *The Shadow of the Wind* is **full of atmosphere** and is part thriller, part love story. Both the **descriptions** and **dialogue** are **beautifully written** and **the plot** is **a real page-turner**. The **first chapter** in particular **took my breath away**. If I have one complaint, it is that the ending feels rather sudden, but perhaps that's just because I **couldn't put it down**.

Film
The Twilight Saga: New Moon

The Twilight Saga, based on the books by Stephenie Meyer, tells the story of a young girl whose boyfriend is a vampire. Robert Pattinson **plays the role of** the vampire, Edward Cullen, and Kristen Stewart **stars as** the heroine, Bella. In this **sequel** to the first film, *Twilight*, Bella is abandoned by Edward and starts a relationship with Jacob, a werewolf. Robert Pattinson is a well-established **heart throb**, and the film seems to be aimed very much at teenage girls, with plenty of romantic scenes. **Fans** of the books will love it, of course, but in my opinion the **performances** are rather dull, and the film failed to make me care about any of the **leading characters**. Some people have compared elements of the story to Shakespeare's play *Romeo and Juliet*, suggesting that the vampires and werewolves in the film are like the rival families the Montagues and the Capulets in the play. However, I don't think Shakespeare would approve of the **plot** – it's completely absurd. In fact the only thing I would recommend about the film is the **soundtrack**, which includes songs from The Killers and Editors, and makes a great **album**.

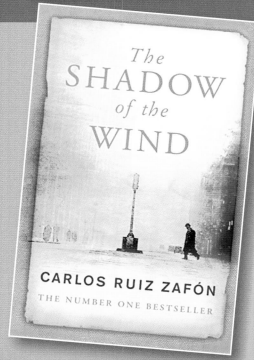

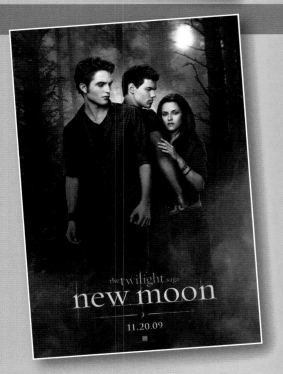

Vocabulary | describing pastimes

9 Look at the Lifelong learning box and read the tip. Then complete the table with the words and phrases in **bold** from the reviews.

Noticing vocabulary

! When you read a text about a particular topic, you will often find words and phrases that you could use yourself to speak or write about this topic.

	Noun or noun phrase	Verb or verb phrase	Adjective or adjectival phrase
Books	*best-seller* *author*	*The book is set in …*	*beautifully written*
Theatre/ Musicals			
Film			

Pronunciation | sounds and spelling: 'a'

10 a 🔊 1.43 Listen to the words in the box. Decide if the underlined letter 'a' is pronounced /æ/ or /eɪ/, and put the words in the correct column.

> ab<u>a</u>ndoned   <u>a</u>lbum   b<u>a</u>sed   ch<u>a</u>pter   ch<u>a</u>racter
> cl<u>a</u>ssic   d<u>a</u>nger   p<u>a</u>ge   soundtr<u>a</u>ck   v<u>a</u>mpire

/æ/	/eɪ/

b 'a' is often pronounced /eɪ/, when the pattern is 'a' + consonant + 'e'. What other spelling patterns with 'a' make the sound /eɪ/?

see Pronunciation bank page 163

Speaking

11 a Think about a book you have read or a play or film you have seen. Then make notes about the topics below. Try to use some of the words and phrases in the Lifelong learning box.

- when/why you read or saw it
- the plot
- the characters
- why you enjoyed it

b Work in pairs and describe your book, film or play to your partner. Use your notes to help you. Answer your partner's questions.

Grammar	countable and uncountable nouns
Can do	describe a restaurant

Vocabulary | food

1 **a** Do you know anything about food in Argentina? If not, what do you think the food is like?

b ● 1.44 Listen to Julia talking about some typical Argentinian dishes. Complete the notes.

'Asado' is *grilled* (1) _____ , on a kind of barbecue.

'Chimichurri' is *a kind of* marinade, *made with* (2) _____ .

(3) _____ are a kind of pie, baked in the oven. They are *stuffed with* (4) _____ and *can be served* (5) _____ .

'Dulce de leche' is a kind of (6) _____ . It's *made by* (7) _____ . It is usually *served with* (8) _____ .

c Work in pairs. Use the words in *italics* in exercise 1a to describe some typical dishes from your country.

Reading

2 **a** You are going to read about a strange restaurant experience. First, try to match these words from the story.

1	long	a	café
2	roadside	b	existed
3	delicious	c	road
4	hungry	d	soup
5	never	e	imagination
6	wonderful	f	and tired

b Work in pairs. What do you think happens in the story? Use the phrases in exercise 2a and the photos to help you.

3 Read the story to check your ideas. Why do you think the man never found the café again?

4 Read the summary of the story below. Find eight mistakes and correct them.

While two engineers, who were hungry, were driving through a busy area in Iran, they stopped in a small city. They found a little café. The owner of the café, who spoke a little English, offered to serve the men a meal. The meal, which was delicious, was surprisingly expensive. After they had finished eating, the restaurant owner asked the engineers to recommend his restaurant to their friends. They did this, but the engineer's friends didn't believe it was possible to find such a poor restaurant in such a remote area. In the end, the engineer returned to the village with his wife. However, when they arrived, they couldn't find the train station. Eventually, they asked a local man about the restaurant. He said he had never heard of it, and he had been there for thirty years.

The world's best restaurant

When I was working as a civil engineer in Iran I had to visit a factory in Marinjab – the centre of a recent earthquake. Marinjab is about 150 miles from Tehran and is a quiet and isolated place. As we drove back along the long road, my colleague and I were both hungry and tired. We didn't have much hope of finding anything to eat, however, as the next town was 80 km ahead. Our only hope was of finding a small roadside café, where you are unlikely to get more than some weak tea and a little sugar to eat.

Just then we came to a village made of small huts with flat roofs. Outside one of the many huts was a sign, 'ghahvehkhaneh' (café) so we went in. It was cool inside, and there were men sitting around smoking pipes. The owner, a proud man, came in from the back and greeted us. 'Good afternoon,' he said, in perfect English. 'My name is Hosseini. My wife is Russian. We do not usually get any foreigners here. It will be a pleasure and an honour to prepare a meal for you.'

A pale-faced lady appeared with a tablecloth, and some knives and forks, shortly followed by Mr H himself, carrying a couple of bowls of soup. Made with spinach and yoghurt, and served hot, it was the most delicious soup I have ever eaten. Soon, the next course arrived – dolmas, stuffed vine leaves. These were so delicious I asked Mr H for the recipe. He replied, 'vine leaves and rice'. It is not an Iranian dish.

The next course was a chelo kebab – the national dish of Iran. The meat was marinated in yoghurt and spices. We ate in silence, and finished with Turkish coffee. There was something almost unreal about the atmosphere of the place. When it was time to go, we asked Mr H how much it cost, and I can tell you the price was astonishingly cheap. It was a fantastic meal – the best I have ever had, and I told him so. Mr H blushed. 'I am glad,' he said. 'As I told you, we do not see many foreigners here. Do come again, and tell your friends.'

I told a lot of friends about the meal I had, yet no one believed me. 'How could you get such a meal in such a remote place?' an English engineer friend asked me.

A few months later, I returned on exactly the same route with this engineer friend and was determined to show him my special restaurant. We reached the village – I recognised the flat roofs – but there was no sign of the café. It was as if the building had never existed. I asked a villager. 'Ghahvehkhaneh?' he said. 'There has never been one here in all the time I have been here. And that is forty years.' We drove away disappointed. Naturally, my companion laughed at me. 'You have a wonderful imagination,' he said. I don't have any explanation. I only know that I definitely had a meal in this village, in a café which, ever since, I have called 'the world's best restaurant'.

Grammar | countable and uncountable nouns

5 **a** Read the Active grammar box. Then complete part A with the words in the box.

> and countable counted restaurant rice uncountable

b Complete part B of the Active grammar box using the underlined examples in the story on page 70.

Active grammar

A Separate objects which we can count are usually (1) _____ nouns. (2) _____ nouns are often liquids, substances or abstract qualities, but some just need to be learnt.

Examples:

Countable	Uncountable
village café	*sugar water money* (4) _____ *coffee*
meal (3) _____	*soup luggage travel information news*
	advice furniture weather hair bread

Some nouns can be countable (5) _____ uncountable. This is either because we understand how much someone is talking about:

Can I have a (cup of) coffee please?
Sure. Do you take one (spoonful of) sugar or two?

Or it might be because we can look at the noun both as something that can be (6) _____ and as a substance.

chocolate (a bar)   *a chocolate* (in a box)
ice cream (in a bowl)   *an ice cream* (in a cone)

B Quantifiers

	None	A small amount	A large amount
Countable		*A _____ months later ...* *A _____ of bowls of soup ...*	*Outside one of the _____ huts ...*
Uncountable		*We didn't have _____ hope ...* *a _____ sugar ...*	
Countable and uncountable	*We do not ... get _____ foreigners here.*	*_____ weak tea ...*	*I told _____ friends about the meal ...*

Note that *any*, *much* and *many* are usually used in negatives and questions.

---

6 Some of the following sentences are incorrect. Decide which ones and correct them.

1 How many money do you have?
2 We need to buy a new furniture.
3 Sam ate almost all the chocolates in the box.
4 She has a beautiful long blonde hair.
5 I don't have some luggage.
6 Would you like some rice with that?

7 Complete the questions with a suitable quantifier from the Active grammar box.

1 Do you drink more than a _____ of cups of coffee a day?
2 How _____ vegetables can you name? Which ones do you eat most often?
3 Do you eat _____ meat? Why/Why not?
4 Some people only eat _____ meat. Do you think this is a good idea?
5 How _____ portions of fruit and vegetables should you eat a day?
6 Some people only eat _____ different kinds of fruit. Do you think it's better to eat a larger variety?

Speaking

8 Work in pairs and discuss the questions in exercise 7.

see Reference page 75

Listening

9 🔵 1.45 Listen to Helen describing a restaurant. Tick (✓) the correct summary.

1 The food was good, but it was much too expensive. ☐
2 The service wasn't very good but the food and the atmosphere were great. ☐
3 The atmosphere was good but there was no vegetarian food. ☐
4 The food was very good but the live music made it very noisy in the restaurant. ☐

10 Listen again and complete each sentence with between one and three words.

1 The speaker went to Bruges to celebrate _____ .
2 The restaurant they chose used to be _____ .
3 It was summertime, so they decided to _____ .
4 She had vegetarian lasagne and her boyfriend chose _____ .
5 The restaurant was famous for _____ .

11 Look at the How to... box. Then listen again and tick (✓) the expressions the speaker uses.

How to... describe a restaurant

Location	It's on the river/on the main square/on a small street/in the centre of ... It's near ...
Atmosphere	Very lively/busy/noisy/romantic/peaceful/relaxing ... It has a bar/live music ...
Menu	It specialises in ... It's famous for ... The menu is varied/traditional. The (food) is fresh/good-quality/beautifully-prepared.
Service	The service is quite slow. The waiters are very friendly/efficient.
Prices	The prices are reasonable. It's quite expensive.

Speaking

12 **a** You are going to talk about a restaurant you like. Plan what you want to say using the phrases in the How to... box.

b Work in groups. Take it in turns to describe your restaurants. Which would you most like to visit?

1 a Think of situations in which you need to explain something ...

1 to visitors.
2 to family/friends.
3 to colleagues.
4 to other students.

b Work in pairs and compare your ideas.

In a restaurant, I sometimes have to explain the local dishes to visitors to my country.

2 a 🔊 1.46 Listen to five descriptions and guess what the speakers are describing. Then check your answers on page 148.

b Read the Lifelong learning box. Then listen to the descriptions again and complete the sentences (1–5).

Paraphrasing

❗ You will not always know the words you need in English. But you can communicate your meaning by using alternative words to explain what you mean.

1 It's a type of ...
2 It's a kind of ...
3 It's the stuff you ...
4 It's something you use for ...
5 They're usually made of .../They're a useful thing to ...

Lifelong learning

---

c Which word, *thing* or *stuff*, do we use for countable nouns and which do we use for uncountable nouns?

3 Put the words in the correct order. Then match the descriptions (1–6) to the pictures (A–F).

1 in/windows/something/find/of/you/front/it's .
2 you/a/pasta/it's/type/cheese/which/on/of/put .
3 you/opening/wine/use/bottles/it's/something/for .
4 Spain/it's/kind/a/dish/of/from/rice .
5 your/for/use/stuff/you/hair/it's/washing/the .
6 large/made/stone/figure/it's/of/a .

A

B

C

D

E

F

4 a Work in groups. Complete the notes below. Which group can finish first?

SHAPE – draw something that's ...
rectangular
oval
round
square

WEIGHT – name an animal that's ...
heavy
light

SIZE – name something that's ...
enormous/huge – The Grand Canyon,
tiny
wide
narrow

TEXTURE – name a type of material or a thing that's ...
smooth – soap
rough
sticky
soft
hard

b 🔊 1.47 Listen to the sentences. Do they mention the same things as you?

c 🔊 1.48 Listen and repeat the adjectives in exercise 4a.

5 Work in pairs.

Student A: turn to page 149.

Student B: turn to page 152.

You have the same crosswords but with different words completed. Take it in turns to describe your words and complete the crossword.

1 a What are the people in the photo doing?

b 🔘 1.49 Listen to Paul talking about Capoeira. Put the sections below in the right order (number 1–5) as you hear them.

2 Listen again and complete the phrases in each section.

3 Choose a skill (it could be anything you enjoy or are good at) and prepare to tell other students about it. Use the phrases in **bold** below to help you plan your ideas.

4 Work in groups and describe your skills. As you listen to the other students, think of one or two questions to ask them when they finish.

Capoeira

---

1 Background information/History

Capoeira **is a kind of** _____ .

It was started by _____ .

The music **is important because** _____ .

☐ Afterwards

You can relax and _____ .

We often spend _____ .

☐ Other information/Future plans

I have been doing Capoeira for _____ .

I have improved a lot since _____ .

I would like to become _____ .

☐ Personal qualities necessary

You need to be _____ .

You have to _____ .

You should _____ .

☐ Main actions/Activity

Everyone _____ , singing and playing music. Two people fight in the centre.

As soon as _____ , you have to move away quickly.

You **must** be careful the other person _____ .

If the other person kicks you, **then** _____ .

If the white costume is still clean at the end of the game, **that shows** _____ .

5 | Reference

Present Perfect Continuous and Present Perfect Simple

We use both the Present Perfect Simple and Present Perfect Continuous to talk about actions, states or activities which happened in an unfinished period of time and have some connection to now.

I've been to Paris. (some time before now)

I've lost my keys. (it happened some time before now and they are still lost)

I've been waiting for him. (I started in the past and I'm still waiting)

We use the Present Perfect Continuous ...

1. to emphasise how long something has taken.
   I've been waiting for ages.

2. to indicate that an activity or situation is temporary.
   I've been living here for a few months now.
   Compare with
   I've lived here all my life.

3. to emphasise the repetition of an activity.
   I've been ringing and ringing you!

Verb patterns with -ing and infinitive

1. Verbs followed by -ing: verbs of feeling, e.g. *can't stand, like, love, enjoy, don't mind, hate, adore*

2. Verbs followed by the infinitive: verbs about future plans, e.g. *agree, promise, want, choose, decide, hope, expect, plan, would like, refuse, prefer*

3. Many verbs can use the pattern: verb + *somebody + to* + infinitive, e.g. *allow, help, want, remind, would like, advise, invite, tell*

4. Some verbs can be followed by both forms but the meaning may change.

Countable and uncountable nouns

Countable

A countable noun can be singular or plural. We can count countable nouns (one apple, two apples, etc.).

*She eats **an apple** a day. I love eating **apples**.*

Uncountable

Uncountable nouns have only one form, no singular or plural. We cannot count uncountable nouns.

*In Asia, people eat **rice** with every meal.*

We cannot say *a rice*, so we specify *a ... of ...*

a bowl of rice, a bottle of water ...

Uncountable nouns are generally not used in the plural, e.g. *information, advice, furniture, equipment, travel*.

Can I have some information? NOT: ~~informations~~

Some uncountable nouns are used only in plural form, e.g. *scissors, jeans, news*.

I bought some jeans/a pair of jeans. NOT: ~~a jeans~~

Some uncountable nouns can be used as both countable and uncountable. Sometimes this is because we understand a certain quantity is meant.

Can I have a (cup of) coffee?

Sometimes the meaning changes, e.g. *chocolate, ice cream, hair, noise, room, time, chicken, lamb, potato*.

Quantifiers

Before countable nouns, we use *a few, a couple, some, a lot of* and *many* in positive sentences.

Before uncountable nouns, we use *a little, some* and *a lot of* in positive sentences.

Any, much and *many* are usually used in negative sentences and questions.

Key vocabulary

Leisure activities

aerobics a musical instrument athletics camping cards climbing computer games dancing drawing exercise jogging karate painting photography sailing skiing snowboarding socialising squash surfing volleyball

Equipment

belt board boots brush canvas costume goggles helmet net poles racquet rope saddle trainers

Responding to a picture

colourful depressing disturbing intriguing odd sad striking unusual vivid

Describing pastimes

Theatre: adapted from amazing spectacle applause audience lighting lyrics melody on stage puppet score sound effect steal the show tell the story of well-rounded

Books: a classic atmosphere author beautifully written best-seller chapter character couldn't put it down description dialogue is set in out of print page turner plot take your breath away

Film: album fan heart throb leading character performance play the role of plot sequel soundtrack star as

Describing food

It's ... grilled/baked/boiled/fried/made with .../made by + verb + -ing/stuffed with .../served with .../hot/cold.

Listen to the explanations and vocabulary.

ACTIVEBOOK

see Writing bank page 157

5 Review and practice

1 Choose the correct words in *italics*.

1. I haven't bought your present yet because I've *worked/been working* all morning.
2. How long have you *known/been knowing* Sally?
3. **A:** Why are you looking so happy?!
   B: I've *danced/been dancing*.
4. Hi. I don't think we've *met/been meeting*. I'm Tim.
5. Have you *finished/been finishing* the report yet?
6. How long have you *learned/been learning* to play golf?
7. How many matches have you *played/been playing* this season?
8. Molly hasn't done her homework. She's *watched/been watching* TV all afternoon.

2 Complete the dialogues with the correct form of the verbs in brackets.

1. **A:** You look exhausted. What _____ you _____ (do)?
   B: I _____ (play) squash.
2. **A:** You're late! I _____ (wait) for nearly an hour.
   B: I'm sorry. I _____ (work) late in the office.
3. **A:** I'm really hungry. I _____ (not/eat) all day.
   B: Sit down. I _____ just _____ (finish) making dinner.
4. **A:** I haven't seen you for hours. What _____ (do)?
   B: I _____ (play) with the dog.
5. **A:** _____ you _____ (leave) any messages for him?
   B: Yes, I _____ (leave) four messages.
6. **A:** There's paint on your clothes! _____ you _____ (decorate)?
   B: Yes, I _____ (paint) the living room. It's nearly finished.

3 Complete the email with the correct form of the verbs in brackets.

Hi Virginia,

I'd like to (1) _____ (check) a few things with you about next week. I am really looking forward to (2) _____ (see) you here in New York. The good news is that my flatmate, Matt, has agreed (3) _____ (give) you his room for the week. He said he would prefer (4) _____ (stay) at his girlfriend's place because he can't stand (5) _____ (listen) to us talking about university all night!

The other thing is that on Thursday I have been invited (6) _____ (go) to dinner with a new colleague from work. I am sure you can manage (7) _____ (entertain) yourself for one night. There is a lot you can do around here if you don't mind (8) _____ (go out) on your own. Remember (9) _____ (bring) your mobile phone, so you can contact me if you get lost. I forgot (10) _____ (ask) you what time your train arrives. Let me know and I'll try (11) _____ (leave) work early so I can meet you.

Speak soon,

Love Felipa

P.S. I need to warn you (12) _____ (bring) some warm clothes with you because it is freezing here!

4 Complete the following pairs of sentences using the countable and uncountable form of each noun. Add an article or plural ending if necessary.

chocolate
I'm trying to give up <u>chocolate</u>, it isn't good for me.
He bought her a huge box of <u>chocolates</u> .

1. coffee
   _____ is produced in Kenya.
   Would you like _____ ?
2. hair
   Waiter! There's _____ in my soup!
   He has short spiky brown _____ .
3. noise
   I jumped when I heard _____ coming from the bathroom.
   There's a lot of _____ in this street.
4. room
   The hotel has 100 _____ .
   Is there _____ for me at the table?
5. chicken
   Susie keeps _____ in her garden.
   I had _____ for dinner.

5 Correct the mistake in each sentence. There may be more than one mistake and more than one way to correct it.

We went to buy a furniture
We went to buy some furniture.

1. In the evening I love listening to a music.
2. We went out to lovely restaurant.
3. Hurry up! We don't have many time.
4. I don't think I can come to the theatre, because I only have a few money.
5. Would you like a milk in your coffee?
6. I've got a bad news – the show has been cancelled.
7. I'm going to the market to buy some breads.

6 Choose the correct words in *italics*.

1. The first film was a great success, so they're making the *sequel/chapter/performance*.
2. To play volleyball you need *a racquet/a net/goggles*.
3. The film is *starred/set/played* in Paris in 2001.
4. I love going *aerobics/cooking/climbing*.
5. I don't understand this song because the *melody/lyrics/album* are in German.
6. The *dialogue/plot/description* is really good – they say such funny things!
7. Flour is the *stuff/thing/type* you use to make bread.
8. Pierogi is *made by/made with/served* potato flour.

6

Lead-in

1 **a** Work in pairs and look at the photos. What type of holidays do they show? Describe them using words and phrases from the box.

> adventure holiday   beach holiday   camping holiday
> (river) cruise   package holiday   safari   sailing holiday
> sightseeing tour

b Which of these holidays are romantic/convenient/dangerous/expensive/relaxing?

2 Cross out one adjective which does not collocate with the noun.
1 rocky/pebbly/snow-capped/scenic mountains
2 dramatic/sandy/scenic waterfall
3 snow-capped/green/lush/scenic valley
4 unspoilt/scenic/pebbly/rocky coastline
5 sandy/pebbly/tropical/rocky/lush beach
6 tropical/snow-capped/desert island
7 sandy/unspoilt/dramatic scenery

3 Work in pairs and discuss the questions.
1 Could any of the places in the photos be in your country? What kind of places do tourists visit in your country?
2 Have you ever been to any of the types of places in exercise 2?
3 Do you prefer holidays somewhere remote, or in a busy city? Why?

6.1 Across Africa

Grammar	Past Perfect Simple
Can do	describe a memorable photo

TRAVELS ACROSS AFRICA

For six hours we shot through the barren landscape of the Karoo desert in South Africa. Just rocks and sand and baking sun. Knowing our journey was ending, Daniel and I just wanted to remember all we had seen and done. He
5 used a camera. I used words. I had already finished three notebooks and was into the fourth, a beautiful leather notebook I'd bought in a market in Mozambique. Southern Africa was full of stories. And visions. We were almost drunk on sensations. The roaring of the water at Victoria
10 Falls, the impossible silence of the Okavango Delta in Botswana. And then the other things: dogs in the streets, whole families in Soweto living in one room, a kilometre from clean water.

As we drove towards the setting sun, a quietness fell
15 over us. The road was empty – we hadn't seen another car for hours. And as I drove, something caught my eye, something moving next to me. I glanced in the mirror of the car; I glanced sideways to the right, and that was when I saw them. Next to us, by the side of the road, thirty,
20 forty wild horses were racing the car, a cloud of dust rising behind them – brown, muscular horses almost close enough to touch them, to smell their hot breath. I didn't know how long they had been there next to us.

I shouted to Dan: 'Look!' but he was in a deep sleep,
25 his camera lying useless by his feet. They raced the car for a few seconds then disappeared far behind us, a memory of heroic forms in the red landscape. When Daniel woke up an hour later I told him what had happened.

30 'Wild horses?' he said. 'Why didn't you wake me up?'

'I tried. But they were gone after a few seconds.'

'Typical,' he said. 'The best photos are the ones we never take.'

We checked into a dusty hotel and slept the sleep of
35 the dead.

Reading

1 **a** Complete the phrases with the words from the box.

> diary   emails   ~~home~~   photos   souvenirs

phone *home*
1 keep a _____
2 take _____
3 buy _____
4 send postcards/letters/_____

b Do you do any of the things in exercise 1a when you travel?

2 Work in pairs and discuss the questions.
1 Have you been/Would you like to go to Africa?
2 What you would expect to see/experience there?

3 Read the extract from *Travels Across Africa* by Sophie Van Ranst, and answer the questions.
1 Where are Sophie and Daniel?
2 Do they experience the things you talked about in exercise 2?
3 How do they like to remember their travels?

4 Read the extract again. Write true (T), false (F) or not given (NG).
1 They drove slowly through the busy desert. ☐
2 Sophie wrote about her experiences in a notebook. ☐
3 Daniel took photos of the Victoria Falls. ☐
4 They had seen a lot of things, and heard many stories. ☐
5 Daniel was driving when they saw the horses. ☐
6 They had seen other animals, but they hadn't seen wild horses before. ☐
7 The horses didn't come near the car. ☐
8 Sophie woke Daniel so that he could take photos. ☐

78

Vocabulary | descriptive language

5 Look at the descriptive language from the extract. Choose the correct words in *italics* and answer the questions.

We shot through the barren landscape (line 1)

This means we moved very fast. Normally we use the word 'shoot' when guns are involved – 'He shot someone!'

1 *drunk on sensations* (line 9)
This means that you have seen and heard so much that you feel *incredible/bored*.
What normally makes people drunk?

2 *roaring of the water* (line 9)
This means the water *makes a loud noise/ is quiet*.
What animal normally roars?

3 *quietness fell over us* (lines 14–15)
This means that as they drove *they had a small accident/it became silent*.
Give some more everyday examples of things that fall.

4 *caught my eye* (line 16)
This means that she had *something in her eye/noticed something and looked at it*.
What else can you catch?

5 *slept the sleep of the dead* (lines 34–35)
This means that they slept *very well/very badly*.

Grammar | Past Perfect Simple

6 a Look at the Active grammar box and answer the questions. Then choose the correct <u>underlined</u> words.

b Find other examples of the Past Perfect Simple in the extract on page 78.

Active grammar

(Past Simple)   (Past Perfect Simple)
*We **wanted** to remember all we **had seen** ...*

Which action happened first?
1 *We saw things ...*
2 *We wanted to remember ...* (the experience)

We use the *Past Perfect*/*Past Simple* to make it clear that one event happened before another one in the past.

We make the Past Perfect Simple with *had*/*hadn't* + *past participle*/*infinitive*.

---

see Reference page 89

7 Read the text and put the verbs in brackets into the Past Simple or the Past Perfect.

I had been warned about the dangers in Peru, but no one (1) _____ (tell) me how incredibly beautiful it was. The mountains (2) _____ (be) all shades of green and purple and as we arrived at Machu Picchu early in the morning, I was glad we (3) _____ (decide) to walk there rather than take the tourist train. The sun had only just come up and the air (4) _____ (smell) very fresh and sweet.
Machu Picchu (5) _____ (be) built in around 1450 but archeologists think it (6) _____ (be) abandoned by the time the Spanish (7) _____ (arrive) in the area a hundred years later.

8 a Complete the sentences using the Past Perfect and your own ideas.

1 I got lost in the city because ...
2 My first evening on holiday went well because ...
3 I missed the flight because ...
4 I decided to travel overland because ...
5 There was a traffic jam because ...

b Have you ever been in any of the situations in exercise 8a? Work in pairs and discuss.

A

C

B

Listening and speaking

9 Work in pairs. Look at the photos and answer the questions.

1 What can you see in the photos?

2 Where do you think the photos might have been taken?

3 What do you think the people who took the photos had done earlier that day?

4 How do you think they are feeling?

10 **a** 🔵 2.1 Listen to three people describing the photos. Match the speakers, Helen, Matthew and Tracy with the photos (A–C).

b Listen again. For each speaker make notes about ...

• where they took the photo.

• what the weather was like.

• what else they had done that day.

c Look at the How to... box. Then listen again and tick (✓) the phrases you hear.

How to... describe a memorable photo	
Say when and where the photo was taken	*This photo shows ...* *This is a photo I took in ...*
Describe what you can see in the photo	*In the background/foreground, you can see ...* *On the left-hand side/right you can see ...* *I think this is ...*
Give background information/talk about the people in the photo	*I/We had been (there) for ...* *I was staying ...* *We suddenly stumbled upon ...* *Afterwards, we ...* *We had always wanted to see ...* *We had a really amazing day.*

11 Think of a favourite photo, or choose a photo from page 148. Work in pairs and describe the photo to your partner, using the phrases in the How to... box.

Vocabulary | places in a city

1 **a** Work in pairs. Discuss the differences in meaning between each pair of words.

1   a castle/a palace
2   a museum/an art gallery
3   a pub/a café
4   a park/a garden
5   a lake/a fountain
6   a bookshop/a library
7   a shop/a market
8   a square/a roundabout
9   a hostel/a hotel
10 a canal/a river

A palace is a large building where a king or queen lives (or lived), but a castle is an old building, built to defend people from attack.

b Tell your partner your top three choices of things to do when you visit a new city.

Number one for me is visiting markets, because the atmosphere is usually very friendly. You can meet local people and buy presents too.

Listening

2 🌐 2.2 Mark and Kate are travelling around Australia. Listen to their dialogues (1–5). Where do you think they are in each instance?

3 Listen again and answer the questions for each dialogue.

1   What do they want or need?
2   What is the problem?

4 🌐 2.3 Listen and complete the sentences in the How to... box.

> ### How to... get around a new place
>
> | Ask about places in a town | *What time does the museum _____ ?*
Is there a _____ near here?
Can you recommend a good restaurant? |
> | --- | --- |
> | Ask for travel information | *How much is a _____ to the city centre?*
_____ this bus go to the airport? |
> | Sound polite | *Excuse me. Could you tell me what time the train _____ ?*
Excuse me. Do you know where _____ is? |
> | Ask/Give directions | *Can you tell me the way to the _____ ?*
Just go straight on. It's on your _____ . |

Pronunciation | intonation in questions

5 **a** 🌐 2.4 Listen to the questions (1–3) and match them with the intonation patterns (a–c).

1   *Wh-* question:
    What time does the museum open?
2   Indirect question:
    Could you tell me what time the train leaves?
3   *Yes/No* question:
    Is there a bank near here?

a   ☐ ☐ ☐
b   ☐ ☐ ☐
c   ☐ ☐ ☐ ☐

b Which type (*Wh-*, *Yes/No* or Indirect) is each question in the How to... box? Practise asking the questions with the correct intonation.

see Pronunciation bank page 164

Speaking

6 Work in pairs.

Student A: turn to page 148.

Student B: turn to page 152.

Ask and answer questions to find out the information you/your partner needs. Try to use expressions from the How to... box in exercise 4.

Reading and speaking

7 **a** What country do you think is shown in the photos? Why?

b If you went to this country, which of these things would you like to do?

1 eat food from many different cultures
2 visit a rainforest
3 go to the beach
4 see wildlife
5 go deep-sea diving
6 visit a vineyard

c Read the article. Which of the things above did Dannii do on her trip?

8 Read the article again and answer the following questions.

1 Why does Dannii think Melbourne has become more cosmopolitan?
2 What does Dannii think is 'a wonderful challenge'?
3 What is St Kilda well known for?
4 What does the Queen Victoria Market sell?
5 What can you see as you drive along the Great Ocean Road?
6 What area of Australia does Dannii still hope to visit?
7 Why is it quite difficult to visit some of the resort islands?
8 What is Dannii's tip for making the long flight to Australia more comfortable?

Dannii Minogue loves travelling the world as much as her sister Kylie, but after working away she says there's no place like home ...

Melbourne is where I grew up so it obviously means a lot to me. It's a city that is constantly evolving. Melbourne people, like all Australians, enjoy travelling and their increasing experience of other countries means local tastes have changed. The city has become much more cosmopolitan.

One of the best places to visit is the Crown Casino, which features more than forty eating places all under one roof. Someone told me that in Melbourne you can sample the cuisines of seventy-five different countries; I haven't managed to eat my way through them all, but it's a wonderful challenge. And besides the top-class restaurants, you mustn't miss Melbourne's vibrant cafe culture, with wonderful beachside places at St Kilda.

If you enjoy your food, you will love exploring local produce markets. One I really like is the Queen Victoria Market on the corner of Queen and Elizabeth streets, which is open five days a week and sells a huge variety of fruit and vegetables.

My boyfriend joined me for my most recent trip home. It was fun showing him all the familiar landmarks, but also going to places I've never been before. From Melbourne, we took the Great Ocean Road, a 150-mile highway that is a scenic delight. You pass through an area that includes the world-famous Twelve Apostles rock formations, the Otways rainforest and Bells Beach along with resort towns such as Torquay and Apollo Bay. We loved spending time on the beach, as well as visiting vineyards and taking in jazz music. It really was an amazing summer.

That said, we've still got a pretty extensive 'to do' list, including a trip to Queensland and the Barrier Reef. And although I've been to Hayman Island a couple of times, I'd like to get to know some of the more exclusive resort islands that can be reached only by private boat or helicopter.

The flight to Australia is a long one but perfectly comfortable if you follow a routine like mine. I get on board and immediately change into my flight pyjamas – one day I'm going to work out how to accessorise them with fashion items, but until then I just look like someone wearing pyjamas!

I just love to travel. It's an Aussie thing: as a people we are up for jumping on a plane and going off to explore. I can't wait to see where I'll go next.

Grammar | uses of *like*

9 **a** Do these extracts from the article use *like* as a verb or as a preposition?

Do you like it? (verb)   *What's it like?* (preposition)

1   There's no place like home.
2   Melbourne people, like all Australians …
3   One I really like is the Queen Victoria Market …
4   I'd like to get to know some of the more exclusive resort islands …
5   … if you follow a routine like mine.
6   … I just look like someone wearing pyjamas!

b Complete the Active grammar box with the example sentences (1–6) in exercise 9a.

Active grammar

The word *like* can be used as a verb or a preposition.

As a verb

A   To enjoy something or to think that something is nice, good or right.
    e.g. sentence __3__

B   To say what you want or to ask someone what they want.
    e.g. sentence _____

C   To suggest or offer something.
    *We could go to the art gallery if you **like**.*

As a preposition

D   Similar to something else or happening in the same way.
    e.g. sentence _____ and _____
    We often use *look* with this meaning.
    e.g. sentence _____
    We also use *sound/feel/taste*.
    *What's that noise? It **sounds like** an aeroplane.*
    *What does papaya **taste like**?*
    *It's so warm, it **feels like** summer.*

E   Used to give an example of something, instead of using *such as*.
    e.g. sentence _____

F   Used to ask someone to describe or give their opinion of something.
    *What is it **like**? It's very cosmopolitan.*

see Reference page 89

10 Complete the dialogues using expressions with *like*.

1   A: I have never been to Paris. What _____ ?
    B: Oh, it is a wonderful city.

2   A: What _____ do today?
    B: I don't mind. You decide.

3   I love old buildings _____ castles and churches.

4   A: What _____ most about Krakow?
    B: I love the market square with all the cafés and restaurants.

5   A: I am not sure if I will recognise Mr Williams. What _____ he _____ ?
    B: He is tall, with dark hair.

6   A: Why didn't you like the food?
    B: Because it was horrible! It _____ rubber.

7   A: I _____ really _____ modern art.
    B: Neither do I. The paintings often _____ the work of children.

8   A: Shall we go out tonight?
    B: We can _____ .

Speaking and writing

11 **a** Work in pairs. Tell your partner about your home town or a place you know well. Answer the following questions.

1   What is it like?
2   What are the people like?
3   Why do you like/dislike it?
4   What do you like doing there?
5   What would you like to change about it?
6   Does it look like any other cities/places that you know?

b Write a short article about a city or place you know well, recommending things a visitor should do. Use expressions from the article on page 82.

One of the best places to visit is …
You mustn't miss …
If you enjoy …, you will love …
One I really like is …

c Read other students' articles. Which city/places would you like to visit? Why?

6.3 Travellers' tales

Grammar	articles
Can do	talk about unexpected events

Vocabulary | travelling

1 **a** Complete the texts with the adjectives in the box.

> barren   cultural   famous
> independent   local   new
> package   sandy
> unforgettable   tropical

A

Tourists … are not so interested in (1) _____ experiences and sensations. When they go abroad, they either go sightseeing to see (2) _____ landmarks like St Mark's Square in Venice, or to (3) _____ beaches where they do nothing but sunbathe. Many tourists prefer (4) _____ holidays, which include travel, accommodation, and sometimes even food. Tourists just want to have fun and relax.

B

Travellers … go to the (1) _____ capitals, just like tourists. However, travellers also explore (2) _____ rainforests, (3) _____ deserts and other places where tourists never go. Travellers try to experience the (4) _____ culture and meet the people who live there. They prefer (5) _____ travel to package tours and hope to experience an (6) _____ journey.

b Work in pairs. Read the texts in exercise 1a again. Do you agree with the definitions of *traveller* and *tourist*? Why/Why not?

2 Work in pairs and discuss the questions. Try to use the vocabulary from exercise 1.

1   Do you prefer to be a tourist or a traveller? Why?
2   What are the advantages and disadvantages of being a traveller rather than a tourist?

Listening and vocabulary

3 **a** Work in pairs. Look at the painting of Lady Mary Wortley Montagu and discuss the questions.

1   When do you think she lived?
2   Where do you think she lived?
3   What do you think she was like? Describe her using words from the box.

> adventurous   aggressive   arrogant   beautiful   brave
> clever   confident   intelligent   open-minded   well-off

b ● 2.5 Listen to a radio programme about Lady Mary and check your ideas.

4 **a** Listen again and complete the notes using between one and three words or a number in each gap.

Joanne Bright is the author of a book about (1) _____ in the eighteenth and nineteenth centuries.

Lady Mary Wortley Montagu went to Istanbul, with (2) _____ in (3) _____ . She wrote a series of (4) _____ which were published (5) _____ .

Lady Mary was unusually open to the new (6) _____ . She thought the Turkish ladies were much more (7) _____ than English ladies. She also copied the Turkish women in having her (8) _____ inoculated against smallpox and brought the idea back to England.

b Listen again and correct the following sentences.

1   Most women travellers went abroad to accompany their children.
2   Lady Mary didn't enjoy living in Turkey.
3   She wore English clothes.
4   She caught smallpox as a child.
5   She had her son inoculated against smallpox in England.
6   She helped to introduce inoculation to Turkey.

Pronunciation | sentence stress

5 **a** 🌐 2.6 Listen to the answers to exercise 4b and write down which word is most stressed in each sentence.

*Most women travellers went abroad to accompany their **husbands**.*

b Why are these words stressed? Practise saying the sentences in exercise 4b with this stress pattern.

6 **a** Turn to page 148 and read about another traveller. Write four sentences about them. Include an incorrect fact in each sentence.

b Work in pairs. Take it in turns to read your sentences. Try to correct your partner's mistakes, paying attention to your intonation.

see Pronunciation bank page 164

Reading and speaking

7 **a** Work in pairs. Describe what is happening in the pictures (A–C).

b Read the article. What strange event does each picture (A–C) show?

8 Work in pairs. Read the article again and answer the questions.

1 Is the article very serious, semi-serious or not serious? How do you know?
2 In your opinion, which are the most amazing events/coincidences in the article? Which are lucky? Which could have logical explanations?
3 Have you experienced a strange event/ coincidence? What happened?

9 Work in pairs. Retell the stories from the article using the key words below to help. Try to use some of the words and phrases in the box.

> amazingly ...   ... didn't expect to ...   Luckily, ...
> turned out ...   unbelievably, ...

1 family/Australian coast/whale/boat
2 Roger/drowning/saved/beach/Alice/beach/ husband
3 dog/Indiana/3,000 miles/Rocky Mountains
4 Karen/beach/ring

Strange things happen when you travel ...

The Johnson family expected to see some whales when they chartered a boat to sail around the Australian coast. But they didn't expect a 30-foot humpback whale to leap out of the ocean onto their boat. Amazingly, no one was seriously hurt, not even the whale.

If you think that's unbelievable, how about the story of Roger Lausier? Aged four, he had wandered away from his mother on Salem beach, Massachusetts and was saved from drowning by a woman called Alice Blaise. Nine years later, the thirteen-year-old Roger was on the same beach when he saw a man fall overboard. Roger saved his life. The man turned out to be Alice Blaise's husband.

Some of the most incredible travel stories, it seems, are about a pet. In August 1923 the Brazier family, holidaying in Indiana, lost their dog, Bobbie, and had to return home to Oregon, 3,000 miles away, without him. Unbelievably, Bobbie travelled across icy rivers, climbed the Rocky Mountains and, six months later, arrived back home in Oregon.

Or more recently, Charlie, a cat who decided to take a nap inside the engine of his neighbour's car and ended up being driven 160 miles away. Luckily for him, he was completely unhurt.

What about the things people lose and find when they are travelling? Rings are top of the list. In Hawaii, Ken Da Vico, who is a professional diver, claims to find about fifteen wedding rings a year in the sea. He returns many of them to their owners. Even if a fish eats the ring, there is still hope. There are many cases of rings being found years later inside the stomachs of sharks, mussels and other kinds of fish. Less common is when the loser finds the lost ring, as happened when Karen Goode went to a beach in Wales and found a ring she had lost there ten years before.

Grammar | articles

10 Look at the Active grammar box and match the example phrases/sentences (1–8) below with the rules (A–H).

1 Ken de Vico, who is **a** professional diver, says …
2 In Hawaii, …
3 Some of **the** most incredible travel stories …
4 **Rings** are top of …
5 They didn't expect **a** 30-foot humpback whale to leap out of the ocean …
6 They didn't expect a 30-foot humpback whale to leap out of **the** ocean.
7 No one was seriously hurt, not even **the** whale.
8 Some of the most incredible travel stories are about **a** pet.

Active grammar

A We use *a/an* when something is one of many. e.g. sentence _____

B We use *a/an* when it's the first time something has been mentioned. e.g. sentence _____

C We use *a/an* with jobs. e.g. sentence _____

D We use *the* when something is the only one. e.g. sentence _____

E We use *the* when something has been mentioned before. e.g. sentence _____

F We use *the* with superlatives. e.g. sentence _____

G We use no article (–) when we make generalisations with plural or uncountable nouns. e.g. sentence _____

H We use no article (–) with most names of people and places. e.g. sentence _____

We use *the* in names if the title includes *States, Kingdom* and *Republic*: **the** *United States,* **the** *United Kingdom,* **the** *Republic of China.*

We use *the* if the name is a plural: **the** *Netherlands,* **the** *Andes,* **the** *Falkland Islands.*

We say **the** *south of Spain,* but *southern Spain* and **the** *north of Africa,* but *North Africa.*

We use *the* with rivers, seas, oceans and deserts: **the** *Pacific Ocean,* **the** *River Thames.*

see Reference page 89

11 Find and correct the mistake in each sentence.

1 The travellers should always respect other people's culture.
2 The Europe is not most beautiful continent.
3 The good way to see a country is to go by train.
4 It'd be really relaxing to go on trip along a river, like River Nile, for example.
5 The delayed flights are one of greatest problems travellers face these days.
6 Before going abroad, you should learn a few words of a local language.
7 The travel is a bit boring for me.
8 I hate travelling in the aeroplanes.

12 Complete the stories with *a/an/the* or – (no article).

Alvaro Cortez met his girlfriend, (1) _____ musician called Pilar, at college in Madrid, and she showed him her favourite guitar. (2) _____ guitar was (3) _____ same instrument that Alvaro's grandfather had played fifty years earlier. It had been lost when his grandfather moved to (4) _____ new house in (5) _____ Valencia, Spain.

Michael and Tamara Weisch went on (6) _____ two-week holiday to Warsaw. One evening, in (7) _____ restaurant of (8) _____ small hotel where they were staying, they started talking to another couple, who, they soon realised, were also called Michael and Tamara Weisch, also from (9) _____ New York City. But (10) _____ best coincidence of all: both couples had been to (11) _____ same hotel in Prague exactly a year before.

Speaking

13 Read the corrected sentences in exercise 11 again. Write *yes* (Y) if you agree completely, *no* (N) if you disagree, or *don't know* (DK). Then work in groups and discuss your answers.

I agree with sentence 1 because … What do you think?

6 Vocabulary | expressions with *get*

1 Look at the mind map and tick (✓) the expressions with *get* that you know. Can you add any more expressions to the map?

7 fetch/collect:
*He's gone to **get** Janice from the station.*

1 buy/receive/obtain:
*Shall we **get** some drinks for our journey?*
*She **got** the tickets through the post.*

2 *get* + past participle:
*Luckily, the cat didn't **get** burnt or scalded.*
*I don't know how we **got** lost.*

6 become: (often used with the present continuous for describing changes)
*I'm **getting** hungry.*
*It's **getting** dark.*

GET

3 Phrasal verbs:
*I **get on** board and immediately change into my pyjamas.*
*I'll call her as soon as I **get back** from holiday.*
*You might have to wait over an hour to **get in**.*

5 have the opportunity to do something:
*I'd like to **get to** know some of the more exclusive resorts.*
*I hope I **get** the chance **to** travel next year.*

4 travel/go/arrive:
*Can you tell me how to **get** to the airport?*
*What time did you **get** here?*

2 Read the Lifelong learning box. Then match each phrase (a–e) to a section of the mind-map (1–7).

Maps for the mind

❗ Don't always write new vocabulary in a list. Use maps like the one above to put related words together. This will help you to remember them.

a How did you **get away with** that? *(section 3)*
b I forgot my umbrella so I **got** really wet.
c I **got** some directions to the hotel in an email.
d It's quite easy to **get around** the city.
e I **got** really **lost** in the old part of town.

Lifelong learning

3 Complete the story with the words/phrases in the box.

get away with   get it into   get off   get on   getting on
got   got out of

The funniest thing that ever happened to me on an airplane was about twenty years ago, in Brazil. My boyfriend and I were (1) _____ a flight from Recife to Brasilia. In front of us in the queue to (2) _____ board was a woman carrying a large cardboard box. She tried to (3) _____ the overhead locker, but it was too big, so she sat down directly behind us with the box on her lap.

Before we could take off, there was a squawking noise and all of a sudden a parrot landed on my boyfriend's head! Honestly! It had (4) _____ the cardboard box and the cabin crew had to chase it round the plane for quite some time before they caught it. The lady and the parrot both had to (5) _____ the plane. She (6) _____very angry, but I don't know how she thought she would (7) _____ it!

4 **a** Work in groups. Write a story using the phrases from the box, and other *get* phrases you know.

get a taxi   get back   get bored
get married   get cold
get directions   get divorced
get home   get ill   get lost
get on (with)   get to the airport late
get to the hotel   get someone a drink
get wet

b Write your story for other students to read. Leave spaces where there is an expression with *get*. Can the other students guess which word/phrase is missing?

Jim was planning to get _____ but on the way to the church ...

6 | Communication

Can do | suggest and respond to ideas

1 Work in groups. When you visit another city, what do you like/not like doing? Tell your group.

2 You are going to plan a day trip for your group in London. Look at the *What's on in London* leaflet and find …

1 a tour which lasts for half a day.
2 the time it takes to go round the London Eye.
3 a musical you could see.
4 where the piano concert is playing.
5 two museums you could visit.
6 an exclusive shop to buy souvenirs.

3 **a** 🔵 2.7 Listen to three people planning a day trip. What do they decide to do …

1 during the day? 2 in the evening? 3 if it rains?

b Look at the audioscript for track 2.7 on page 171. <u>Underline</u> the phrases the speakers use to make suggestions and respond to ideas. Then work in pairs and compare.

4 **a** Work in groups. Plan your day in London, using the leaflet.
• You can spend £100 each.
• Plan activities for the morning, the afternoon and the evening.
• Try to include activities for everyone in your group.

b Tell the class about your plans.

What's on in LONDON

G General

Tour around London on a Big Red Bus. Enjoy the views from the top of this famous London bus, as you learn about the sights from one of our friendly guides. Half-day tour, £25 per person.

London walks – Experience London on foot with one of our specialised walking tours. £5 per two-hour walk.

Camden market – the perfect place to walk around and visit shops, eat in a local café, buy some arts and crafts and just sit with a coffee and watch London go by. Colourful, fun and cheap – this is real London.

Buckingham Palace – Entrance ticket: £12 per person. Watch the Changing of the Guard outside Buckingham Palace at 2 p.m. every afternoon.

The London Eye – the Giant Observation Wheel became operational in January 2000. The Wheel is the largest of its kind ever to be built and visitors to London from abroad are delighted by this new way of seeing the city. Tickets £12.50, duration 30 minutes.

Theatre

Les Misérables – Palace Theatre 020 7494 5555. 'This musical has been playing for eighteen years, and it is still like going to a first night'. Eves 7:30, Mats Thu and Sat 2.30. Tickets from £40.

Music

Philharmonic Orchestra Hear Rachmaninoff's first piano concerto (with Michael Pletnev) accompanied by the Philharmonic Orchestra. Free. The Royal Festival Hall.

M Museums and Galleries

Madame Tussaud's – Visit the museum to see their world-famous wax models of famous stars, past and present. A very popular attraction, you might have to wait over an hour to get in. £24.50.

The British Museum – has outstanding collections that cover world cultures from pre-history to the present day. Free.

The National Gallery – The National Gallery, London, houses one of the greatest collections of European painting in the world, with over 2,300 paintings covering the period from about 1250 to 1900. Free.

Shopping

Shop at Harrods – the most famous department store in the world. Buy exclusive souvenirs for family and friends, and enjoy afternoon tea and wonderful views across London in our sky-view café.

Past Perfect Simple

We use the Past Simple to talk about something that happened in the past, e.g. *I was ill.*

We use the Past Perfect Simple to talk about what happened before that, e.g. *I had eaten something bad.*

We use it to make the order of events clear.
I was ill because I'd eaten something bad.

```
I had eaten
something bad        I was ill        now
————————x————————————x————————x————————►
```

We don't need to use the Past Perfect Simple when the sequence of events in the past is clear:
I came home and turned on my computer.

The Past Perfect uses many of the same expressions as the Present Perfect (*since, for, already*).

Uses of *like*

As a verb

1 To enjoy something or think that something is nice, good or right.
   I like fresh coffee. Harry doesn't like swimming.

2 To say what you want or ask someone what they want.
   I'd like a non-smoking room please.

3 To suggest or offer something.
   I'll help you, if you like.

As a preposition

1 Similar to something or happening in the same way.
   He eats like a horse.

   We often use *look, sound, feel, taste* with this meaning.
   Sam looks like a popstar.

   We can also use *look like* and *feel like* with a more idiomatic meaning.
   It looks like Rachel is going to be late again!
   I don't feel like going.

   ! When *like* is a preposition and is followed by a verb we use *-ing*.

2 Used to give an example (instead of *such as*).
   Big cities like London can be expensive.

3 Used to ask someone to describe or give their opinion.
   What's London like? It's enormous.

Articles

a/an is used ...

1 when something is one of many.
   I went to an island in the Pacific.

2 when it's the first time we've mentioned the subject.
   I went to an island in the Pacific. The island was completely isolated.

3 with jobs.
   She's a doctor, he's a cook.

the is used ...

1 when the subject is unique (there's only one).
   The President of the US

2 when we already know which one we are talking about.
   I went to an island in the Pacific. The island was completely isolated.

3 with superlatives: *It's the best holiday I've ever had ...*

No article

We use no article when we make generalisations with ...

plural nouns: *Trousers are warmer than skirts.*

uncountable nouns: *Progress is possible.*

Articles in place names

We use no article with ...

1 most place names: *Warsaw, Spain*

2 names with South/East, etc. *South America*

We use *the* for ...

1 countries with the word *State, Kingdom* or *Republic*:
   the United States, the United Kingdom.

2 plural names: *the West Indies.*

3 rivers, seas, oceans, deserts: *the River Seine.*

4 describing where in a country: *the south of France, the west coast of Scotland.*

Key vocabulary

Holidays and travelling

(river) cruise   cultural and historical capitals   barren deserts   famous landmarks   go abroad   go sightseeing   have fun and relax   independent travel   adventure/package/beach/camping/sailing holiday   local culture   safari   sightseeing tour   unforgettable journey

Describing landscape

beach   coastline   desert   dramatic   green   island   lush   mountains   pebbly   rocky   sandy   scenery   scenic   snow-capped   tropical   unspoilt   valley   waterfall

Places in a city

bookshop/library   canal/river   castle/palace   hostel/hotel   museum/art gallery   lake/fountain   park/garden   pub/café   shop/market   square/roundabout

Expressions with *get*

get a letter/an email/a distinction/a job/directions   get a newspaper/a drink   get away with something   get hungry/dark/worse/cold/wet/ill/bored   get home/to the airport   get someone from the station/a taxi   get on/get back/get on (with)   get married/dressed/lost   get (the chance) to + infinitive

 Listen to the explanations and vocabulary.

ACTIVEBOOK

 see Writing bank page 158

1 Choose the correct words in *italics*.

1 When I got to the restaurant I realised that I *left/had left* her phone number at home.

2 By the time she was eighteen she *lived/had lived* in six cities.

3 On my birthday, when I *got/had got* home I found that my husband *had cooked/cooked* dinner.

4 That morning, she got up, had breakfast and *went/had gone* to work, as normal.

5 Tibet was incredible. I *never saw/had never seen* such a beautiful country before.

6 He called twice but no one answered. They *all went/had all gone* to bed.

7 When I arrived in France, my cousins *kissed/had kissed* me on the cheek.

8 When I returned a month later, I found that the weather *grew/had grown* cold and I *had/had had* to buy a new jacket.

9 It was Max! I *hadn't seen/didn't see* him for twenty-five years.

2 Correct the mistakes in the sentences. Four of the sentences are correct.

1 I don't feel like to go tonight.

2 A: What's he like?
   B: He's like really nice.

3 It tastes like coffee.

4 Would you like having a drink?

5 What Madrid like?

6 We could eat out tonight, if you like.

7 I like going to restaurants.

8 Can you hear that noise? It sound likes Joe's car.

9 I'll come round tomorrow and help clear up, if you're liking.

10 I like two tickets please.

3 Complete the names with *the* or – (no article).

the Black Sea

1 ___ Canary Islands
2 ___ Africa
3 ___ Czech Republic
4 ___ Andes (mountains)
5 ___ River Nile
6 ___ Canada
7 ___ United Arab Emirates
8 ___ northern Europe
9 ___ Atlantic Ocean
10 ___ Mount Kilimanjaro
11 ___ Sahara Desert
12 ___ Mediterranean Sea

4 Choose the correct words in *italics*.

1 A: Why do you like this hotel so much?
   B: It's *a hotel/the hotel* where I met Dave.

2 A: How was the restaurant?
   B: *The food/Food* was wonderful.

3 A: Why don't you go to Australia for your holiday?
   B: I don't like *the aeroplanes/aeroplanes*.

4 A: Who was Alexander Fleming?
   B: He's *a/the* man who discovered penicillin.

5 A: Why didn't you buy a dog?
   B: *The cats/Cats* are easier to look after.

6 A: What happened yesterday?
   B: *The/A* strange man knocked on our door and asked for water.

7 A: Why does Mariana always win prizes?
   B: Because she is *the most/most* intelligent person in the class.

8 A: What did you do last night?
   B: I went to *a/the* club.
   A: Oh really, which one?

5 Complete the advertisement with the words from the box. Some words may be used more than once.

get   getting   go   sandy   travel   tropical   unforgettable

Would you like to (1) _____ abroad? Would you like to (2) _____ the world? If you are only interested in (3) _____ a tan and lying on a (4) _____ beach with all the other tourists, then AMAZ Tours are not for you. We organise trips to the (5) _____ rainforest in Brazil. We offer a truly (6) _____ journey where you (7) _____ the chance to experience something truly different. The Amazon is (8) _____ smaller and smaller. See it before it disappears. We fly every Saturday. It takes fifteen hours to (9) _____ there and a whole lifetime to leave! (10) _____ your ticket before 12th July and we will give you a fifteen percent discount!

6 Choose the correct words in *italics*.

1 It was a lovely day so I decided to do some digging in the *park/garden*.

2 George took a boat out on the *lake/fountain*.

3 I bought a new paperback at the *library/bookshop*.

4 *Hostels/Hotels* are good places to stay if you're on a budget.

5 There's a market in the *square/roundabout* every Friday.

Lead-in

1 Work in pairs and discuss the questions.

1 Which of the learning situations in the photos have you experienced? When and where did you experience them?
2 Do you prefer learning alone or with others? Why?

2 Make as many verb/noun collocations as possible using the nouns in the box and the verbs in the table below.

> a course a decision   a degree   an exam   from university   good marks
> a mistake   notes   progress   some research
> a subject (History, Law, Architecture, etc.)   a suggestion   to a lecture
> to class   your best   well at something

Get	Take	Do	Pass	Fail	Revise	Go	Make	Graduate
	a course							

3 **a** Complete the sentences with verbs from exercise 2.

1 Before exams do you usually _____ alone or with friends? Which is better?
2 Do you think that to learn anything you have to be willing to _____ mistakes? Why/Why not?
3 What other courses have you _____/done in the past? What was good/bad about them?
4 If you _____ to a lecture, do you make lots of notes or just listen?
5 How can you _____ good marks in your English test?
6 What is more important? To _____ well at something or to _____ your best?

b Work in pairs and discuss the questions in exercise 3a.

7.1 Learning from experience

Listening

1 🔊 2.8–2.12 Listen to five speakers describing a learning experience. Match the speakers (1–5) with the pictures (A–E). What are they doing in each picture?

2 a Listen again and complete the sentences with between one and three words.

1 Natalie started playing the drums when she was _____ . When she was _____ she was given her first drum kit.

2 Philip started learning Yiddish about _____ ago. He found it quite easy because he had studied _____ at school.

3 When Rachel got a job at a kids' camp she was surprised that she had no _____ herself.

4 Sean asked for a parachute jump for his _____ birthday. He went on a one-day course with _____ other students and made his jump at the end of the day.

5 Yvette went to work in Indonesia about _____ years ago. The job was challenging because she had to manage _____ as well as teach classes.

b Which learning experience do you think was the most interesting/difficult/exciting?

Vocabulary | learning

3 a Complete the phrases with the words in the box.

> crash   heart   picking   steep   thrown

1 That was one thing that I had to **learn by** _____ .
2 I was amazed how quickly I started _____ **it up.**
3 An occasion where I **had a really** _____ **learning curve** was …
4 I **was just** _____ **into** everything.
5 I took a one-day _____ **course** in parachuting.

b Match the phrases in **bold** in exercise 3a with the definitions (a–e).

a a short learning programme in which you study a subject very quickly

b to memorise something so you can do or say it without referring to anything written down

c made to deal with something difficult without being prepared for it. We also say 'someone was _____ in at the deep end'.

d when you had to learn something really quickly to succeed

e learning something without really trying

4 Look at the How to... box. Then listen again to the speakers from exercise 1 and tick (✓) the expressions you hear.

How to... describe a learning experience

What you did/learnt	*About a year ago I took an interest in …* *I was studying (for) …* *I was training for …* *I needed to learn the basics of …* *I had to revise for …* *I took a one-day crash course in …* *I used to practise … over and over …*
How you felt about it	*I was amazed how quickly I started picking it up.* *It was important/difficult/easy/ useful/a waste of time.* *What surprised me was …* *I'm not sure I'd want to do it again.* *It was a great experience, even though it was hard work.* *I really didn't know what to expect …*

5 **a** Think about a good (or bad) learning experience you have had. Make questions from the prompts below.

1 What/you/learning? Why?
2 Why/experience/good(or bad)?
3 How/you/learn?
4 Learn/in a group/on your own?
5 It/easy/difficult to learn?
6 How/you/make progress?
7 You/learn/useful techniques?

b Answer the questions in exercise 5a. Make notes.

c Work in pairs and tell each other about the experience. Use the How to... box in exercise 4 and give as much detail as possible.

Reading

6 What do you think is the connection between light bulbs, crisps, bread and post-it notes? Read the article to find out.

Mistakes that work ...

People who don't make mistakes are unlikely to learn anything.

The best way to learn something is to make mistakes first. Thomas Edison, who invented the light bulb, told his colleagues: 'Of the 200 light bulbs that didn't work, every failure told me something I was able to incorporate into the next attempt.' Benjamin Franklin, the US statesman and scientist once said: 'I haven't failed, I have had 10,000 ideas that didn't work.'

Both these people understood that failures and false starts are the condition of success. In fact, a surprising number of everyday objects had their beginnings in a mistake or a misunderstanding. Post-it notes, packets of crisps and even bread are all unexpected inventions. In 2600 BC, a tired Egyptian slave invented bread when the dough rose during his sleep. And crisps were first cooked by a chef in the USA when a customer complained that his fried potatoes were not thin enough.

In 1968 Spencer Silver was trying to develop a strong adhesive when he accidentally invented a very weak glue instead. His colleague, Art Fry, decided to use it six years later, in 1974, to hold his bookmarks in his books and the post-it note was invented.

Successful businesspeople have often made big, expensive mistakes in their past. When an employee of IBM made a mistake that cost the company $600,000, Thomas Watson, the chairman, was asked if he would fire the man. 'Of course not,' he replied. 'I have just spent $600,000 training him. I am not going to let another company benefit from his experience.'

The important thing to remember is that you need to learn from your mistakes. If you don't, then there is no sense in making them.

7 Write the questions for the following answers.

200
How many of Edison's lightbulbs didn't work?

1 10,000
2 2600
3 1968
4 1974
5 600,000

8 Work in pairs and discuss the questions.

1 Do you agree with what the article says about mistakes?
2 Give an example of a time when you did/didn't learn from your mistakes.

9 Read the Lifelong learning box and complete the exercise.

Using a correction code

! Sometimes you can learn by correcting your own mistakes. Your teacher could use a correction code to help you.

WW – wrong word
WT – wrong tense
WF – wrong form
WO – wrong order
Sp – spelling
P – punctuation
M – something is missing

Use the correction code in the text below. Then correct the mistakes.

I started learning drive (WF) when I am seventeen. I very nervous. My father tort me in his car to drive and everyctime I did a mistake he shouted to me it took me long time to learn.

Lifelong learning

Grammar | subject/object questions

10 Work in pairs and discuss the questions.

1 What is the main purpose of education? To learn facts or to learn how to learn?

2 Do you think you learn more useful things through experience or through classroom learning?

3 Do you think it is important to have good general knowledge now that facts can be easily looked up online? Why/Why not?

11 You are going to test your general knowledge by writing and answering some questions. First look at the Active grammar box and choose the correct <u>underlined</u> words.

Active grammar

Object questions

Thomas Edison invented the **light bulb**.
What *did Thomas Edison invent?*

The light bulb is the <u>subject</u>/<u>object</u> of the question.

Subject questions

Thomas Edison *invented the light bulb*.
Who *invented the light bulb?*

Thomas Edison is the <u>subject</u>/<u>object</u> of the question.

When a *Wh-* word refers to the subject in a question we do not use an auxiliary verb. The word order is the same as the affirmative.

Subject + verb + object
Who wrote *The Lord of the Rings?*

---

see Reference page 103

12 a Work in pairs.

Student A: write questions for the statements in quiz A. Then look at the answers on page 149.

Student B: write questions for the statements in quiz B. Then look at the answers on page 152

b Ask each other your quiz questions. Give one point for each correct answer.

13 Work in pairs and write your own quiz questions. Ask and answer the questions in groups.

Quiz A

1 A famous artist painted *Guernica* in 1937. (Who?)

2 Mozart started composing music. (When?)

3 A scientist discovered penicillin in 1928. (Who?)

4 One of the world's greatest scientists lived from 1879–1955. (Which?)

5 A famous city is nicknamed *The Big Apple*. (Which?)

6 Guglielmo Marconi is responsible for an invention. (What invention?)

7 This is the largest desert in the world. (Which?)

8 This man wrote the best-sellers *The Da Vinci Code* and *The Lost Symbol*. (Who?)

9 This country is the oldest surviving republic in the world. (Which?)

10 Tom Daley became Britain's youngest ever male Olympics competitor. (When?)

Quiz B

1 Christopher Columbus discovered these islands in 1492, before he discovered America. (Which?)

2 An Italian artist painted the Sistine Chapel. (Who?)

3 This song about London was a huge hit for Lily Allen in 2006. (What?)

4 This country has the smallest area of all European countries. (Which?)

5 This team bought Cristiano Ronaldo for $163 million. (Which?)

6 A famous Beatle wrote the song *Imagine* in 1971. (Who?)

7 Laszlo Biro invented something. (What?)

8 This is the world's longest river. (Which?)

9 One of the world's most famous writers lived from 1564–1616. (Which?)

10 Hong Kong became part of China again. (When?)

Reading and speaking

1 What can you remember about your first day at school? How did you feel? What did you do? What did you think of the teachers?

2 **a** Look at the picture below. What do you think this teacher is like?

b Now read the extract from *Matilda* by Roald Dahl. Were you right about Miss Trunchbull?

3 Read the text again and write true (T) or false (F).

1 Miss Honey reads the names of all the children. ☐

2 The school provides pencils for the children. ☐

3 All the children are new to the school. ☐

4 They will stay at the school for eleven years. ☐

5 Miss Trunchbull is the class teacher. ☐

6 Miss Honey tells the children how to behave in front of the headmistress. ☐

7 Miss Honey advises the children not to argue with each other. ☐

8 The children are happy about being at school. ☐

4 Look at the words/phrases from the extract and underline the correct definition.

1 strict discipline (line 13): *making people obey rules/have fun*

2 take my advice (line 14): *do what I suggest/give me a suggestion*

3 behave yourselves (lines 14–15): *act like a good/bad child*

4 argue (line 15): *agree/disagree* with someone by talking or shouting

5 answer back (line 16): *reply politely/rudely* (especially for children)

6 deals severely with (lines 20–21): *punishes/rewards*

1 After the usual business of going through all the names of the children, Miss Honey handed out a brand-new exercise book to each pupil.

'You have all brought your own pencils, I hope,' she said.

5 'Yes, Miss Honey,' they chanted.

'Good. Now this is the very first day of school for each one of you. It is the beginning of at least eleven long years of schooling that all of you are going to have to go through. And six of those years will be spent right
10 here at Crunchem Hall, where, as you know, your headmistress is Miss Trunchbull. Let me for your own good tell you something about Miss Trunchbull. She insists upon strict discipline throughout the school, and if you take my advice you will do your very best to behave
15 yourselves in her presence. Never argue with her. Never answer her back. Always do as she says. If you get on the wrong side of Miss Trunchbull she can liquidise you like a carrot in a kitchen blender. It's nothing to laugh about, Lavender. Take that grin off your face. All of you
20 will be wise to remember that Miss Trunchbull deals very severely with anyone who gets out of line in this school. Have you got the 'message?'

'Yes, Miss Honey,' chirruped eighteen eager little voices.

From *Matilda* by Roald Dahl

5 **a** Complete the sentences using some of the words and phrases in exercise 4.

1 I didn't _____ myself when I was at school.

2 I believe that _____ is important when you are bringing up children.

3 I think you should _____ your father's _____ . He is usually right.

4 My brother and I _____ a lot, but we still get on well.

5 My teacher _____ with anyone who arrives late at school.

b Change three of the sentences in exercise 5a so that they are true for you. Work in pairs and compare.

Vocabulary | personal qualities

6 **a** Check you understand the meaning of the words in the box. Is each one the quality of a good or a bad teacher?

> boring   calm   clear   encouraging
> enthusiastic   frightening   imaginative
> inspiring   interesting   knowledgeable
> patient   strict   tolerant   understanding

b Choose the correct words in *italics*.

1 Her classes were so *boring/inspiring* that everyone fell asleep.
2 My teacher is very *patient/knowledgeable*. He explains things many times.
3 When students have problems, our teacher helps them. He is very *understanding/calm*.
4 The students know everything about the topic. They are extremely *patient/knowledgeable*.
5 My teacher is rather *strict/interesting*. No one dares to break the rules.
6 Our teacher is very *encouraging/boring* when we find things difficult, so we don't give up.

Listening

7 **a** ⊕ 2.13 Listen to two people discussing their teachers. Write the subjects the teachers taught.

Mr Halsworth _____
Miss Matthews _____
Mrs Sharp _____
Mr Ford _____

b Listen again. Make notes about each teacher's good/bad qualities. Add any further information.

Vocabulary | word building

8 **a** Complete the table with the missing words.

Verb	Noun	Adjective
1 _____	*imagination*	_____
2 *know*	_____	_____
3 _____	*fright*	_____
4 *encourage*	_____	_____
5 _____	_____	*inspiring*
6 _____	*tolerance*	_____
7 *bore*	_____	*boring*
8 *clarify*	_____	*clear*

b Do these endings usually indicate a noun or an adjective? Write *N* for noun and *A* for adjective.

1 *-tion/sion/cian* N   5 *-ance/ence*
2 *-ment*   6 *-ive*
3 *-ing*   7 *-able*
4 *-dom*

Pronunciation | word stress in word building

9 **a** ⊕ 2.14 Listen to these pairs of words and mark the stress.

1 bored – boring
2 inspire – inspiration
3 encourage – encouragement
4 enthusiasm – enthusiastic
5 fright – frightening
6 imagine – imagination
7 knowledge – knowledgeable

b In most cases adding a suffix to a word does not change the stress. Tick (✓) the suffixes in exercise 9a which change the stress.

c ⊕ 2.15 Practise saying these pairs of words. Then listen and check.

1 electric – electrician
2 scientist – scientific
3 educate – education
4 decide – decision
5 artist – artistic

see Pronunciation bank page 163

Grammar | *used to* and *would*

10 a Complete the sentences (1–5) in the Active grammar box by looking at the audioscript for track 2.13 on page 172. Then choose the correct <u>underlined</u> words to complete rules (A–D).

b <u>Underline</u> other examples of *used to* and *would* in the audioscript.

Active grammar

A We use *used to* + verb and *would* + verb to talk about <u>single actions</u>/<u>repeated actions</u> in the past which don't happen now.

  1 We _____ throw paper at him. (action)

  2 She _____ play us Mozart. (action)

B We only use <u>used to</u> + verb/<u>would</u> + verb to talk about states in the past.

  3 She _____ live in Zimbabwe.

  4 I _____ like her lessons at all. (state)

  NOT: ~~She would live in Zimbabwe.~~ or ~~I wouldn't like her lessons at all.~~

C <u>Used to</u>/<u>Would</u> is usually contracted to *'d* in spoken English.

  5 We' _____ learn about the stars.

D The negative and question form is <u>use to</u>/<u>used to</u>.

---

see Reference page 103

11 Read the text and decide if one or both of the words in *italics* are correct in each case.

Going to school

I didn't (1) *use to/would* like the journey to school. I (2) *used to/would* go by bus, but I was afraid of the other children. They were bigger than me, and they (3) *used to/would* shout at me. I always sat at the back of the bus, even though it (4) *would/used to* be the hottest place, and I (5) *used to/would* hope that no one could see me. It's funny to think that those boys were probably only eight years old, but I (6) *would /used to* be so frightened.

12 Complete the sentences with *use to* or *used to* and a verb from the box.

> be   not behave   do   eat   not go   like   live   not watch

1 Did your life _____ very different when you were a child? How?
2 I _____ playing outside with my friends.
3 I _____ TV in the evenings.
4 We _____ in the countryside, but now I live in Vienna.
5 My family _____ to the seaside at the weekend.
6 Did you _____ ice cream every day?
7 My best friend at school was called Sam. We always _____ our homework together.
8 I _____ very well at school.

13 a Change the sentences in exercise 12 so that they are true for you and answer the questions.

b Work in pairs and compare your sentences.

Speaking

14 a Think about a good (or bad) teacher from your past. Use the questions to help you write notes.

1 What did he/she look like? What clothes did he she use to wear?
2 What subject did he/she use to teach?
3 What did he/she use to do that was so special/bad?
4 Did all the students particularly like/dislike this teacher? Why?
5 How did this teacher treat you personally? Was he/she very different from the other teachers you had?
6 Would you like to meet him/her again? What would you say to him/her now?

b Work in groups. Take it in turns to tell the group about your teacher.

Writing

15 Use your notes from exercise 14 to write an entry for the website below about a favourite teacher from your past.

GREATTEACHERS

The College of Education is compiling stories of great teachers and the qualities that made them memorable. You can help by submitting a memory of your special teacher.

Vocabulary | education

1 Work in pairs. Read the sentences and check you understand the words in **bold**. Then answer the questions.

1 What different **courses** have you taken? Were they all **academic**? What were the **subjects**?

2 Do you prefer **formal assessment**, such as an **exam**, or **continuous assessment** by the teacher? Why?

3 What do you prefer: a **lecture** or a **seminar**? Why?

4 Have you ever tried a **distance learning** or **blended learning** course? What are the advantages/disadvantages?

5 Have you taken, or would you like to take a **degree** at a university? What **subject**?

Listening

2 **a** ⏺ 2.16 Listen to a radio programme about a university. How is it different from other universities?

b Work in pairs. Listen again and answer one set of the questions below.

Student A

1 How many branches around the world does the U3A have?

2 What does the study coordinator do?

3 Give one reason why older people like to study.

4 What did the Prague branch do last year?

5 How do the U3A students in Valencia study?

Student B

1 How many students does the U3A have in the UK?

2 Name one of the more academic courses offered.

3 Give one reason why older people like to study.

4 What did the Cape Town branch do last year?

5 What do the U3A students in Montreal do as well as study?

c Tell your partner what you found out in exercise 2b.

d Listen again and <u>underline</u> the words in **bold** from exercise 1 that you hear. What is said about them?

Reading

3 **a** Work in pairs. You are going to read three articles about remarkable people.

Student A: read the articles below.

Student B: read the articles on page 149.

As you read, make notes about the following:
• name
• current age/age at death
• activity/achievement
• personal philosophy/attitude to being old

b Tell your partner about the people you read about.

Speaking and listening

4 Work in pairs and discuss the questions.

1 At what age is someone 'old'?

2 Do you know any very active elderly people?

3 Are you inspired by them or by the people in the articles?

4 What would you like to do when you are old?

It's never too late

At the age of 100, Rose Hacker started a new career as a journalist after a newspaper editor heard her giving a speech. This career was just one of many she had in her lifetime. Her first job was as a clothes designer, buyer and model for her father's fashion business. She also managed to find the time to do charity work and teach in the evenings. Later she became a marriage counsellor and even a member of parliament. She said of old age, 'You need to keep as interested as you can.' She died at the age of 101.

Joan Collins can't believe she's seventy-seven – she certainly doesn't look it. She made her first films in the 1950s and is still one of Britain's best known actors. Probably most famous for her role in the 1980s classic soap, *Dynasty,* Joan has always been very glamorous.

She recently made a television programme, *Joan Does Glamour,* with the aim of showing younger women how they can dress with a bit more style.

Joan insists that she has never had plastic surgery and that she never will. She claims that her good looks are a result of good skincare and make-up.

5 🔊 2.17 Listen to Eben and Polly discussing the questions in exercise 4. Look at the statements and write Eben (*E*), Polly (*P*) or neither (*N*).

Who …

1 thinks someone in their fifties or sixties is old?
2 knows someone in their seventies who regularly cycles eighty miles?
3 was particularly inspired by Mary Wesley?
4 is looking forward to being a grandparent?
5 plans to write a novel in their old age?

Anna Moses, better known as 'Grandma Moses', began her career as a painter in her seventies after she gave up embroidery because she couldn't hold a needle anymore. She lived until 101 and became very famous in her own lifetime for her pictures of country scenes in America. At first she used to charge $2 for a small painting and $3 for a larger one, but one of her paintings was recently sold for $1.2 million.

Grammar | modals of ability, past and present

6 **a** Complete the sentences with the words in the box. You will need to use some words more than once.

> can   can't   couldn't   managed to   was able to

1 Rose Hacker also _____ find the time to do charity work and teach in the evenings.
2 Rose said of old age, 'You need to keep as interested as you _____ .'
3 Joan Collins _____ believe she's seventy-six.
4 She aims to show younger women how they _____ dress with a bit more style.
5 Grandma Moses gave up embroidery because she _____ hold a needle anymore.
6 Somehow Buster Martin and his wife _____ have seventeen children.
7 Peter Oakley thinks it was lucky that he _____ stay on at school after the age of fourteen.
8 When her husband died, Mary Wesley _____ survive on her small pension.

b Now check your answers by looking at the articles on this page and pages 98 and 149.

7 Look at the Active grammar box and tick (✓) the correct boxes. Use the sentences in exercise 6a to help you.

Active grammar

	General ability	Succeed in actually doing something
can/can't	✓	
could/ couldn't		
be able to/ not be able to (or be unable to)		
manage to/not manage to		

In the present tense we usually use **be able to** after another verb.

*I'd like **to be able** to help you.*

We use *managed to* when the speaker believes that the action is difficult for the person doing it.

*Have you **managed to** finish that essay yet?*

see Reference page 103

8 Underline all the words in *italics* which are possible.

1 Amazingly, Rose Hacker *has been able to/managed to/could* become more active as she has got older.

2 Joan Collins *can't/isn't able to/doesn't manage to* believe she's seventy-six.

3 She would like to *could/can/be able to* help younger women be more stylish.

4 Grandma Moses gave up embroidery because she *wasn't able to/couldn't/didn't manage to* hold a needle anymore.

5 Peter Oakley thinks it was lucky that he *could/was able to/managed to* stay on at school after the age of fourteen.

9 Complete the sentences using *could* where possible, or *managed to* where *could* is not possible.

1 Sir Ranulph Fiennes, aged sixty-five, _____ climb Mount Everest on his third attempt.

2 In 2002, Hakan Sükür _____ score the fastest goal in World Cup history.

3 Usain Bolt _____ win both the 100 m and 200 m World and Olympic titles at the same time.

4 In 1954, Emil Zátopek, _____ break the world record for running 10 kilometres.

5 Mozart _____ compose piano music at the age of four.

6 Grandma Moses _____ paint more than 1,000 paintings.

7 People say that Pavarotti was the only singer who _____ sing better than Caruso.

Pronunciation | connected speech

10 a 🔊 2.18 Listen and tick (✓) the sentence you hear.

1 I **could do** it. ☐
   I **couldn't do** it. ☐

2 He **was able** to stop. ☐
   He **wasn't able** to stop. ☐

3 They **were able** to play. ☐
   They **weren't able** to play. ☐

4 I **managed** to do it. ☐
   I **manage to** do it. ☐

b 🔊 2.19 Listen to all the sentences in exercise 10a. Look at the words in **bold** and find examples of the following:

1 Where a consonant at the end of one word links to a vowel at the beginning of the next word.

2 Where /t/ and /d/ sounds are next to each other and become one sound.

3 When the letter 'r' in a word is pronounced to make linking words easier.

c Listen again. Practise saying all the sentences with connected speech.

see Pronunciation bank page 164

Speaking

11 a Make notes about ...

1 something unusual you can do.

2 two things that you can do now that you couldn't do ten years ago.

3 something that you could do when you were a child, but you can't now.

4 something difficult that you managed to do recently.

b 🔊 2.20 Listen to Jake being interviewed about his abilities. What does he say about the things in exercise 11a?

c You are going to interview your partner about their abilities. Use the How to... box to prepare some questions.

How to... carry out an interview

Initial questions	*Would you mind telling me ... ?* *I wonder if you could tell me ... ?* *Can you give me an example of ... ?*
Follow-up questions	*And how/why did you (learn to) do that?* *That sounds interesting, tell me a bit more ...* *I'd love to hear a bit more about that.*

---

d Work in pairs and interview each other. Try to find out as many details as possible.

1 **a** Which subjects do you associate with the sentences below?

1 I read five novels a week. I'm a complete **bookworm**. *Literature*
2 I **haven't got a clue** about Algebra.
3 The question about bacteria was so difficult. I just **made a wild guess**.
4 I **know** Puccini's operas **inside out**.
5 Simon always gets good grades for his paintings. He's **the teacher's pet**.
6 My teacher **gave me a hand** with my essay about African deserts.
7 I **passed** the vocabulary test **with flying colours**.
8 Learning the table of elements was **a piece of cake!**

b Match the words and phrases in **bold** in the sentences (1–8) in exercise 1a with the definitions (a–h).

a helped someone
b very easy
c don't know anything about something
d the teacher's favourite student
e know a subject or topic very well
f a person who reads a lot of books
g gave an answer without thinking about it (the answer may be completely wrong)
h did very well indeed in an exam

2 Which idioms from exercise 1 do the pictures illustrate?

(A)

(B)

(C)

(D)

3 Look at the Lifelong learning box and follow the instructions.

The history of words

❗ Knowing the origin of an idiom can often help you remember it.

Work in pairs.

Student A: look at page 149.

Student B: look at page 150.

Read about the origin of some idioms. Then tell your partner about them.

Lifelong learning

4 **a** Match the phrasal verbs in **bold** in the sentences (1–5) with their definitions (a–e).

1 I **picked up** a lot of new words when I visited Poland last summer.
2 I need to **brush up on** the theories of Nietzsche and Sartre.
3 I always used to **mess around** in lessons. The teacher got really cross.
4 The exam is in a couple of weeks. I must **get down to** some work.
5 I found the course really difficult. Luckily I **got through** the exam.

a passed
b learned something without trying
c start doing something which needs time or energy
d do things which are silly or not useful
e practise something so you are as good at it as you used to be

b Complete the phrasal verbs with the correct particle(s).

1 I always find it hard to get _____ revising.
2 Stop messing _____ and get ready!
3 Joe watched how they did it to see if he could pick _____ any tips.
4 I must brush _____ my Polish before I go to Warsaw next month.
5 You'll never get _____ the exam if you don't work harder.

5 **a** Choose five of the sentences below and complete them so that they are true for you.

1 I know _____ inside out.
2 I haven't got a clue about _____ .
3 I picked up some _____ .
4 I sometimes make a wild guess if _____ .
5 I've learned _____ by heart.
6 _____ is a piece of cake!
7 I need to brush up on _____ .
8 The teacher's pet in my _____ class was _____ .
9 The last time I gave someone a hand was _____ .

b Work in pairs and discuss your sentences.

1 a You have one minute to look at the photo above. Try to remember as many objects as possible.

b Now close your book and write down all the objects you can remember.

c What methods did you use to try and remember the items? Did you try to picture them, repeat their names or group them in some way?

2 Read the article about memorisation methods. Which of them ...

- do you already use?
- do you think might be useful in the future?

3 Work in small groups. You are going to memorise a list of ten words and phrases. Decide together which memorisation method to use. You must all agree to use the same method.

4 a Turn to page 149. You have three minutes to memorise the list of words and phrases.

b Now test yourselves. How many can you remember?

c Which group(s) did the best? Was it the result of using a particular method?

Some methods for memorisation

Finger Method

Just 'count' new words on your fingers to help you remember them. This technique is useful for things like lists, numbers and days of the week, though it doesn't always help you remember things long term.

Linking Method

To use this method, create sound or sight links between the new word or phrase and a word that actually has a different meaning, but sounds similar in your own language. For example, an English person trying to learn the Spanish word 'banco' (bench) could imagine themselves sitting on a bench outside a bank.

Pictorial Method

Imagine a scene or picture that really reminds you of that word. It doesn't have to mean the same, but it needs to be strongly connected in your mind. Draw the picture.

Mnemonics Method

Take the first letter of a series of words you want to learn and make a new word from the first letter of each one. For example:

Boring, **U**nderstanding, **C**alm, **K**nowledgeable, **E**ncouraging, **T**olerant → BUCKET

Or use the words to make a sentence. For example:

Collect, butterfly, exciting → Karen collects exciting butterflies.

Story Method

Make up a story using the new words in a setting or context that helps you remember them.

7 | Reference

Subject and object questions

Object questions

When a *Wh-* question word is the object of the question, we use the normal question word order.

Form: question word + auxiliary + subject + verb

Who did you shout at?

What did you buy?

Most questions that we ask are object questions.

Subject questions

When a *Wh-* question word is the subject of the question, the word order is the same as an affirmative sentence (there is no 'inversion' and we don't use an auxiliary verb).

Form: question word + verb + object

Who shouted at you? (NOT: ~~Who did shout at you?~~)

What happened? (NOT: ~~What did happen?~~)

used to and *would*

*I **used to** live in Rome.*

*She **didn't use** to like olives.*

*She **wouldn't** return my phone calls.*

***Did** you **use to** live in Italy? Yes, I did./No, I didn't.*

***Would** your parents tell you off for shouting?*

! There is no 'd' in the spelling of *use to* in negatives and questions.

*We didn't **use to** like our teacher.*

*Did you **use to** study art?*

We use *used to* and *would* to talk about repeated actions in the past which don't happen now. We only use *used to* to talk about states in the past.

*They **used to**/**would** meet every day.* (action)

*I **used to** love him.* NOT: ~~I would love him.~~ (state)

We use the Past Simple, not *used to*, to describe how long something lasted.

*I **worked** in Italy for five years.* NOT: ~~I used to work in Italy for five years.~~

We use the Past Simple, NOT *used to*/*would*, to talk about a single event in the past.

*I **broke** my leg skiing.* NOT: ~~I used to break my leg skiing.~~

We use the Present Simple, not *used to*, to talk about habits which are true now.

*I usually **play** football three times a week.*

Modals of ability, past and present

We use *can*, *could* and *be able to* to describe general ability.

*I **can** swim but I **can't** dive.*

*I **could** speak French, but I **couldn't** speak German when I was at school.*

*I **was able to** run much faster when I was younger.*

We do not often use *be able to* in the present tense unless it is after another verb.

*I want to **be able to** help my kids with their homework.*

We use *be able to* to describe when someone actually succeeded in doing something, not *could*.

*She **was able to** visit him every week.*

*She **could** visit him every week.* – This means she had the ability, but NOT that she actually did it.

If we want to emphasise that the action is difficult, we can use *manage to* in the present or past.

*I usually **manage to** visit forty countries every year.*

*I **managed to** finish the book but it was very boring.*

In the negative we can use *couldn't*, *wasn't able to*, and *didn't manage to* for a specific action.

*I **couldn't** book the tickets.*

*I **wasn't able to** book the tickets.*

*I **didn't manage to** book the tickets.*

Key vocabulary

Learning and education

academic   formal/continuous assessment
do a degree/an exam/a course/some research/
a subject/your best/well at something
fail an exam/a subject   get good marks/a degree
go to lectures/to class   graduate from university
make a mistake/progress/notes/a decision/
a suggestion   pass an exam/a subject
revise notes/a subject   seminar
distance/blended learning
take an exam/a course/notes/a subject

Personal qualities (2)

calm   clear   encouraging   frightening   inspiring
interesting   knowledgeable   patient   strict
understanding

Learning idioms

bookworm   crash course   be thrown into something
steep learning curve   give someone a hand
haven't got a clue   know something inside out
learn by heart   make a wild guess
pass with flying colours   piece of cake
practice makes perfect   teacher's pet
throw someone in at the deep end

Learning phrasal verbs

brush up on   pick (something) up   get down to (work)
get through (an exam)   mess around

Listen to the explanations and vocabulary.

ACTIVEBOOK

 see Writing bank page 159

103

1 Make questions using the words in brackets.

Something went wrong. (What?)

What went wrong?

1 Somebody phoned me last night. (Who?)
2 He gets the train at 18:00. (When?)
3 Maria taught her to play the piano. (Who?)
4 He failed the exam. (Why?)
5 Something fell on the floor. (What?)
6 An old man lives in that house. (Who?)
7 She ran into one of the offices. (Which?)
8 They met at a party. (How?)

2 Complete the sentences with *use to*, *used to* or *would* and a suitable verb from the box. Use *would* where possible.

> dream get go out have live love read ~~wake up~~ spend stay (x2) study think

When I was a child, I *would wake up* at 5:30 in the morning, and want to get up. My mother (1) _____ very angry if we went into her bedroom before it was light. So we (2) _____ in bed and sing songs until she came to get us. We didn't (3) _____ much for breakfast, just a piece of toast and glass of milk.

I (4) _____ going to school, and playing with all my friends. We didn't (5) _____ very much, and our exam results were never very good. To be honest, I (6) _____ schoolwork was a waste of time. We (7) _____ in a village and at weekends, I (8) _____ a lot of time at home. We didn't (9) _____ much, instead we (10) _____ at home and help my mother. My father (11) _____ the newspaper, and watch the sport on television. I (12) _____ of being a famous footballer.

3 Correct the mistakes in the sentences. Two sentences are correct.

1 Sam use to smoke but now he has given up.
2 He didn't use to go to the gym, but now he goes every week.
3 Tomas would to go to the market every day with his father.
4 Emil used love riding horses on the beach.
5 They'd leave the keys in the door so I could open it.
6 Tom didn't use have a girlfriend, but now he has lots!
7 Myra used to being a dancer when she was younger.
8 She would dance for me one time when I came to visit.

4 Underline all the words in *italics* which are possible.

1 I'm studying English because I want to *can/ be able to/could* speak to overseas visitors.
2 How many languages *can/do you manage to/ are you able to* speak?
3 When I was younger I *can/could/was able to* touch my toes easily.
4 The door was stuck but finally I *could/ managed to/ was able to* open it.
5 I'd like to help you but I *couldn't/can't/ don't manage to.*
6 Yesterday I *couldn't/can't/wasn't able to* drive home because my car broke down.

5 Complete the school reports by choosing the correct word below (*a*, *b*, *c* or *d*).

Megan Bradman   Form: 7BI

Megan worked hard in History this term. She did very well in the final exam, and she knows the key events *inside out*. She just needs to (1) _____ up on her dates. Megan reads a lot – she is a real (2) _____! – and this has helped her pick (3) _____ a lot of information about the subject. An excellent term!

Dorothy Miller   Form: 7TG

Dorothy got 5 percent in her final exam, and she clearly hasn't got a (4) _____ about Geography. In the exam, she made several (5) _____ guesses about fairly easy questions. Some of the facts are easy to (6) _____ by heart, and she needs to do this quickly. The other students and I can (7) _____ her a hand, but Dorothy must work harder.

(a) perfect (b) inside out (c) inside
(d) up and down

1 (a) push (b) work (c) study (d) brush
2 (a) bookie (b) bookkeeper (c) bookworm (d) book reader
3 (a) up (b) on (c) to (d) over
4 (a) idea (b) hope (c) knowledge (d) clue
5 (a) errors (b) mad (c) wild (d) crazy
6 (a) study (b) memorise (c) know (d) learn
7 (a) give (b) take (c) help (d) get

Lead-in

1 **a** Work in pairs. What different kinds of change do the photos illustrate? Use ideas from the box.

> career change   climate change   image change
> political change

b Have you experienced any of these changes? Which ones? How did they make you feel?

2 Underline the words and phrases in the box which go with the verb *change*.

> an arrangement   direction   places   talking   time   the subject
> your address   your clothes   your hairstyle   your happiness   your head
> your mind   your name   your password   your tune

3 **a** 🔵 2.21 Listen to Stig and Carol talking about when they changed some of the things in exercise 2. What did they each change?

b Listen again and answer the questions.

1 Why did Carol want to take her husband's name?
2 Why did she then decide against changing her name?
3 What three things did Stig not like about his new apartment?
4 How long did he stay there?

4 Work in pairs. Think about when you changed one of the things in exercise 2 and tell your partner about it.

Reading

1 a Work in pairs. Decide if the following facts about New York are true (T) or false (F).

1 More than 8 million people live in New York City.
2 More than half the population of New York was born outside the US.
3 People often refer to New York as the Big Banana.
4 New York is the capital of the US.
5 New York is the most dangerous city in the US.

b Read the first paragraph of the article and check your answers.

2 a Which of the following things are illegal in your country or city?

1 Feeding wild birds.
2 Riding a bicycle without a bell.
3 Letting your mobile ring at the cinema.
4 Putting your bag on a spare seat on public transport.
5 Putting your feet on the seat on public transport.
6 Smoking in bars and restaurants.
7 Smoking in parks and on the street.
8 Keeping a gun at work.
9 Keeping an ashtray on your desk at work.

b Read the rest of the article and find out which of the things in exercise 2a are illegal in New York.

The Forbidden Apple

Home to 8.2 million people, 36 percent of whom were born outside the United States, New York, known as the Big Apple, is the biggest city in America. Nearly twenty times bigger than the capital, Washington DC, you might expect New York to be twenty times more dangerous. Actually, it's safer. Recent figures show that New York now has fewer crimes per 100,000 people than 193 other US cities. It's also healthier than it used to be. For example, the smoking rate has gone down from 21.5 percent a few years ago, to 16.9 percent today.

New Yorkers should be delighted, shouldn't they? In fact, many feel that New York is losing its identity. It used to be the city that never sleeps. These days it's the city that never smokes, drinks or does anything naughty (at least, not in public). The Big Apple is quickly turning into the Forbidden Apple.

If you decided to have a picnic in Central Park, you'd need to be careful – if you decided to feed the birds with the last crumbs of your sandwich, you could be arrested. It's banned. Even riding your bike with your feet off the pedals is now against the law. And you'd better have a bell on your handlebars too, or face a fine.

In many countries a mobile phone going off in the cinema is irritating. In New York it's illegal. So is putting your bag on an empty seat in the subway.

If you went to a bar for a drink and a cigarette, that would be OK, wouldn't it? Er ... no. You can't smoke in public in New York City. In fact, you can't smoke outdoors on the street or in parks either.

Some of the laws are not actually new, but have never been enforced before now, so most people are not actually aware that they are breaking the law.

The result is a lot of fines for minor offences. An elderly woman, advised by her doctor to keep her leg elevated to avoid a blood clot was given a $50 fine for resting a foot on the subway chair opposite her. Her appeal, backed by her doctor, was turned down. Elle and Serge Schroitman were fined for blocking a driveway with their car. It was their own driveway.

The angry editor of *Vanity Fair* magazine, Graydon Carter, says, 'Under New York City law it is acceptable to keep a gun in your place of work, but not an empty ashtray.' He should know. The police came to his office and took away his ashtray.

But not all of New York's inhabitants are complaining. Marcia Dugarry, seventy-two, said, 'The city has changed for the better. If more cities had these laws, America would be a better place to live. Nixon Patotkis, thirty-eight, a barman, said, 'I like the new laws. If people smoked in here, we'd go home smelling of cigarettes.'

The new laws have helped turn the city into one of the healthiest and most pleasant places to live in America – very different from it. old image of a dirty and dangerous city. Its pavements are almost litter-free, its bars clean and its streets among America's safest. Not putting your feet on subway seats might be a small price to pay.

Vocabulary and speaking

3 **a** Work in pairs and discuss the questions.

1 What does the writer think about the new laws in New York? Is the article 100 percent serious? How do you know?

2 Do you think the laws in the article are 'stupid'? Why/Why not?

3 Would these laws be popular in your country? Why/Why not?

b Check the meaning of the following words and phrases from the article on page 106.

> against the law   an appeal   banned   be arrested
> break the law   face a fine   give someone a fine   illegal
> a minor offence

c Work in pairs. Discuss the questions using the vocabulary in the box in exercise 3b.

1 What would happen if you did some of the things in exercise 2a in your country? Do you agree with the punishment?

2 Should smoking be banned in all public places? Even outside?

3 Which is more important – individual freedom, or health and safety for everyone?

Grammar | Second Conditional

4 Read the Active grammar box and choose the correct <u>underlined</u> words.

> ## Active grammar
>
> We use the Second Conditional to describe <u>*an imaginary*</u>/<u>*a real*</u> situation in the present or future and its result.
> *If more cities had these laws, America would be a better place to live.*
> In the *if* clause, use the <u>*Present Simple*</u>/<u>*Past Simple*</u>.
> In the result clause, *would* (or *'d*) is used because the situation is in the <u>*past*</u>/<u>*imaginary (hypothetical)*</u>.
> *If people **smoked** in here, we**'d** go home smelling of cigarettes.*
> It is possible to use a modal verb such as *could* or *might* instead of *would*, if you are <u>*certain*</u>/<u>*not sure*</u> of the result.
> *If you decided to feed the birds with the last crumbs of your sandwich, you **could** be arrested.*
>
> ### First and Second Conditional:
>
> In a real/possible situation we use the <u>*First Conditional*</u>/<u>*Second Conditional*</u>.
>
> In an imaginary situation we use the <u>*First Conditional*</u>/<u>*Second Conditional*</u>.
>
> The <u>*First Conditional*</u>/<u>*Second Conditional*</u> uses the Present Simple + *will*.
>
> The <u>*First Conditional*</u>/<u>*Second Conditional*</u> uses the Past Simple + *would*.

see Reference page 117

5 Make Second Conditional sentences using the verbs in brackets.

1 If you _____ (be) a New York police officer, _____ (arrest) someone for feeding birds?

2 I _____ (not/like) the new laws if I _____ (live) in New York.

3 Where _____ (go) if you _____ (want) a cigarette at work?

4 I _____ (not/be) very happy if I _____ (have to) pay a fine for putting my bag on a seat.

5 If New York _____ (not/have) these laws, tourists _____ (find) it dangerous and dirty.

6 If these laws _____ (exist) in your country, _____ (be) popular?

7 There _____ (be) less crime if the police _____ (have) more power in my country.

6 Work in pairs. Are the situations below real/possible situations in your life or imaginary? In what circumstances would/will you ...

• lie to a police officer?
• miss my English lesson?
• live in another country?
• go away next weekend?
• stay in bed until 12:00 p.m.?
• take a taxi?
• make a long distance phone call?
• write to the government?
• sing in public?
• run a marathon/five km?

Speaking and listening

7 **a** Work in groups. If you could propose five new laws for the town where you are studying, what would they be?

b Tell the class about your laws/proposals and together, choose the five best.

If we could propose one new law, we'd stop cars from entering the city centre.

Vocabulary | cities

8 Complete the table with words and expressions from the box.

> building work   construction   drilling
> exhaust fumes   heatwave   horns honking
> roads being blocked   rush hour   terribly cold
> tower blocks   traffic jams

Noise	
Congestion	
Pollution	
Weather	

9 **a** ⏺ 2.22 Listen to Emma and Kirsten talking about things they would like to change about their cities (Madrid and Edinburgh). Tick (✓) the problems they mention.

	Madrid	Edinburgh
Noise	✓	
Construction		
Congestion		
Pollution		
Weather		
Architecture		

b Listen again and make notes about each problem they mention.

c What do they like about each city?

10 **a** Think about your town or city and use the language in the How to... box to make notes under the following headings.

a   What I like about my town/city

b   What I would like to change

c   How I feel about the town/city overall

> ### How to... discuss problems and suggest changes
>
> | Talking about what you'd like to change | *There are just a few things that I'd like to change ...* |
> |---|---|
> | | *I suppose I'd like to change ...* |
> | | *There always seems to be a lot of ...* |
> | | *It would be nicer perhaps if ...* |
> | Accepting what you can't change | *... but there's not much I can do about that.* |
> | | *But apart from that, ...* |
> | Concluding | *I don't think I'd want to live anywhere else.* |
> | | *I'd rather live in ...* |

b Work in pairs. Use your notes to tell your partner about your town or city.

Comic marathon man raises £200,000

To the cheering of taxi drivers and the honking of horns, the comedian and actor Eddie Izzard ran into London yesterday to complete his 43rd marathon in 52 days. In total he had covered 1,100 miles.

Fighting blisters that have caused the nails on his smaller toes to fall off and his larger toes to swell into 'alien monsters', he ran up The Mall and into Trafalgar Square where he had started 7¹/₂ weeks ago.

In finishing he proved what many thought was an impossible task: that a 47-year-old comedian with no sporting experience could do something a top athlete might find difficult.

His 43 marathons were in aid of the charity *Sports Relief*, which raises money for the poor all over the world. So far Izzard has raised more than £200,000.

After only six weeks' training he started out on a journey that would take him to every corner of the British Isles. 'The first three weeks were the hardest,' he said. The non-stop pressure on his body led to sleepless nights and he would wake exhausted with 'blisters on top of blisters'.

But the people he met along the way cheered him up. 'People stopped their cars and cheered, they gave me money and food.'

More than 500,000 people 'followed' the comedian, in a different sense, on Twitter. Running into London he looked lean and muscular. 'Everyone says my legs look very good but I thought they looked quite good beforehand,' he said.

Simon Blease, 51, a sports doctor and mountain runner who has been following his progress, was waiting on Tower Bridge. 'I didn't think he could do it,' he said. 'Like a lot of people I thought he would have a good try, but his body would break down. Someone with so little training, I find it extraordinary that he has done it.'

Asked what he had gained, Izzard said: 'I know now I can do that. Sport is one of those words that stopped being part of my life when I was about 14. Sporting success was not something I ever associated myself with.' He now plans to continue jogging and hopes to inspire others into sport.

He then excused himself – to take an ice bath. 'I'm going to have a party somewhere that is dry and then I'm going to sleep for a week,' he said.

Reading

1　**a**　Work in pairs. Read the newspaper headline and look at the photo. Before you read the article think of some questions you would like to ask about the story.

　　b　Read the article. Does it answer your questions?

2　Read the article again and answer the questions.

1　What is Izzard's age and usual job?
2　What was his marathon-running in aid of?
3　How much training did he do for the marathon?
4　What effect did the run have on his body?
5　How did it change his view of himself?

3　Work in pairs and discuss the questions.

1　Do you think his run is likely to inspire others? Why/Why not?
2　What other big charity events do you know about/have you participated in?
3　Do you think that raising money for charity can make a real difference to people's lives? Why/Why not?

Vocabulary | global issues

4 Work in pairs and discuss the questions.

1 What can you see in the photo?

2 Do you think this is an effective way to make things change?

5 Put the words and phrases in the box under the following headings. More than one answer may be possible.

- Environment
- Global economic issues
- Global political issues
- Health

> climate change   conflict   cure   debt(s)
> disease   fair trade   global warming
> intensive farming   mortality rate
> organic farming   peace   pollution
> poverty   recycling   solar power
> standard of living   war   wealth

6 **a** Complete the sentences with words and phrases from exercise 5.

1 _____ caused by cars and factories contributes to _____ . What do you think can or should be done about it?

2 People argue that _____ is better for the environment and healthier, but _____ produces more food. Which do you think is better?

3 Are you happy to pay a bit extra to buy goods which are _____ ? Why/Why not?

4 Do you think that doctors will find the _____ for many _____ , such as cancer?

5 Do you think that poorer countries should be forced to pay their _____ ? Why/Why not?

b Work in pairs and discuss the questions in exercise 6a.

Pronunciation | sounds and spelling: 'o'

7 **a** ● 2.23 Listen to the words in the box. How is the letter 'o' pronounced in each one? Put the words in the correct column.

> conflict   global   mortality   organic   poverty   solar

/ɒ/	/ɔː/	/əʊ/

b ● 2.24 Now put the words in the box below in the correct column in exercise 7a, according to the pronunciation of 'o'. Then listen to the words to check.

> coast   cold   floor   hot   open   own   phone
> pocket   road   short   throw   your

c 'O' is often pronounced /ɔː/ when there is an 'r' after the 'o'. The spelling patterns below can also make the sound /ɔː/. Try to think of an example word for each one.

ou	au	al	aw	ar	oo

see Pronunciation bank page 163

Listening and speaking

8 ● 2.25 Listen to two people discussing how the world has changed since they were children. Which issues in exercise 5 do they talk about?

9 Look at the How to... box. Listen again and tick (✓) the phrases you hear.

How to... express attitude and respond to opinions

Express your attitude	*Luckily, ...*
	Unfortunately, ...
	(Not) surprisingly, ...
	Interestingly, ...
Respond to an opinion	**Positive**
	Too right! (informal)
	I completely agree with you.
	That's certainly true.
	You have a point there. (informal)
	Neutral
	Well, that's your opinion.
	Perhaps, perhaps not.
	Negative
	I can't agree with you there.
	I don't know about that.
	Oh, come on! (informal)

Speaking

10 a Work in two groups.

Group 1: you are optimists. Write five things that have made the world better in the last twenty-five years.

Group 2: you are pessimists. Write five things that have made the world worse in the last twenty-five years.

b Take it in turns to read your sentences. Respond to the other group's sentences in a positive, negative or neutral way. Use the How to... box on page 110 to help you.

Grammar | adverbs

11 a Read the Active grammar box and match the example sentences (1–4) with the rules (A–D).

1 The situation has really improved.
2 Luckily, doctors and surgeons can cure so many diseases now.
3 In the future, disease probably won't be such a big problem.
4 The number of cars on the roads is growing quickly.

b Choose the correct <u>underlined</u> words.

Active grammar

To make an adverb we usually add -ly to the adjective.
quiet – quietly; clear – clearly

A Adverbs of manner modify verbs. They describe the way in which something happens.
*She talked **quietly**.*
e.g. sentence ____
These adverbs usually come *before/after* the main verb.

B Adverbs of frequency/probability describe how often something happens or how probable it is.
*She **usually** comes to my house on Fridays.*
e.g. sentence ____
These usually come *before/after* the main verb.

C Adverbs of degree make an adjective or a verb weaker or stronger. They may be used for emphasis.
*I'm **completely** confused.*
*The temperature has **slightly** increased.*
e.g. sentence ____

D Attitude adverbs may be used as discourse markers to describe your attitude.
***Interestingly**, she didn't phone back.*
e.g. sentence ____
These usually come at the *beginning/end* of the sentence because they modify the whole sentence (or clause).

see Reference page 117

12 Match the adverbs in the box with their uses (1–6).

> basically   fortunately
> hopefully   obviously
> personally   surprisingly

1 when something good or lucky happens
2 when something is not as you would expect
3 when you say what you hope will happen
4 when you give your opinion
5 to emphasise the most important fact about something
6 when describing something you can understand easily

Speaking

13 a Work in groups and guess the answers to the questions.

1 Which continent has the most people?
2 What percentage of the world's people don't have enough food to eat?
3 What percentage live in houses without running water?
4 What percentage of people can read/have been to university/own a computer?

b Look at page 150. Check your answers and complete the sentences.

c Compare your sentences with your group and discuss your reactions.

Your life, your decisions

This week's problems

1

After leaving university, Linda got a well-paid job with a big city bank. She has now worked there for eight years and has been **promoted** twice. However, she isn't really happy in her work. She hates having to commute through the rush hour, doesn't enjoy office politics or the stress and long hours.

She has been considering quitting her job and going to work as a **volunteer** overseas. She would like to be doing a job where she is really making a difference to other people's lives. But should she **take the plunge**?

It depends what other responsibilities she has. If she doesn't have a family to support, then why not? You only live once.

Jack, UK

If she is so unhappy then I think she has **no real alternative**. She should leave – if she doesn't, she'll **regret** it.

Vikram, India

I think she has a number of different options. She could, for example, ask for a year's **unpaid leave** so that she could try out her new lifestyle and still come back to her job if it doesn't work out.

Chiara, Italy

2

Jack and his girlfriend Suzie have been together for six years. They were planning to get married and **start a family** in the near future, but Jack has just been offered **a once-in-a-lifetime opportunity** abroad. His employers want him to spend two years at the New York office. Suzie doesn't want to follow him to New York as she has just **landed her dream job** in London. Can they realistically maintain **a long distance relationship**? What should Jack do **for the best**?

If they want to make the relationship work long distance, then it's certainly possible. But maybe Jack secretly wants to put some distance between them. Is he ready for marriage?

Beata, Poland.

I don't think long distance relationships ever work. Maybe for a while at the beginning of a relationship, but not like this. If he wants to stay with Suzie, he shouldn't go.

Ana, Brazil

I don't see the problem. They can talk to each other every day if they want to – it's cheap enough now online. Flights aren't that expensive either, and presumably the salary will be good. Jack should **go for it**!

Katie, Ireland

Reading and vocabulary

1 Read the problems and advice from a website. Do you agree with any of the advice? Do you have any different ideas?

2 Match the words and phrases in **bold** in the texts with the definitions below.

Problem 1

1   decide to do something important and risky, after thinking about it carefully
2   time off work with no salary
3   someone who does work without being paid
4   given a better job, usually with more money
5   no choice
6   feel sorry about something that has happened

Problem 2

1   a relationship when the two people live very far apart
2   try to get or do something you want
3   a chance to do something that may never come again
4   have your first child
5   to have the best result
6   got the perfect job for her

Speaking

3   **a** Work in pairs and discuss the questions.

1   Are you good or bad at making decisions?
2   If you have an important decision to make, who do you talk to about it? Why?

b Choose three or four decisions you have made from the list below, or use your own ideas. Make notes about the decisions you made and how you decided.

- which subjects to study at school/university
- to leave school
- to go to university
- to buy or sell a house/flat
- to get married
- to start or change your career
- to start your own business
- to leave a job
- to take up or give up a hobby/sport
- to retire or give up work

c Work in pairs. Tell your partner about the decisions you made and why.

Listening

4 **a** 🔊 2.26 Listen to these people talking about important decisions they have taken. Which decisions from exercise 3 does each person talk about?

Roger

Tunde

Sarah

b Listen again and answer the questions. There may be more than one answer.

Who ...

1 didn't do what his/her family wanted?
2 went overseas?
3 has started their own business?
4 is planning to get married?
5 had a life-changing holiday?
6 wanted to spend more time with his/her family?
7 has bought a new house?

c Check your answers to exercise 4b in the audioscript for track 2.26 on page 173.

d Work in pairs. Which speaker do you think had the most difficult decision to make? Why?

Grammar | Third Conditional

5 **a** Read the extracts from the listening and answer the questions.

If I had stayed at work, I wouldn't have spent time with Jack when he really needed me.

1 Did Roger stay at work?
2 Did he spend time with Jack?

I wouldn't have met Nancy if I hadn't come to France!

3 Did Tunde come to France?
4 Did he meet Nancy?

b Look at the Active grammar box and choose the correct underlined words.

Active grammar

We use the Third Conditional to talk about a *real*/*imaginary* situation in the *present*/*past*.

We make the Third Conditional with ...

if + subject + past perfect + *would(n't) have*/*could(n't) have* + past participle.

Past condition   Past result (hypothetical)
*If I **had stayed** at work, I **wouldn't have spent** time with Jack.*

or

Past result (hypothetical)   Past condition
*I **would have cooked** dinner **if I'd known** you were coming.*

In spoken English, *have* and *had* are usually contracted to *'ve* and *'d*.

For a hypothetical situation in the present or future we use the *Second Conditional*/*Third Conditional*.

For a hypothetical situation in the past we use the *Second Conditional*/*Third Conditional*.

---

see Reference page 117

6 Match the sentence beginnings (1–8) with the endings (a–h).

1 If I had known the test was today,
2 I wouldn't have missed the last train
3 If I'd known it was you on the phone,
4 If you'd asked me out to dinner,
5 I wouldn't have felt so tired this morning
6 If I hadn't gone on holiday to Greece,
7 I would have organised a party for you
8 I wouldn't have spent so much time with my children

a if I'd gone to bed earlier.
b I'd have said 'yes'.
c I would have done some revision.
d if I'd known you were coming.
e I would've answered it.
f if I hadn't stopped work.
g if I had left home earlier.
h I wouldn't have met my husband.

7 Read the text and complete the sentences using the Third Conditional.

> There was a lot of snow and Rosa's flight was delayed. She decided to go for a cup of coffee. There was a bag on the floor but she didn't see it and tripped over. She spilt her coffee on Paulo. They started talking and a year later they got married.

If it hadn't snowed, Rosa's flight wouldn't have been delayed.

1 If her flight hadn't been delayed, _____ .

2 _____ , she wouldn't have tripped over.

3 _____ tripped over, she _____ her coffee.

4 If _____ , _____ talking to Paulo.

5 _____ talking, they _____ .

Pronunciation | sentence stress in the Third Conditional

8 **a** 🔊 2.27 Listen to this sentence. Which words are contracted?

If I had left home earlier, I wouldn't have missed the train.

b Listen again to the rhythm of the sentence in exercise 8a. Do the stressed words fall with a regular beat in the sentence? How many 'beats' are there in the sentence?

9 **a** Underline the stressed words in these sentences.

1 If I'd known the test was today, I'd have done some revision.

2 If I'd gone to bed earlier, I wouldn't have been so tired.

3 If you'd asked me out to dinner, I'd have said 'yes'.

b 🔊 2.28 Listen and check. Practise saying the sentences using the same rhythm.

see Pronunciation bank page 164

Speaking

10 **a** Draw two large circles in your notebook and label one of them 'Now' and the other 'Ten years ago'. Read the questions and write short answers in the 'Now' circle.

1 Where are you living?
2 What do you do?
3 Who is your closest friend?
4 How do you spend your free time?
5 Do you spend much time with your family?
6 Are you studying anything?
7 Do you play any sports?
8 What music do you enjoy?
9 What are your dreams/ambitions?

b Change the questions in exercise 10a to make questions about the past. Write short answers for these questions anywhere in the 'Ten years ago' circle.

11 Work in pairs and show your circles to each other. Tell your partner about how your life has changed in the past ten years. Ask questions to find out as much information as possible.

12 Work in pairs and discuss the questions.

1 What have been the important turning points (important moments or events which have changed things) in your life?
2 How might your life have changed if these turning points had been different?
3 Do you think you have always made the right decisions?

Writing

13 Write a paragraph describing an important turning point in your life and the effect this had. Think about what happened before/after the event, and how things might have been different.

get married?
back to college?
change job?
move house?
·SOLD·

1 Look at the table and add your own example words.

Prefix	Meaning	Example	Your examples
over-	too much	overcook	
under-	not enough/below	underdeveloped	
dis-	used to make an opposite meaning	dishonest	
in-/im-	not or no	inhuman	

2 Complete the text with prefixes from exercise 1.

Life CHANGE

Many people dislike their job. Maybe they are (1) _____worked or (2) _____paid. Maybe they feel (3) _____valued in the company or they (4) _____agree with the company's methods. If you are one of these people, why not change things? LifeCHANGE workshops show you how to be (5) _____ dependent. You will see (6) _____credible differences in your life as your problems (7) _____appear. Change is never (8) _____possible, but you have to make the first move.

Call us on **0879 997 5543** for an (9) _____formal chat.

3 Look at the table and add your own example words.

Suffix	Example	Rules	Your examples
-tion/-ation	creation civilisation	If the verb ends in -e, cut the -e. If the verb ends in -se, the suffix is usually -isation.	
-ence/-ance	intelligence ignorance	There are no clear rules about which words end -ence or -ance. You have to learn them.	
-ment	movement	Add -ment to the verb.	
-ness	darkness	If the word ends in -y, change the -y to -i. happy → happiness	

4 Correct the sentences by changing the form of the words in bold. Use suffixes from exercise 3.

Vote for the Perfect Party

1 Our priority is **educate**.
2 We will increase **employ**.
3 We promise to give free **accommodate** to people over sixty-five.
4 There will be free hospital **treat** for everyone.
5 We promise proper **punish** for criminals.
6 We believe in the **important** of free speech.
7 Giving you, the voter, your **independent**.
8 A **govern** for the twenty-first century.
9 Taking the country in a new **direct**.
10 Your vote can make a **different**.

5 **a** Choose one of the topics below and make some notes about it.

- an inspiration
- new forms of entertainment
- globalisation
- a great achievement/my greatest achievement
- what happiness means to me
- cultural differences
- my development

b Work in small groups. Speak about your topic using your notes to help you.

c Change groups. Either speak about the same topic more fluently, or speak about a different topic. What new things did you learn about your classmates?

8 Communication

Can do express and respond to feelings

1 Work in pairs. If you could change one thing in your life, what would you like to change? Why?

I'd like to have a bigger flat so that I could invite my friends to stay.

2 **a** 🔘 2.29 Listen to the people in the photos answering the questions above. Which question does each person answer? Write the number (1–5) next to each photo (A–E).

1 Your house is too small for your needs. Would you …
  A put up with it for as long as possible because you hate moving?
  B be anxious about it, as it is a big decision to make and you might get it wrong?
  C draw up a checklist of things to do and plan the move for the future?
  D love the idea of moving and rush off to the estate agent during your lunch break?

2 Someone you know suggests that you should change your image. Would you …
  A make an appointment at the hairdresser's and arrange to go shopping with a friend?
  B feel very offended as the way you look has suited you for a long time?
  C feel you would like to change, but what to? You'll probably go back to how you always look anyway.
  D look through magazines for a few days before making any decisions?

3 At an interview, you are offered promotion. It means moving to another city. Would you …
  A say no immediately as you'd never leave the city where you grew up?
  B ask for time to think about it and start researching the new city?
  C feel you should accept the offer because it is a better job, but be a bit worried that you might regret it later?
  D say yes immediately as you are always up for a new challenge?

4 You get on well with one of your friend's guests at a party. Would you …
  A take the plunge and suggest meeting for a coffee later that week?
  B ask colleagues and friends about them before starting a friendship?
  C know you have too many friends already, so you really don't want another?
  D worry that they might not find you interesting enough for a further meeting?

b Listen again and make notes about what each person says. Then work in pairs and compare your notes.

c How would you respond to what each speaker says? Use the responses below or your own ideas.

That sounds fascinating!
I wish I could do that!
I know just what you mean.
I wouldn't want to do that.

d Work in groups. Take it in turns to answer the questions in exercise 3. Respond to what the people in your group say.

3 Read the questions below and note down your answers.

1 Does your job/lifestyle give you enough new, interesting experiences?
2 What changes do you think you might make in the future?
3 Has anything in your life changed for the better recently? Think about your friends/family/town/country.
4 Is it important for people to change their routine?
5 Do you think you like change?

4 **a** Complete the questionnaire below about how you deal with change.

b Look at page 150 to find out what your answers mean.

c Work in pairs and compare your results. Do you agree with them?

8 Reference

Second Conditional

To talk about an unreal/imaginary/hypothetical situation and its consequences, we use:

If + Past Simple + *would('d)/wouldn't*
*If I **had** a car, I'**d** drive to work.*

We can use *would*, *could* or *might* in the result clause.

*I'**d** live in Jamaica if I **could** live anywhere.*

The '*if* clause' can come first or second in the sentence. If it is first, there is a comma before the result clause.

If I could live anywhere, I'd live in Jamaica.

When the subject is *I* and the verb is *to be*, we often say *If I **were***.

*If I **were** you, I **wouldn't** wear that dress again!*

Adverbs

We usually make an adverb by adding *-ly* to the adjective.

interesting – interestingly   *quick – quickly*

Some adverbs are irregular.

good (adj) – *well* (adv)   *hard* (adj) – *hard* (adv)
*Do you feel **well**?*   *Natasha works **hard**.*

1   **Adverbs of manner** describe how something happens – they modify the verb. They usually come after the verb.
    *The news spread **quickly** around the office.*
    *Drive **carefully**!*

2   **Adverbs of frequency/probability** describe how often something happens or how probable it is. They usually come before the main verb.
    *Newspapers **rarely** report on these important issues.*
    *She'll **probably** arrive at six o'clock.*

3   **Adverbs of degree** modify an adjective or a verb. They make it weaker or stronger.
    *It was **totally** unexpected.*
    *He's **quite** late.*

4   **Attitude adverbs** describe the speaker's attitude towards the information in the clause.
    ***Luckily**, the money was still there when I returned.*
    ***Surprisingly**, he waited until the bus had left.*
    (These can come at the beginning/end of the sentence because they modify the whole sentence or clause.)

There is usually a comma after a sentence adverb.

! Some adjectives look like adverbs because they end in *-ly*, but they are not, e.g. *silly, lovely, lively.*

Third Conditional

We use this form to talk about imaginary or hypothetical past situations, and imagine different consequences.

*If there **hadn't been** so much traffic on the motorway, I **would have got** to the meeting on time.*

Form: *If* + past perfect + *would have* + past participle

To indicate possibility, rather than certainty, we can use *might have/could have* instead of *would have*.

*If she'**d studied** harder, she **might have passed** her exams.*

These unreal past situations have unreal past results.

*If I'**d studied** Art I **would have been** happier.*

Sometimes the hypothetical past situation has a present result.

*If I'**d finished** my university degree, I'**d be** an architect now.*
(*If* + Past Perfect + *would* + verb)

Key vocabulary

Expressions with *change*

career change   climate change   image change
political change   change an arrangement/direction/places/
the subject/your mind/your address/your clothes/
your hairstyle/your name/your password/your tune

The law

against the law   an appeal   banned   be arrested
break the law   face a fine   give someone a fine   illegal
a minor offence

Cities

architecture   building work   congestion   construction
drilling   exhaust fumes   heatwave   horns honking
noise   roads being blocked   rush hour   terribly cold
tower blocks   traffic jams

Global issues

climate change   conflict   cure   debt(s)   disease
fair trade   global warming   intensive farming
mortality rate   organic farming   peace   pollution   poverty
recycling   solar power   standard of living   war   wealth

Life decisions

be promoted/be offered a promotion
have no real alternative   quit   regret something
take the plunge   take unpaid leave   volunteer

 Listen to the explanations and vocabulary.
ACTIVEBOOK

 see Writing bank page 160

8 Review and practice

1 Make Second Conditional sentences beginning with the words in brackets

I am too old. I can't learn to play rugby. (If)

If I was/were younger, I would learn to play rugby.

1 She doesn't have Dave's number. She wants to call him. (If)

2 I can't go out. I have an exam tomorrow. (I'd)

3 We want to buy a new car. We don't have enough money at the moment. (If)

4 There isn't time. They can't see the show. (They'd)

5 I don't have a choice. I want to live in the city. (If)

6 We want to go swimming. The sea is polluted. (We'd)

7 It's raining heavily. We want to go for a walk. (If)

2 Complete the First and Second Conditional sentences with the correct form of the verbs in brackets.

1 She's coming tomorrow so when she _____ (arrive), I _____ (pick) her up.

2 If I _____ (win) a million euros, I _____ (buy) an enormous house.

3 I _____ (leave) my job if I _____ (have) enough money. Sadly, I don't.

4 If you _____ (cook) dinner, I _____ (do) the washing-up. Thanks for the offer.

5 If he _____ (study), he _____ (pass) the test. But he's very lazy.

6 If he _____ (study), he _____ (pass) the test and we can have a big party to celebrate.

7 If you _____ (live) nearer, I _____ (give) you a lift, but it's just too far.

3 Make adverbs from the words in brackets. Write the adverb in the correct space to complete the sentences.

_____ we will see _____ them at the party. (*hopeful*)
Hopefully we will see them at the party.

1 I _____ go _____ to the supermarket on Saturdays. (*usual*)

2 Susana is so _____ busy that I _____ ever see her any more. (*hard*)

3 Steve _____ drives when we _____ go on long journeys. (*normal*)

4 I exercise _____ in _____ the gym. (*regular*)

5 We _____ don't _____ want to damage the relationship. (*certain*)

6 _____ , I can't see _____ how we can do it any other way. (*personal*)

7 He did a very poor interview. _____ , he got the _____ job. (*surprising*)

4 Complete the sentences with the phrases in the box.

> had decided ~~had gone dancing~~ hadn't gone
> had known hadn't listened to the radio
> wouldn't have heard wouldn't have met
> ~~wouldn't have woken up~~ wouldn't have gone
> wouldn't have worked

If I *had gone dancing* all night, I *wouldn't have woken up* this morning.

1 If I _____ to university, I _____ Sam.

2 If I _____ that England was so cold in the summer, I _____ there.

3 If I _____ to study medicine, I _____ in an office all my life.

4 If I _____ this morning, I _____ the news.

5 Complete the Third Conditional sentences using the verbs in brackets.

1 If she _____ (ask) me to help her, we _____ (finish) the job yesterday.

2 If I _____ (know) you were coming, I _____ (cook) some more supper.

3 If Ken _____ (leave) five minutes earlier this morning, he _____ (miss) the train.

4 If you _____ (tell) me you needed to get up early, I _____ (wake) you.

5 If she _____ (see) the mess, she _____ (be) angry.

6 If I _____ (not/drink) that coffee, I _____ (fall asleep) during the film.

7 If I _____ (not/lose) my camera last week, I _____ (take) some photos of the children.

6 Complete the sentences with the words and phrases from the box.

> banned cure environment fine ~~mind~~
> password pollution standard subject

I planned to study Art, but I changed my *mind* and studied French.

1 He didn't want to talk about politics so he changed the _____ .

2 Smoking in the office is _____ .

3 All the traffic in the city causes _____ .

4 Waste from industries is bad for the _____ .

5 We haven't found a _____ for AIDS yet.

6 You should change your computer _____ every month.

7 Most African countries have a very low _____ of living.

8 If you park your car in the wrong place, you may face a _____ .

Lead-in

1 Work in pairs and discuss the questions.

1 Describe the working environments in the photos.
2 What are the pros and cons of working in each place?
3 What would be your ideal working environment? Why?

2 **a** 2.30 Listen to someone answering the following questions. Number the questions in the order you hear them.

a When you **apply for** a job, do you normally **send a CV**? Do you need to include **references**? `1`

b Do you do a **nine to five job** then?

c Would you like to **work flexitime**?

d What are the **perks** of your job?

e How do you hear about **job vacancies** in your profession?

f How often do you **work overtime**?

g Would you like to be **self-employed** or **work freelance**? Why/Why not?

h Are you **employed** or **self-employed**?

i How often do you expect to **get a pay rise** in your job? Is it easy to **get promoted**?

b Work in pairs. Discuss the meaning of the words and phrases in **bold** in exercise 2a.

c Listen again and check your answers.

3 Work in pairs. Think about your job or a job you would like to have, and discuss the questions.

9.1 Freedom at work

Grammar	*make, let, allow*
Can do	ask for clarification

Speaking and listening

 a Read the quotes. Write *A* (agree), *D* (disagree), or *N* (not sure).

> 'People who work sitting down get paid more than people who work standing up.' (Ogden Nash)

> 'The longer the title, the less important the job.' (George McGovern)

> 'Most workplaces have too many rules. Employees aren't children, and the office isn't a junior school.' (Araba Green)

> 'Most managers spend their time making it difficult for workers to work.' (Paul Shorter)

b Work in pairs and compare your ideas.

c 🔘 2.31 Listen to James, Carol and Verity discussing the quotes in exercise 1a. Tick (✓) the opinions (1–7) that you hear.

1 Teachers work standing up and don't get paid that much.
2 Some people, such as admin staff, work sitting down but are not well paid.
3 Companies like to give people longer job titles instead of raising their pay.
4 Some bosses just enjoy making up more and more rules.
5 Some people abuse rules at work and everyone else suffers.
6 The person who does the job usually knows more about it than their manager.
7 Managers are usually too busy to make things difficult for other people.

d Work in pairs. Which of the opinions (1–7) do you agree with?

Reading

 Which workers (e.g. managers, receptionists, secretaries, ...) normally do the things below? Write answers, then compare in pairs.

- decide start/finish times/working hours
- do the photocopying
- meet guests in reception
- set salaries
- type emails
- wear uniforms

3 **a** Read the introduction to the article. Who is Ricardo Semler? What problem did he have?

b Work in groups. What changes do you think Semler made? Write a list. Then read the rest of the article to check your ideas.

Semco

At twenty-one, Ricardo Semler became the boss of his father's business in Brazil, Semco, which sold parts for ships. Knowing his son was still young, Semler senior told him, 'Better make your mistakes while I'm still alive.'

Semler junior worked like a madman, from 7:30 a.m. until midnight every day. One afternoon, while touring a factory in New York, he collapsed. The doctor who treated him said, 'There's nothing wrong with you. Yet. But if you continue like this, you'll find a new home in our hospital.' Semler got the message. He changed the way he worked. In fact, he changed the way his employees worked too.

He let his workers take more responsibility so that they would be the ones worrying when things went wrong. He allowed them to set their own salaries, and he cut all the jobs he thought were unnecessary, like receptionists and secretaries. This saved money and brought more equality to the company. 'Everyone at Semco, even top managers, meets guests in reception, does the photocopying, sends faxes, types letters and dials the phone.'

He completely reorganised the office: instead of walls, they have plants at Semco, so bosses can't shut themselves away from everyone else. And the workers are free to decorate their workspace as they want. As for uniforms, some people wear suits and others wear T-shirts.

Semler says, 'We have an employee named Rubin Agater who sits there reading the newspaper hour after hour. He doesn't even pretend to be busy. But when a Semco pump on the other side of the world fails and millions of gallons of oil are about to spill into the sea, Rubin springs into action. He knows everything there is to know about our pumps and how to fix them. That's when he earns his salary. No one cares if he doesn't look busy the rest of the time.'

Semco has flexible working hours: the employees decide when they need to arrive at work. The employees also evaluate their bosses twice a year. Also, Semco lets its workers use the company's machines for their own projects, and makes them take holidays for at least thirty days a year.

It sounds perfect, but does it work? The answer is in the numbers: in the last six years, Semco's revenues have gone from $35 million to $212 million. The company has grown from eight hundred employees to 3,000. Why?

Semler says it's because of 'peer pressure'. Peer pressure makes everyone work hard for everyone else. If someone isn't doing his job well, the other workers will not allow the situation to continue. In other words, Ricardo Semler treats his workers like adults and expects them to act like adults. And they do.

4 Read the article again and answer the questions.

1 What do employees at Semco do that they probably wouldn't do in other companies?
2 How does Semco and its staff look different from other companies?
3 Who is Rubin Agater and why is he important at Semco?
4 How does Semco show that it trusts its workers?
5 Do Semco's methods work? How do we know?
6 What is 'peer pressure' and why is it important at Semco?

5 Work in pairs and discuss the questions.

1 What do you think of Semco's policies?
2 Would you like to work in a company with these policies?
3 Would any of the 'rules' at Semco be possible where you work/in your country? Why/Why not?

Grammar | *make, let, allow*

6 Read the Active grammar box. Then complete the sentences/phrases in A and B with the correct form of *make, let* or *allow*.

Active grammar

Semco **lets** its workers use the company's machines ...

Semco **makes** the workers take holidays.
The workers **are made to** take holidays.

Semler **allowed** the workers **to** set their own salaries.
The workers **are allowed to** set their own salaries.

A Meaning

_____ and _____ mean *give permission to do something.*
_____ means *force to do something.*

B Form

_____ someone do something
Passive: be _____ to do something

_____ someone to do something
Passive: be _____ to do something

_____ someone do something
_____ cannot be used in the passive.

see Reference page 131

7 Rewrite each sentence, using *make, let* or *allow* so the meaning stays the same.

He allowed his workers to take more responsibility.
He let *his workers take more responsibility*.

1 The managers have to do the photocopying.
Semler makes _____ .
2 Semler doesn't let the bosses shut themselves away.
The bosses aren't _____ .
3 The workers are free to decorate the workspace as they want.
The workers are _____ .
4 The workers don't have to wear suits.
Semler doesn't _____ the workers _____ .
5 The workers can use the company's machines for their own projects.
Semler _____ the workers use the company's machines for their own projects.

8 Complete the sentences with a suitable ending.

1 Our boss is very relaxed. She lets _____ .
2 The employees have great holidays. They're allowed _____ .
3 He was wearing dirty clothes in the office. So the boss made _____ .
4 It wasn't a very good job. The workers were made _____ .
5 It's my favourite airline. They allow _____ .
6 Don't go near the computer! You're not allowed _____ .

Speaking

9 a Work in pairs. Do you agree with the following statements? Why/Why not?

1 Companies should allow people to work flexitime.
2 Businesses shouldn't let people smoke in the workplace.
3 Businesses should allow workers to set their own salaries.
4 Companies shouldn't make workers retire at sixty-five.

b How would you improve your current place of work/study? Complete the sentence beginnings below.

I'd let ...
I'd allow ...
I'd make ...

Listening

10 **a** ● 2.32 Listen to a talk about a new business and answer the questions.

1 What type of business is it?
2 What is special about this business?
3 What will the chefs be allowed to do?
4 How many people will they employ?
5 What perk will employees get?
6 What is the name of the business?

b Listen again. Note down phrases the speaker uses to …

1 greet people.
2 introduce the topic.
3 emphasise the key points.
4 conclude.
5 say that the talk is finished.

11 ● 2.33 Listen to three questions the speaker is asked at the end of the talk. What are the questions and answers? Make notes.

Pronunciation | intonation for pausing

12 **a** Look at the extracts from the listening (1–3). Divide each of them into three sections, showing where the speaker pauses.

1 We'll allow the chefs to choose the dishes / and the menu will be very big, with something for everybody.

2 We won't make the waiters wear a uniform, and they will have one special perk: we'll let them eat free at our restaurant.

3 To sum up, our restaurant will be small and friendly but with a great international menu.

b ● 2.34 Listen and check your ideas.

c Listen again and mark where the speaker's intonation goes up or down. How do we know when the speaker has finished his point, or is going to continue?

see Pronunciation bank page 164

13 Read the How to… box and listen again to the questions and answers in exercise 11. Tick (✓) the phrases you hear.

How to… ask for clarification and deal with difficult questions

Asking for clarification or more information	*What I'd like to know is … ?* *Could you say that again?* *I wonder if you could explain …* *Could you tell me a bit more about … ?* *I didn't quite follow what you said about …* *Are you saying … ?* *Would it be true to say you agree … ?*
Dealing with difficult questions	*Well, let me think about that …* *That's a very interesting question …* *I'm not really sure …* *I'll have to get back to you on that.*

Speaking

14 **a** Imagine you are going to set up a new company. Work in groups and complete the company profile.

COMPANYPROFILE

Name: _____

Location: _____

Type of business: _____

_____

Number of employees: _____

Future plans: _____

_____

_____

Holidays: _____

b Think about how you will treat your employees. Will you …

1 let them work flexitime?
2 make them work long hours/overtime?
3 allow them perks? Give examples.
4 let them take lots of responsibility? How?
5 make them wear uniforms?

c Present your ideas to the rest of the class. Listen to the other groups' ideas and make notes and ask questions. Which company would you want to work for? Why?

Listening and speaking

1 **a** Look at the picture. What kind of boss do you think this is? Have you ever known a boss like this?

b 🔊 2.35 Listen to descriptions of the different management styles (1–3) below. Which style do you think the boss in the picture has?

1 autocratic   2 democratic   3 laissez faire

c Listen again and complete the notes.

Autocratic

What it means: _____
How the speaker feels about it: _____
When it works well: _____

Democratic

What it means: _____
How the speaker feels about it: _____
A disadvantage: _____

Laissez faire

What it means: _____
When it works well: _____
A disadvantage: _____

2 Think about a boss or a teacher you have had. Then work in pairs and discuss the questions.

1 Was he/she more autocratic or democratic?
2 Do you think his/her style worked well in the circumstances? Why/Why not?
3 What kind of boss or teacher would you like to be? Why?

Vocabulary | -ed and -ing adjectives

3 Look at the examples and choose the correct words in *italics*.

I find that style of management annoying.

I'm much more motivated.

1 We use *-ed* adjectives to talk about *feelings/ situations that cause the feelings.*
2 We use *-ing* adjectives to talk about *feelings/ situations that cause the feelings.*

4 Choose the correct adjective in *italics* to complete the sentences.

1 I'm going to watch the World Cup final tonight. I'm so *excited/exciting*!
2 I'm *exhausted/exhausting*. I've just been for a long run.
3 Can we stop talking about politics? It's very *bored/boring*.
4 I'm not watching that horror film. It's too *frightened/frightening*.
5 I hate getting up early every day. It's so *tired/tiring*.
6 I don't watch the news on television, because I find it too *depressed/depressing*.
7 I don't walk on my own at night. I'm too *frightened/frightening*.
8 I love sitting in a café and reading the newspaper in the morning. I find it very *relaxed/relaxing*.
9 I find English grammar a bit *confused/confusing*.

5 **a** Read the questions below and note down your answers. Think about when you are working/ studying and your freetime.

1 What do you find interesting?
2 What do you find confusing?
3 What makes you motivated?
4 What do you do when you are bored?
5 What do you find relaxing?

b Work in pairs and discuss the questions.

Reading

6 a Work in pairs. Look at the words in the box from the story below. What do you think the story is about?

> come down   engineer   hot air balloon   lost
> manager   problem   promise

b Read the story and check your ideas.

c Work in pairs. Do you agree with what the story says about managers and technicians/engineers? Why/Why not?

The Engineer and the Manager

A man flying in a hot air balloon realised he was lost. He started to come down until he could see a man on the ground who might hear him. 'Excuse me,' he shouted. 'Can you help me? I promised my friend I would meet him a half hour ago, but I don't know where I am, or where I am going.'

The man below responded: 'Yes. You are in a hot air balloon, approximately 30 feet above this field. You are between 40 and 42 degrees North Latitude, and between 58 and 60 degrees West Longitude.'

'You must be an engineer,' responded the balloonist. 'I am,' the man replied. 'How did you know?' 'Well,' said the balloonist, 'everything you have told me is technically correct, but I have no idea what to do with this information, and the fact is I am still lost.'

Whereupon the man on the ground responded, 'You must be a manager.' 'I am,' replied the balloonist, 'but how did you know?' 'Well,' said the man, 'you don't know where you are, or where you're going. You've made a promise which you can't keep, and you expect me to solve your problem. The fact is you are in the exact same position you were before we met, but now it's my fault.'

Grammar | reported speech

7 Look at the sentences (1–4) and write what the people actually said.

1   The manager asked if the engineer could help him.
    '_____?'

2   The manager said (that) he didn't know where he was going.
    '_____.'

3   The manager told the engineer that everything he had said was technically correct but that he was still lost.
    '_____.'

4   The engineer told the manager that he had made a promise which he couldn't keep and that he expected him to solve his problem.
    '_____.'

8 Read the Active grammar box and complete the examples (1–5).

Active grammar

With reported speech we usually use *say* or *tell*. Note that *say* cannot have a person as its object.

He **said** (that) he was lost./He **told** me (that) he was lost.

When you report speech, you usually change the tense one step back to show that the words were said in the past.

'*I'm going* for a job interview.'

*She said she **was going** for a job interview.*

Present Simple	Past Simple
Carly is in a meeting.	1 She told me Carly _____.
Present Continuous	**Past Continuous**
I am going to meet Marc.	2 He said _____.
Present Perfect/ Past Simple	**Past Perfect**
Tom has been late every day.	3 He told me _____.
He didn't buy it yesterday.	4 She told me he _____ the day before.
will/can	***would/could***
I'll help you.	5 He said he _____ help me.

see Reference page 131

9 Complete the sentences with the correct form of *say* or *tell*.

1 Please _____ Jenny I'll call tomorrow.
2 Excuse me. Can you _____ me the time?
3 The guide _____ that the museum was closed.
4 I _____ you that we'd be late.
5 I didn't hear you. Can you _____ that again?
6 _____ me what the interviewer _____ .
7 She _____ that we should wait here.
8 They _____ me not to go to Moscow.

10 Write the sentences in reported speech.

1 'I'm the new technician.' He said …
2 'I'll be back tomorrow.' Mum said …
3 'I've been stuck in traffic.' Mara told us …
4 'He won't be away for long.' She said …
5 'I'll carry your bag for you.' He said …
6 'We're going on holiday next week.' He told me …
7 'I went shopping yesterday.' He told us …
8 'I'm feeling better.' She told him …

Listening

11 a Work in pairs. What questions might you be asked in a job interview? Make a list.

b Look at the job profile below. What is the difference between 'essential' and 'desirable'?

c Put the headings in the box in the correct section (1–4) of the profile.

> Experience and knowledge   Personal qualities
> Qualifications and training   Skills

Job profile: Marketing Assistant

	Essential	Desirable
1 ___	A degree	A degree in marketing
2 ___	An understanding of marketing	Experience of working in marketing
3 ___	Excellent communication skills Organisation skills	Ability to negotiate
4 ___	Self-motivated Good team member	Creative

d 🔊 2.36 Listen to two people being interviewed for this position. Which things listed in the job profile do they each have? Who would you choose, and why?

I think he would be good because he had a degree in marketing.

12 a Put the words in the correct order to make questions from the interviews.

1 you/do/want/why/this/job ?
2 work/experience/have/do/any/you ?
3 good/communicating/people/with/at/are/you ?
4 weakness/biggest/is/what/your ?
5 skills/have/do/what/you ?
6 work/others/with/do/well/you ?

b Read the Active grammar box and complete the direct questions.

Active grammar

'What are your strengths?'
She asked what his strengths were.

'Are you good at listening to people?'
She asked if he was good at listening to people.

We use the verb *ask* to report questions.

We use *if* or *whether* to report *Yes/No* questions/*Wh-* questions and drop the question word (*why*, *who*, etc).

Direct question	Reported question
'_____ you like working in an office?'	I asked her if/whether she liked working in an office.
'_____ is your name?'	I asked her what her name was.

see Reference page 131

c Write the questions (1–6) from exercise 12a in reported speech.

She asked him …

Speaking

13 a Work in pairs. Write five questions to ask your partner to find out if he/she would suit the job of marketing assistant.

Do you like … ?
Are you good at … ?
What … ?
Can you … ?
Do you … ?

b Interview your partner and make notes. Would he/she suit the job of marketing assistant? Why/Why not?

c Report what your partner said in the interview to the class.

Grammar	past obligation/permission
Can do	describe job skills

Reading

1 Work in pairs and discuss the questions.

1 What do you think are the best and worst things about being famous?

2 Would you like to be famous? What for?

2 Read the article and answer the questions.

1 What was Jane and Denise's dream job?

2 How did they achieve it?

3 What problems did they have?

Operatunity

A _____

Operatunity is a TV talent show for amateur opera singers. The winners get the chance to sing with the English National Opera. When two housewives, Denise Leigh and Jane Gilchrist won in 2002, their lives changed forever. As they sang Verdi's *Rigoletto* at the Coliseum in Rome, they were transformed from working mothers into opera celebrities.

B _____

'I live in the village I was born in,' says Denise, who is blind and was a full-time mother. 'Lots of my neighbours are family, and my life revolved around my three children.' Jane, who worked as a cleaner and a shop assistant, was in a similar situation. She says, 'All I had to look forward to was seeing my four children grow up, and I love that, but ... you think "there must be more to life". Winning *Operatunity* has opened up avenues I never knew existed.'

C _____

'This last year has been amazing,' Denise continues. 'Last month was Paris, before that we were recording at Abbey Road, in London, and recently we had our album launch at the Royal Opera House.' 'We've been treated like princesses,' laughs Jane. '... champagne, chocolates, five-star hotels ...'

D _____

But it hasn't all been about being treated like royalty. For Denise, the worst part was waiting at the beginning. 'After I'd sent in my application form I worried for a month. Then I had to wait ten days after my first audition. That was awful.' Even when they won the competition they were allowed to tell their close family, but they weren't allowed to tell anyone else until later. Denise and Jane also found the travelling difficult. They couldn't take their children with them while they were away singing so they had to organise childcare.

They also had to learn to deal with the media. 'The kids loved the fact that they could stay up and watch us on TV, but I just couldn't understand why some newspapers were more interested in the fact I divorced at 21, rather than the fact I had just sung at the Coliseum,' says Denise.

E _____

When asked if they'd recommend the experience, Denise says, 'It's been the most fantastic thing I've ever done. I wake up in the morning and think I must be the luckiest person in the world. My profession is something I used to do as a hobby.' And their advice to other hopeful singers out there? 'Live your dream,' says Jane.

3 a Match the headings (1–5) with the paragraphs (A–E) in the article. Underline the phrases in the article that helped you.

1 The difficult parts

2 Living the new life

3 The competition

4 Their lives before

5 Advice

b Summarise each paragraph in just one sentence.

4 Read the summary. Find nine mistakes and correct them.

Jane and Denise won a pop singing competition on the radio, even though Denise is blind. The competition gave them the opportunity to sing a famous Beatles' song at Wembley Stadium, and it changed their lives forever. Although they are both housewives with families – Denise has three children, and Jane has two – they now get the chance to travel and see the world, singing. Their new lives have not been very exciting, and they have been treated very well. They found the travelling easy because their children were grown-up. They would recommend the experience to other singers, and say that if your dream is to sing, you should keep it as a hobby.

5 Work in pairs. Would you ever enter/consider entering a competition like *Operatunity*? Why/Why not?

6 Look at the Lifelong learning box and find the related words in each paragraph in the article.

Lexical cohesion

Vocabulary can be used to make a text 'stick together', using synonyms, antonyms or lexical sets.

1 Paragraph A: find another word which means the same as 'changed' (synonym).

2 Paragraph B: find three words or phrases which describe occupations (lexical set).

3 Paragraph C/D: find another word which means the same as 'princesses' (synonym).

4 Paragraph D: find three adjectives to describe something negative (lexical set).

5 Paragraph D: find two examples of media (lexical set).

6 Paragraph E: find a word which means the opposite of 'profession' (antonym).

Grammar | past obligation/permission

7 Look at the example sentences (1–6) in the Active grammar box and complete the sections (A–G) with the appropriate verbs in **bold**. Some verbs are used more than once.

Active grammar

1 They **had to** organise childcare.
2 We **didn't have to** worry about that.
3 They **were allowed to** tell their close family.
4 They **weren't allowed to** tell anyone else.
5 They **couldn't** take their children with them.
6 They **could** stay up to watch us on TV.

	Present	Past
Obligation	have to/must	A _____
No obligation	don't have to	B _____
Permission	be allowed to	C _____
	can	D _____
No permission	not be allowed to	E _____
	can't	F _____
	mustn't	G _____

Form

have/had + verb with to

allowed + verb with to

could (n't) + verb without to

see Reference page 131

8 Complete the sentences with modal verbs from the Active grammar box. More than one answer may be possible.

1 Martin wasn't in the office, so I _____ phone him on his mobile. (I was obliged to.)

2 When I was at school, we _____ run inside the building. (It was not permitted.)

3 In my last job, we _____ work from home for two days a week. (It was permitted.)

4 Luckily, we had our passports with us, so we _____ go back to the hotel. (It wasn't necessary.)

5 We _____ smoke in the restaurant, so we _____ go outside. (It was not permitted/It was necessary.)

6 I stayed up all night, because I _____ finish my assignment by today. (It was necessary.)

7 As a young child, I was _____ travel alone on buses. (It was permitted.)

8 The flight was delayed, but we _____ wait very long before take-off. (It wasn't necessary.)

9 **a** Correct the mistakes in the sentences.

1 I wasn't be allowed to stay out late.

2 We could to eat chocolate all day long.

3 Did you were allowed to buy new clothes?

4 We didn't allowed to watch television.

5 I couldn't to use the telephone because it was too expensive.

6 We didn't had to help with the housework.

7 We had to studying very hard.

b Work in pairs. Are the sentences in exercise 9a true for you when you were a child? Tell your partner.

Speaking

10 Work in groups and discuss the questions.

1 Are there more rules for children now, or when you were a child? Give examples.

2 Do schools and universities give students more or less freedom than in the past? Give examples.

3 What are some of the rules where you work/study?

Vocabulary | job requirements

11 Match the activities in the box with the definitions (1–8).

> controlling budgets   delegating   explaining things clearly
> making decisions   persuading people   prioritising
> solving problems   working in a team

1   giving jobs to others to do
2   deciding which jobs are more/less important
3   getting people to do things they don't want to do
4   working with others
5   finding answers to problems
6   saying what will happen
7   giving good explanations
8   managing money

12 a Match the qualities in the box with the definitions (1–9).

> creative   fit   flexible   formal qualifications
> good communication skills   methodical
> positive and encouraging   stamina

1   able to change easily
2   able to continue doing something for a long time
3   careful and well-organised
4   good at talking to people
5   good at thinking of new ideas
6   healthy and strong
7   something to show you have passed an examination or course
8   wanting and helping others to succeed

b Complete the sentences with appropriate words from the box in exercise 12a.

1   In our company we work very long hours, so you need _____ .
2   Supply teachers work in a lot of different schools, so they need to be _____ .
3   You don't need _____ to be a good salesperson.
4   My boss is great to be around – he's very _____ .
5   Postal delivery workers have to walk a lot and carry heavy bags, so they must be _____ .
6   _____ are important in most jobs.
7   Accountancy is a job where's it's important to be _____ .
8   I'd like to be a designer or an architect – I'm very _____ .

c Think of students in the class who you think have the qualities in exercise 12a. Write a name next to each quality. Then ask them questions to find out if you are right.

Magda, are you creative?

Yes, my job involves solving problems, which I really enjoy.

Listening

13 a ● 2.37–2.39 Listen to three people talking about jobs. What job does each speaker talk about?

b Listen again and make notes in the table.

Speaker	Job	Activities	Abilities/skills
1 Jonathan			
2 Polly			
3 Rachel			

c Work in pairs and compare your notes. Which job would you most like to do? Why?

Speaking

14 a Think about your job, or a job you would like to do in the future. Make notes about the following:

- the activities involved
- place of work
- main tasks
- skills/abilities needed
- experience/qualifications needed
- good and bad things about the job

b Work in pairs and describe your jobs. Do you think you would be good at your partner's job? Why/Why not?

1 **a** 🔊 2.40 Listen to an American living and working in the UK. What does she say about the things in the photos?

b Listen again and answer the questions.

1 What other difference did she notice about the way in which the Americans and the British communicate?

2 What did she misunderstand about a colleague?

c Work in pairs and discuss the questions.

1 In which other countries is English spoken?

2 What other languages are used in more than one country? Do you know about any cultural or language differences?

2 Match the US English words in the box with the UK English words in **bold** in the sentences (1–15) below.

> apartment   cell   check   freeway   fries
> gas   mail   mall   movie   restroom   resumé
> round trip   soccer   subway   vacation

1 Can I use your **mobile** phone?
2 Can we have the **bill**, please?
3 Do you want **chips** or a baked potato?
4 Was there any **post** today?
5 We need to stop for **petrol**.
6 Turn left to get onto the **motorway**.
7 See you in the **shopping centre** at 4:30.
8 When did you buy your **flat**?
9 I sent in my **CV** with the application form.
10 How much is a **return ticket**?
11 The **underground** is so expensive.
12 We like watching **football**.
13 Let's see a **film**.
14 I'm on **holiday**!
15 Where's the **toilet**?

3 **a** Is the speaker using UK or US English in the sentences below? Complete the sentences with a word from exercise 2.

1 Getting fired did not look very good on his _____ .
2 A: How are you getting to the mall?
   B: On the _____ .
3 For my holiday I bought a _____ to Paris.
4 There's a place on the _____ where we can stop and buy gas.
5 If you want to use the toilet, we can go to my _____ . I live close to here.
6 I never get any mail, only stupid text messages on my _____ .
7 Let's get some burgers and fries and go watch a _____ .
8 We went to a restaurant near the shopping centre. As usual, I paid the _____ .
9 Excuse me. I'd like the check, and could you show me where the _____ is, please?

b 🔊 2.41 Listen and check your answers.

4 **a** Look at the table showing differences in spelling between UK and US English. Can you add any more examples?

UK	US	Explanation
centre	*center*	UK words ending in *-tre* are usually spelled *-ter* in US English
organise	*organize*	Where UK English uses *-ise* at the end of some verbs, US English generally uses *-ize*. There are some exceptions, e.g. *advertise* uses *-ise* even in US English.
colour	*color*	UK nouns (with two syllables) often lose the *-u* in US English.

b Change the spelling of the words in the box to US English.

> criticise   flavour   humour   metre   neighbour
> prioritise   summarised   theatre   realised

Pronunciation | UK and US English

5 🔊 2.42 Listen to the following words said first by a British person and then by an American person. What differences can you hear?

1 new   tune
2 bath   laugh
3 caught   saw
4 butter   letter

see Pronunciation bank page 164

9 | Communication

1 **a** Look at the photos. What do you think is happening in each one?

b Work in pairs. Which of these things do you think would be a good idea to do before, or at a job interview? Why/Why not?

1 Look the company up online.
2 Practise some possible answers to interview questions.
3 Dress in comfortable, casual clothing.
4 Try to arrive on time.
5 Don't leave any silences during the interview.
6 Be honest about why you left your last job.
7 Prepare some questions to ask about the company.

c Read the text and check your ideas.

A successful job interview starts long before you walk in the interview room. The first thing to do is to research the company. Have a look at their website and find out as much as you can. Then practise some common interview questions, and most importantly, think of examples to back up what you say.

On the day of the interview, dress smartly and try to arrive at least 10–15 minutes early. This shows you are punctual and gives you time to calm down.

During the interview, make sure you listen carefully to the questions. It's OK to think for a few seconds before you answer. If you are asked about why you are leaving your current job, think of a positive reason even if the truth is that you hate your boss.

Finally, when they ask you if you have any questions about the job make sure you have prepared something intelligent to ask about the company.

2 Read the common interview questions (1–8) and think about your answers.

1 What has been your greatest achievement?
2 How do you deal with stress?
3 What is the most difficult situation you have had to face and how did you deal with it?
4 What are your ambitions for the next five years?
5 Describe a situation where you worked in a team.
6 What are your strengths?
7 What kind of people do you find it difficult to work with?
8 What are your weaknesses?

3 **a** Read some advice from top managers about the best answers to the questions in exercise 2.

Student A: turn to page 148 and read about questions 1–4.

Student B: turn to page 150 and read about questions 5–8.

b Work in pairs. Tell your partner what you learned about successful job interviews.

c Interview each other using the questions in exercise 2a. Try to follow the advice from exercise 3a.

make, let, allow

We use *make* + object + verb (without *to*) to talk about obligation imposed by another person or set of rules.

*My father **makes me** clean my room.* (She doesn't want to clean the room, but she has to clean it.)

She didn't make/never made us work very hard.

Passive form: *be + made + verb with to.*

*We **were made to** clean the whole house.*

We use *let* + object + verb (without *to*) to talk about permission.

*Mum **lets**/**doesn't let me** drive.* (She says it's OK/not OK.)

It is not possible to use *let* in the passive form.

We use *allow* + object + verb with *to* to talk about permission. The meaning is similar to *let.*

*My parents **allow me to** stay out late.*

Passive form: *be + allowed + verb with to.*

*They **weren't allowed to** borrow the money.*

Reported speech

When we report what someone said, we usually change the tense one step back to show that the words were said in the past.

Present Simple → Past Simple

*'I **live** in São Paolo.' She said she **lived** in São Paolo.*

Present Continuous → Past Continuous

*'I**'m working** for a fashion company.'*
*He said he **was working** for a fashion company.*

Present Perfect/Past Simple → Past Perfect

*'I**'ve been** here for three months.'*
*She told me she **had been** there for three months.*

will → *would*

*'I**'ll** go tomorrow.' He said he **would** go the next day.*

Time references can also change in reported speech.

'Call me later today or tomorrow.'
*She told me to call her later **that day** or the **next day**.*

Pronouns can also change in reported speech.

*'I'll see you soon.' He said **he** would see us soon.*

If what the person said is still true, we can keep the present tense.

*'I still love you.' She said she still **loves** me.*

Look at the verb patterns for *say* and *tell.*

Say cannot have a person as its object.

*She **said** (that) it was late.* NOT: ~~She said me ...~~

Tell must be followed by a person.

*He **told me** I was special.* NOT: ~~He told that ...~~
*He **told me** to lock the door.* NOT: ~~He told to me ...~~

Reported questions

'What time is it?' He asked me what time it was.
'Do you understand Spanish?' She asked me if/whether I understood Spanish.

In reported questions the word order is the same as in affirmative statements because they are not actually questions.

The auxiliary verb (*do/does/did*) is not used.

'What do you do?' He asked me what I did/I do.

NOT: ~~He asked me what do I do.~~

In *Yes/No* questions we use *if/whether.*

'Do you live in Italy?' She asked if I lived in Italy.

Tenses may shift back, as for reported statements.

'What time is it?' She asked what time it was.

Pronouns and time/place references may change.

'Will you still be here tomorrow?'
He asked if I would still be there the next day.

Past obligation/permission

To talk about obligation in the past, we use *had to* + verb. We cannot use *must* in the past.

*We **had to** be smart, but we **didn't have to** wear suits.*

To talk about permission in the past, we use:

allow (see above) and *could* + verb.

*We **could** watch TV, but we **couldn't** stay up late.*

Key vocabulary

Work

apply for   do a nine to five job   employed
get a pay rise   get promoted   job vacancies
overtime   perks   references   self-employed
send a CV   work flexitime/freelance/overtime

-ed and -ing adjectives

annoyed/-ing   bored/-ing   confused/-ing
depressed/-ing   excited/-ing   exhausted/-ing
frightened/-ing   interested/-ing   motivated/-ing
relaxed/-ing   tired/-ing

Job requirements

controlling budgets   creative   persuading people
delegating   explaining things clearly   fit   flexible
formal qualifications   good communication skills
making decisions   methodical   organising/prioritising
positive and encouraging   solving problems   stamina
working in a team

UK and US English

bill/check   chips/fries   CV/resumé   film/movie
flat/apartment   football/soccer   holiday/vacation
mobile phone/cell phone   motorway/freeway
petrol/gas   post/mail   return ticket/round trip
shopping centre/mall   toilet/restroom
underground/subway

 Listen to the explanations and vocabulary.

ACTIVEBOOK

 see Writing bank page 161

9 Review and practice

1 Complete the text with the correct form of the verbs in brackets.

What makes a great employer?

A great employer allows their employees (1) _____ (work) flexible hours and doesn't make them (2) _____ (do) too many hours over the week. In fact, the employer shouldn't let the employee (3) _____ (do) too much overtime. Employees should be made (4) _____ (take) proper holidays and allowed (5) _____ (take) time off sick when it is needed.

2 Complete the second sentence so it has the same meaning as the first.

1 In my last job I wasn't allowed to make personal phone calls.
   My boss didn't let ...

2 My boss also made me work weekends.
   I was ...

3 I wasn't allowed to use the Internet
   My boss didn't allow ...

4 But when I was sick she allowed me to have as much time off as I needed.
   But when I was sick she let ...

5 And she let me take my holiday when I wanted too.
   And she allowed ...

3 Report what Jim said yesterday.

1 'I've just started at Manchester University.'
   Jim said he ...

2 'I'm studying Engineering.'
   Jim told me ...

3 'I've made lots of new friends.'
   Jim told me ...

4 'We went to a fantastic concert last weekend.'
   Jim told me that they ...

5 'We're going to the Lake District at the weekend.'
   Jim told me that ...

6 'I'll call you tomorrow.'
   Jim said ...

7 'I went to a brilliant lecture this morning.'
   Jim said ...

8 'I live in a flat with three other students.'
   Jim told me ...

9 'We're having a party tonight.'
   Jim said ...

4 Report the questions.

1 'Do you know where the post office is?'
   She asked ...

2 'Where can I change some money?'
   He asked ...

3 'Have you been here before?'
   She asked ...

4 'What time did the meeting finish this morning?'
   He asked me ...

5 'Will you look after the plants for me?'
   She asked ...

6 'Did you go to the cinema last night?'
   They asked if we ...

7 'What time did you arrive?'
   She asked ...

8 'Are you meeting anyone here?'
   He asked ...

5 Complete the text using *had to*, *didn't have to*, *could*, *couldn't*, *were allowed* and *weren't allowed*.

Working from home has changed my life. Before, I (1) _____ be in my office by 9:00 a.m., but now I work when I want to. And I can wear whatever I like. I (2) _____ wear pyjamas in the office! In fact, we (3) _____ wear a suit, which I hated. Another good thing is that I don't have to travel. Before, I didn't use to get home before 8:00 p.m. because we (4) _____ to leave the office before 6:00 p.m. and I (5) _____ spend two hours a day travelling. Working at home is a bit lonely. In the past I used to talk to my colleagues in the office. Also, now I have to pay for computer software. Before, I (6) _____ buy anything. And if my computer goes wrong, I have to fix it. Before, I (7) _____ ask the IT technician to do it. And the Internet is very expensive too. In the office I didn't pay anything and we (8) _____ to use the Internet as much as we wanted. Now I have to pay for every minute!

6 Choose the correct words in *italics*.

1 The workers are *confused/confusing* about the company's new rules.

2 When I'm busy I always *delegate/persuade* some of the work to my colleagues.

3 My job can be very *tired/tiring*.

4 Eventually we *prioritised/persuaded* the boss to give us a pay rise.

5 It was very *annoyed/annoying* when my computer stopped working.

6 Accountancy is a job where you need to be very *creative/methodical*.

7 A successful business executive doesn't necessarily need *good communication skills/formal qualifications*.

8 I find swimming very *relaxed/relaxing*.

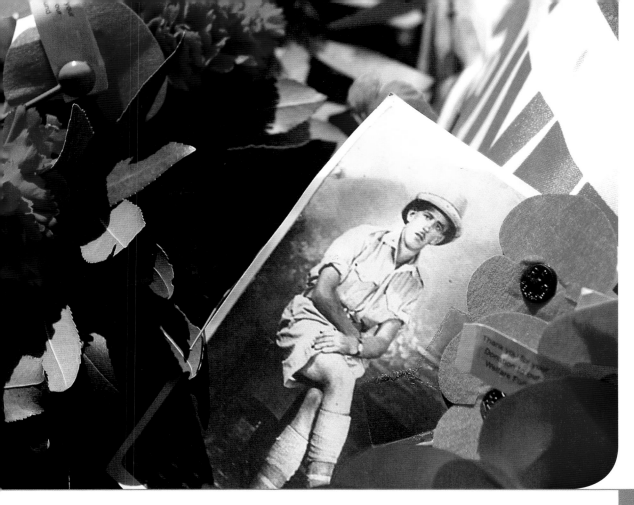

Lead-in

1 **a** Complete the sentences with words and phrases from the box.

> in memory   to commemorate   remind us   remember
> homesick   nostalgia   memento   memorial

1 The Princess Diana _____ was built _____ Princess Diana and her work.
2 People wear poppies each November to _____ the soldiers who died in the First World War.
3 This bench was placed here to _____ of a local person.
4 People who live abroad can sometimes feel _____ .
5 Childhood is a time that most of us look back on with _____ .
6 The Taj Mahal was built by Emperor Shah Jahan _____ of his wife.
7 People often take photos to keep as a _____ of a special day or trip.

b Which sentences (1–7) in exercise 1a can you match with the photos?

ARTHUR FOWLER
HE LOVED THIS PLACE

2 **a** 🔊 2.43 Listen to Sean talking about the Princess Diana Memorial and complete the summary below.

The Princess Diana Memorial, in Hyde (1) _____ , London, was opened in (2) _____ , seven years after Princess Diana (3) _____ . The Memorial is a (4) _____ in the shape of a large ring. The design is very (5) _____ and not at all traditional. It is very popular, especially with families with (6) _____ .

b Listen again. Why would Princess Diana have liked the fact that the fountain is popular with families?

c Work in pairs and discuss the questions.

1 What kind of memorial would you choose for someone you admire? Why?
2 Where would you build the memorial? Why?

It was long ago

I'll tell you, shall I, something I remember?
Something that still means a great deal to me.
It was long ago.

A dusty road in summer I remember,
A mountain, and an old house, and a tree
That stood, you know,

Behind the house. An old woman I remember
In a red shawl with a grey cat on her knee.
Humming under a tree.

She seemed the oldest thing I can remember,
But then perhaps I was not more than three.
It was long ago.

I dragged on the dusty road, and I remember
How the old woman looked over the fence at me
And seemed to know

How it felt to be three, and called out, I remember
'Do you like bilberries and cream for tea?'
I went under the tree

And while she hummed, and the cat purred, I remember
How she filled a saucer with berries and cream for me
So long ago

Such berries and such cream as I remember
I never had seen before, and never see
Today, you know.

And that is almost all I can remember
The house, the mountain, the grey cat on her knee,
Her red shawl, and the tree.

And the taste of the berries, the feel of the sun I remember,
And the smell of everything that used to be
So long ago.

Till the heat on the road outside again I remember,
And how the long dusty road seemed to have for me
No end, you know.

That is the farthest thing I can remember.
It won't mean much to you. It does to me.
Then I grew up, you see.

Reading

1 **a** Look at the picture and describe the old woman. What is she wearing and doing?

b Read the poem and answer the questions.

1 Who is the narrator of the poem?
2 What happened between her and the old lady?
3 What is the effect of the poet using the words 'you know' and 'you see'?
4 How does the poem make you feel?

c Read the poem again and make notes. What can the narrator see, hear, smell, taste and feel?

2 Read the Lifelong learning box and answer the question.

Lifelong learning

Make it rhyme!

! When a word is difficult to pronounce, e.g. *though*, think of other words that have a similar pronunciation, e.g. *ago / know*. This will help you to remember.

Which words in the poem rhyme with *me*?

Listening and speaking

3 **a** Think about one of your earliest memories and make notes about what you could see, hear, smell, taste and feel.

b Work in pairs and describe your memories.

4 **a** 🔵 2.44 Listen to Sarah talking about a childhood memory and answer the questions.

1 Where did the event take place?
2 Who was she with?
3 How old was she?
4 How did she feel at the time? Why?
5 What did she realise when she grew up?

b Put the sentences (a–j) from the story in the correct order. Then listen again and check.

a Later I realised that they were probably cows at the end of the shed and they were completely harmless.

b And there was a very, very strong smell coming from the sheds and I could hear scuffling, hear noises at the end of the sheds.

c There was a dark doorway up some steps into some sheds and I really wanted to go up there, and I went to the doorway, and it was very dark.

d And my cousin told me there were monsters there.

e I have a very vivid memory of being a child and visiting a farm with my cousins.

f It was a very, very strong memory.

g But for a long time I thought there were monsters there.

h I was probably four at the time.

i I was terrified and I remembered it for many years.

j You couldn't see anything.

c Which sentences in exercise 4b are part of ...

a the introduction?
b the main sequence of events?
c the big or surprising event?
d the conclusion?

5 **a** From whose viewpoint is the following version of Sarah's story?

I was in the kitchen, making some tea. It was a lovely sunny day and the kids were playing happily outside in the yard. Suddenly I heard Sarah scream. I dropped what I was doing and ran outside. What would I tell my sister if anything had happened to Sarah when I should have been watching her?! I ran over to her. She was standing by the cowshed, crying and shaking. It turned out that the kids had told her there were monsters in there. Little devils! They were always teasing her like that.

b Write another version of Sarah's story from the viewpoint of her cousin. Use the structure in exercise 4c to guide you. Think about what the cousin could see, hear, smell, taste or feel.

Listening

6 **a** Erma Bombeck was an American columnist who wrote humorously about everyday life. Read this extract from one of her most famous columns. Do you agree with any of the points she makes?

Someone asked me the other day if I had my life to live over, would I change anything. My answer was no, but then I thought about it and I changed my mind.

If I had my life to live over, I would have talked less and listened more.

I would have invited friends over to dinner, even if the carpet was stained and the sofa faded.

I would have taken the time to listen to my grandfather ramble about his youth.

I would have sat cross-legged on the lawn with my children and never worried about grass stains.

I would have cried and laughed less while watching television … and more while watching real life.

I would have eaten less cottage cheese and more ice cream.

There would have been more I love yous … more I'm sorrys … more I'm listenings … but mostly, given another shot at life, I would seize every minute of it … look at it and really see it … try it on … live it … exhaust it … and never give that minute back until there was nothing left of it.

b ● 2.45 Listen to Matt and Claire talking about Bombeck's column. Make notes in the table of some things they would like to change about their lives.

	Present	Past
Claire		
Matt		

Grammar | I wish/If only

7 Read the Active grammar box. Then choose the correct underlined words to complete the rules.

Active grammar

Wish	Actual situation
'I **wish** I **was** better at listening.'	He isn't good at listening.
'I **wish** I **had eaten** more healthily.'	She didn't eat very healthily.
'I **wish** I **could** sing.'	He can't sing.

We use *wish* + Past Simple to talk about imaginary things we would like in the *past*/*present*.

We use *wish* + Past Perfect to talk about imaginary things we would like in the *past*/*present*.

We use *wish* + *could* to talk about ability in the *past*/*present*.

We use *wish* + *someone*/*something* + *would* when you want someone or something to change.
I wish they would be quiet! (They refuse to be quiet.)

You can't say: *I wish I would* (Because you can control what you do.)

We can also use *If only* instead of *I wish*. The meaning is a little bit stronger than *I wish*.
If only I could dance! (I can't dance.)
If only you hadn't left your bag on the bus! (You did leave it on the bus.)

see Reference page 145

8 Rewrite the sentences using *wish* so that they have a similar meaning. Different answers are possible.

I'm hungry. I didn't eat earlier.
I wish I had eaten earlier/I wish I had some food.
1 I'm bad at Maths. I want to be better.
2 You're late again.
3 We went to a boring museum.
4 I'd love to be a good dancer, but I can't do it.
5 You always leave your dirty plate on the table!
6 I'm lonely. I'd like to have more friends.
7 I don't want to smoke any more, but I can't quit.

9 Write down three wishes about your life (past or present). Then work in pairs and compare your ideas.

Grammar	review of past tenses
Can do	briefly describe a famous person

Marie Curie

Marie Sklodowska Curie's family had lost all their money so Marie worked as a governess so her sister could go to (1) _____ . Marie fell in love with her employer's (2) _____ , but they were not allowed to (3) _____ . She paid for her education in Paris by (4) _____ in the evenings. She married Pierre Curie in (5) _____ and they discovered radium together. She won the Nobel Prize in 1903 and (6) _____ .

Tanni Grey Thompson

As a child, Baroness Tanni Grey Thompson enjoyed a variety of sports, including swimming, archery and horse-riding. She entered her first wheelchair race aged (1) _____ . Two years later she won a national event. She won her first Paralympic medal in (2) _____ but had to stop racing because she needed surgery on (3) _____ . She returned to racing and won eleven (4) _____ .

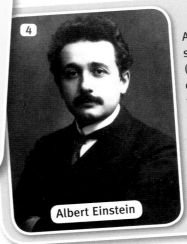

Pelé

Pelé was born into (1) _____ in Minas Gerais, Brazil. He started work aged (2) _____ , as a shoe shine boy. He was so poor that he (3) _____ a proper football. Nevertheless, he became one of the greatest footballers of all time.

Albert Einstein

Albert Einstein did not speak well until (1) _____ and one of his teachers thought that he would never be (2) _____ . Despite this, Einstein went on to publish more than (3) _____ scientific works, including his theories of relativity.

Listening

1 **a** Do you know anything about the people in the photos? What memorable things do you think they did?

b ⬤ 2.46 Listen and check your ideas.

c Listen again and complete the texts above about each person.

Vocabulary | biographies

2 Match the phrases (1–6) from the listening with the meanings (a–f).

1 a difficult start in life
2 one of the greatest ... of all times
3 against the odds
4 from an early age
5 is widely considered to be
6 is best known for

a although it seemed very unlikely
b most people agree this person is
c one of the best ... ever
d problems in childhood
e from childhood or youth
f is famous because of

3 Complete the sentences with a suitable word or phrase (1–6) from exercise 2.

1 Tanni Grey Thompson was interested in sport _____ .
2 Marie Curie _____ discovering radium.
3 Pelé had _____ because he was born into a very poor family.
4 Einstein _____ the father of modern physics.
5 Pelé is _____ footballers _____ .
6 Despite some problems, all four people succeeded _____ .

4 **a** Think of another famous person, or someone you know who succeeded against the odds. Make notes about what they did, using words and phrases from exercise 2.

b Work in groups. Tell each other about the person you chose and why.

THE MAKING OF [   ]

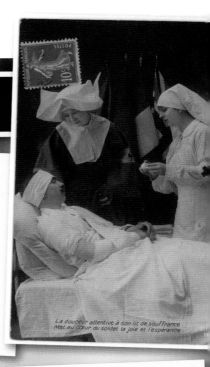

La douceur attentive à son lit de souffrance
Met au cœur du soldat la joie et l'esperance

1 She was born in a home for poor people in Saumur, France, on 19 August 1883, and christened Gabrielle. Her mother died when she was just six years old. This left her father with Gabrielle and four other young children. What happened next?

a) The father brought them up alone.

b) The children became film stars.

c) The father sent them away.

Read 5 to find out ····>

7 She had worked for a short time as a nurse in World War I, but during World War II she went to Switzerland. She returned to France in 1953 and dressed many Hollywood stars, such as Liz Taylor and Katharine Hepburn. What happened next?

a) She acted in a film about her life.

b) She died in the 1970s.

c) She moved to the West Indies.

Read 4 to find out ····>

4 She was still working up until her death on 10 January, 1971, when her fashion empire brought in over $160 million a year. Before that, in 1969, Katharine Hepburn had starred in a Broadway musical about her life. She is considered one of the most influential fashion designers of the twentieth century.

THE END

5 He sent them away to grow up with relatives. In her early twenties, while she was working as a singer in cafés, she met two wealthy men, one a soldier, the other an Englishman called Arthur Capel. What did the men do?

a) They shot each other because they loved her.

b) They helped her start a clothes business.

c) They paid for her to travel around the world.

Read 3 to find out ····>

3 With the men's money and contacts, she opened a hat shop in 1913. She soon expanded her business to include clothes, and opened a fashion shop at 31 rue Cambon, Paris. What happened next?

a) She married a politician.

b) She became a singer.

c) She designed clothes for women.

Read 6 to find out ····>

6 She began to design clothes for women. She said, 'Most women dress for men and want to be admired. But they must also be able to move, to get into a car. Clothes must have a natural shape.' What was her other famous product?

a) Shoes.

b) Perfume.

c) Furniture.

Read 2 to find out ····>

2 In the early 1920s she introduced Chanel No. 5, which became one of the world's favourite perfumes. Throughout the 1920s and 30s her clothes were becoming more and more popular. But then, in 1939, World War II began. What happened to her?

a) She moved to Switzerland.

b) She designed uniforms for soldiers.

c) She worked as a nurse.

Read 7 to find out ····>

Reading and listening

5 **a** Work in pairs. Read about another person who succeeded against the odds. Stop at each question and guess the answer. Then follow the instruction to the next stage of the story.

b When you know who the famous person is, complete the title with her name.

6 **a** 🔊 2.47 Listen to a summary of the woman's life. Which three facts does the speaker get wrong?

b Work in pairs. Retell the woman's life story using the numbers/dates in the box.

> 19 August, 1883   six years old   two men
> 1913   31 rue Cambon   No.5   1920s and 1930s
> 1939   1953   1969   10 January, 1971
> twentieth century $160 million

Grammar | review of past tenses

 a <u>Underline</u> the different tenses that are used to describe the woman's life in the article on page 138.

b Read the Active grammar box and complete the rules with *Past Perfect*, *Past Continuous* and/or *Past Simple*.

Active grammar

We use the _____ to describe the main events of a story.

We use the _____ to make it clear that something happened before the main events in the past.

*I felt ill because I **had eaten** bad food.*

We use the _____ to describe actions that were already in progress when the main events happened.

We often use the _____ and _____ together when one action was in progress and the other action happened suddenly.

*He **was sleeping** when the storm **began.***

---

see Reference page 145

 a Read about Gianni Versace. Put the verbs in brackets into the correct tense. There is one passive.

b Find three things Versace had in common with the woman in the article on page 138.

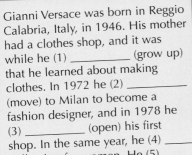

GIANNI VERSACE

Gianni Versace was born in Reggio Calabria, Italy, in 1946. His mother had a clothes shop, and it was while he (1) _____ (grow up) that he learned about making clothes. In 1972 he (2) _____ (move) to Milan to become a fashion designer, and in 1978 he (3) _____ (open) his first shop. In the same year, he (4) _____ (present) his first collection for women. He (5) _____ (already/design) a leather collection for a company called Complice, but now, he worked for himself.

His designs (6) _____ (be) brightly coloured and sexy, and he used celebrities like Madonna, Tina Turner and Bon Jovi as models. In 1984 he (7) _____ (bring out) his own fragrance for men, Versace l'Homme.

On 16th July 1997, while he (8) _____ (walk) outside his apartment in South Beach, Miami, he (9) _____ (shoot) dead by an unknown killer.

During his life, his fashion empire (10) _____ (become) so successful that it was worth over $800 million.

Pronunciation | pronouncing numbers

 a Read the information in the How to... box. Then look back at the numbers/dates in the box in exercise 6b and say them aloud.

How to... say numbers

	Written	Spoken
Dates	02/12/03	*The second of December, two thousand and three*
	1750s	*The seventeen fifties*
	C19th	*The nineteenth century*
Percentages	21.2%	*Twenty-one point two percent*
Money	£78.32	*Seventy-eight pounds, thirty-two pence*
Big numbers	1,265	*One thousand, two hundred and sixty-five*
	1,000,000	*A million/One million*
Fractions	1 ½	*One and a half*
	¾	*Three-quarters*

---

b Say the numbers.

1	54½	**4**	2010	**7**	€1,300,000
2	4,076	**5**	$4,375	**8**	7¾
3	9.3%	**6**	12/04/13	**9**	21st May

10 6.2%

11 1920s

c 🔊 2.48 Listen and check. When do we use *and*? When do we use *the*?

see Pronunciation bank page 164

10 Work in pairs.

Student A: turn to page 151.

Student B: turn to page 152.

You have the same ideas but with different information missing. Ask and answer questions to complete your information.

Speaking

11 **a** Write down five numbers that are important to you. They could be dates, years, code numbers, prices, etc.

b Work in pairs and show your partner your numbers. Ask your partner questions to find out why each number is important. Then ask follow-up questions.

A: *Why did you write July 1997?*

B: *I graduated in July 1997.*

A: *What did you study?*

Reading and speaking

1 **a** What types of goodbye are shown in the photos (A–E)?

b What do you think are the best and worst ways to say goodbye? Think about the situations shown in the photos.

2 **a** Work in pairs.

Student A: read the article on this page.

Student B: read the article on page 151.

Answer the questions below.

1 What type of goodbye is described in your article?
2 How did the companies/people say goodbye?
3 What is the conclusion at the end of the article?
4 What do you think of the behaviour described in the article?
5 Is there a 'good' way to say goodbye in these situations?

b Explain your article to your partner. Use your answers to exercise 2a to help you. Then quickly read your partner's article.

3 Work in pairs. Match the phrasal verbs in bold in the article on this page and on page 151 with the meanings in the box.

> arriving   became   continue   cancelled   discover experienced (something bad)   finished a relationship happening   tolerate   think of/invent   recover from returned

We're letting you go.

One company text-messaged its employees, asking them to check their email to see if they had been retained. Those who had lost their jobs were not contacted at all. It's probably not the nicest way to **find out** that you are now unemployed. But it's maybe better than some. A recent survey in New Zealand found that several people claimed to have been fired by post-it note.

Or, using a newer technology, an employee in the North of England was recently fired for **turning up** late. Fair enough, you might think, but was it really acceptable to sack her by sending her a message on Facebook?

A receptionist for a certain company was asked to train up a new assistant. One day she **came back** from lunch and found that her security card didn't work. 'What's **going on**?' she asked. The reply? She had been replaced by her new 'assistant'.

It is impossible to **come up with** a 'nice' way to fire someone, but managers should at least do it in private and show respect for the employee. The problem is that bosses often panic. They are worried that the fired employees will steal important information. And they are sometimes right: in one company, the fired staff stole computers and other equipment and nearly destroyed the company's offices as an argument **turned into** a riot.

Grammar | phrasal verbs

4 Read the Active grammar box. Match the phrasal verbs in **bold** from the articles on pages 140 and 151 with the phrasal verb types (A–D).

Active grammar

There are four different types of phrasal verb:

A The verb takes no object (intransitive).
   *I **turned up** late.*

B The verb takes an object (transitive) and the verb and particle can split.*
   *I **called off** the wedding.*
   *I **called** the wedding **off**.*
   *I **called** it **off**.*

   *When the object is a pronoun (he/she/it, etc.) the verb and particle must split. NOT: ~~I called off it.~~

C The verb takes an object but the verb and particle cannot split (transitive, inseparable).
   *He's **going through** a difficult time.*
   NOT: ~~He's going a difficult time through.~~

D The verb has two particles and doesn't split (transitive, inseparable).
   *We **came up with** a new idea.*
   NOT: ~~We came up a new idea with.~~

see Reference page 145

5 Put the words in the correct order to make sentences and questions.

1 girlfriend/I/up/split/my/with .
2 we/until/out/didn't/later/find .
3 back/when/you/coming/are ?
4 carry/couldn't/I/tired/because/I/was/on .
5 always/she/late/up/turns .
6 with/good/they/up/did/any/ideas/come ?
7 going/is/here/on/what ?
8 match/because/rain/the/called/off/was/of .
9 period/is/company/going/the/a/difficult/through .
10 anymore/I/him/up/can't/with/put .
11 ice/water/the/turned/into .
12 it/get/over/a/serious/illness/take/weeks/can/to .

6 Use words from boxes A and B to complete each sentence below. Change the tense if necessary.

A

carry   come   go (x2)   put   split   turn (x2)

B

into   on (x2)   up (x4)   through   with (x2)

1 I won't _____ this noise! If it continues, I'll call the police!
2 The book was _____ a film.
3 I don't need a break. I'm going to _____ .
4 It was a quiet party. There were only six of us, though later more people _____ .
5 Can someone explain? I have no idea what's _____ .
6 She _____ a difficult period when she lost her job, but she's OK now.
7 Couples usually _____ because of jealousy or boredom, or because they find other partners!
8 You need to _____ a plan to improve your business, because you are losing money.

Pronunciation | word stress in phrasal verbs

7 **a** 2.49 Listen to the sentences from exercise 6. Which part of the phrasal verb is the main stress on?

b Which phrasal verbs in exercise 6 have the main stress on the verb? Which type (A–D) are they?

see Pronunciation bank page 163

8 Work in pairs. Make a sentence about a picture (A–F) using a phrasal verb. Can your partner guess which picture it is?

Listening

9 a ⊕ 2.50 Listen to four goodbyes. Number the situations below in the order you hear them.

a father and daughter before she goes away ☐
friends at the end of a party ☐
a speaker at the end of a conference ☐
two colleagues at the end of the day ☐

b Listen again. In which situation (1–4) in exercise 9a …

a might some people meet again the following weekend? ☐
b will someone wait for an email? ☐
c is someone in a hurry? ☐
d will someone wait for a phone call? ☐

c Look at the How to… box. Then listen again and tick (✓) the phrases you hear. Which phrases are more formal?

How to… say goodbye (in person)

Signalling that you're going	*Right then, it's time I made a move.* *… I'm off.* *(Is that the time?) Sorry, I've got to dash.*
Thanking (if appropriate)	*Thank you very much for coming.* *Thank you and goodbye.* *Thanks for everything. I really enjoyed it.*
Pre-closing	*We'll see you in a couple of weeks.* *Maybe see you next weekend.* *Have a safe trip/nice weekend.*
Saying goodbye	*Take care.* *See you.* *Catch you later.*

10 a You are going to listen to two friends saying goodbye. First try to complete B's part of the dialogue using the phrases in the box.

> Yes, that sounds good.   See you then.
> Yes, me too.   I've got loads to do.
> Yeah, bye.   You too.

A: Right well, I'd better be going.
B: _____ .
A: Maybe see you next Wednesday then?
B: _____ .
A: Have a good weekend.
B: _____ .
A: See you.
B: _____ .

b ⊕ 2.51 Listen and check your answers. Which phrases do they use …

1 to signal they are going?
2 just before they say goodbye?
3 to say goodbye?

c British and American speakers tend to take a long time to say goodbye, to make sure that the other person has definitely finished. Is it the same in your country or different?

11 Work in pairs. Look at the role cards and roleplay each situation. Then swap roles and repeat.

Situation 1

Student A: You have been to a friend's house for dinner. You have just realised that you need to go or you will be late for the babysitter. Say goodbye appropriately.

Student B: You are hosting a dinner party. Say goodbye appropriately to your guest.

Situation 2

Student A: You have been speaking on the telephone to your best friend for an hour. Now you need to go. Say goodbye appropriately.

Student B: You have been talking to your best friend on the phone for an hour. Now they need to go. Say goodbye appropriately.

10 | Vocabulary | the senses

1 **a** Which senses – sight, sound, smell, touch or taste – do you associate with the photos (A–E)?

b Which senses do you first associate with the words in the box?

> a cold wind   a cotton shirt   a mountain stream
> a stone floor   drums   fish   fresh bread
> olives   petrol   red roses   sunshine   the sea

c Complete the phrases below with words/phrases from the box in exercise 1b.

1   The look/sight of ...
2   The sound of ...
3   The feel of ...
4   The smell of ...
5   The taste of ...

d Work in pairs. Tell your partner which things in exercise 1b you like/dislike.

I love the taste of olive oil and fresh coffee.

2 **a** Look at the table below. Then match sentences from A and B to make dialogues.

It	looks feels sounds smells tastes	+ adjective	*It* **looks** *beautiful.* *It* **tastes** *delicious.*
		+ *like* + noun phrase	*It* **sounds** *like a* *mechanical problem.* *It* **looks** *like a nice day.*

A	B
1 I love this dress.	a Yes, he looked terrible.
2 Shall we go to the cinema?	b Yes, the roses smell beautiful.
3 I cooked the soup myself.	c Yes, touch it. It feels very soft.
4 Can you hear the birds singing?	d Yes, it looks great on you.
5 Miguel went home early.	e That sounds like a great idea.
6 Have you been in the garden?	f Yes, they sound lovely.
7 Are you sure this fish is fresh?	g It tastes delicious.
8 Is the skirt made of silk?	h No, it smells a bit strange.

b Work in pairs and practise the dialogues.

c 🔊 2.52 Listen to someone reacting to five different situations. What do you think has just happened in each instance? Which sense is she using?

3 **a** Work in pairs. Discuss the difference in meaning between the following verbs.

1   see/look at/watch
2   listen to/hear
3   touch/hold

b Complete the sentences with the verbs from exercise 3a.

1   Can you _____ this bag for me? It's very heavy.
2   Have you _____ Jo's car? It's very fast.
3   Can you speak up, please? I can't _____ you.
4   Don't _____ that wire! It looks dangerous.
5   I was just _____ these beautiful photos.
6   Shall we _____ some music on the radio?
7   Did you _____ that TV programme last night?

4 **a** Read the poem below. Then write your own version by changing the words in *italics*.

> I love the look of *mountains with snow on top,*
> I love the smell of *fresh coffee beans,*
> I love the taste of *pasta with garlic,*
> I love the sound of *a young boy singing,*
> But most of all I love the feel of *a warm wind on my face,*
> It reminds me of *walking by the sea.*

b Work in groups. Take it in turns to read your poems.

143

1 Spend a few minutes thinking about the topics in the game below. Then read the instructions on how to play the game.

2 Work in groups and play Memory Blockbusters.

How to play...

1 Play in two teams: A and B. Teams can have one or more members.

2 The teams take it in turns to choose a block. When a team has chosen a block, one of the team members must try to talk about the topic in the block for one minute. If they succeed they win the block.

3 The aim of the game is to win a line of blocks from top to bottom (team A) or side to side (team B). When a block has been won, it cannot be used by the other team.

4 The first team to make a line of blocks is the winner.

MEMORY BLOCKBUSTERS

Happy memories from your childhood (U10)

An older person you admire (U7)

A special day you remember (U10)

A city you know well (U3)

Your favourite food and the first things you learned to cook (U5)

The best film you have ever seen (U2)

Music you used to listen to (U5)

How you met your best friend (U1)

Jobs you had to do as a child to help round the house (U9)

Your best birthday (U10)

A beautiful place you have been to (U6)

How your home town has changed in your lifetime (U8)

A teacher you remember (U7)

The most precious thing you own (U4)

A place you didn't like in the past (U6)

The first time you earned some money and what you did with it (U4)

You ten years ago (U10)

A TV programme you used to watch as a child (U2)

An interesting person you met (U1)

A sport or hobby you don't do any more (U7)

A story you have heard in the news recently (U2)

A favourite book (U5)

The house you lived in when you were younger (U3)

Something you loved learning as a child (U7)

Your first school (U7)

10 | Reference

I wish/If only

We use *wish* to say we would like something to be different from the reality.

To talk about a wish in the present, or a permanent wish, use *wish* + Past Simple. The most common verbs are *wish* + *was/were* and *wish* + *had*.

*She **wishes** she **was** taller.*

*I **wish** I **had** a pen.*

With the verb *to be* you can also say *I wish I were/she wishes she were*.

*She **wishes** she **were** taller.*

To talk about a wish in the past, use *wish* + past perfect.

*He **wishes** he **had gone** to the exhibition yesterday.*

*I **wish** I **hadn't eaten** that sandwich.*

We use *wish* + object + *would* to show you want something to change. We often use this structure to show anger or annoyance.

*I **wish** she **would** come on time.*

*I **wish** you **wouldn't** make that noise.*

! We can't say: *I wish I would*.

We use *wish* + *could* to talk about an ability that you want but don't have.

*I **wish** I **could** play chess as well as you.*

*I **wish** I **could** fly.*

! We don't usually use *wish* + *couldn't*.

We can also use *if only* instead of *I wish*. The meaning is a little bit stronger than *I wish*.

If only we could go home!

If only they hadn't taken the money!

Review of past tenses

We often use the Past Simple, Past Perfect and Past Continuous for narratives.

The Past Simple is used for the main completed events of a story.

*I **took** the money and **ran**.*

The Past Perfect is used to make it clear that one action happened before another action.

*I knew I**'d seen** him before.*

The Past Continuous is used for an action in progress when the main events happened. It's often a background action in the narrative.

*When I got outside, it **was raining** hard.*

*I **was living** in Paris when I **married** Lily. I'd **met her** in Austria.*

Phrasal verbs

There are four main types of phrasal verbs:

1 Intransitive
The verb takes no object.

*I **grew up**.*

2 Transitive – separable
The verb takes an object and the verb and particle can split.

*I **turned off** the light.*

*I **turned** the light **off**.*

*I **turned** it **off**.*

When the object is a pronoun (*he/she/it*, etc.) the verb and particle must split.

NOT: ~~I turned off it.~~

3 Transitive – inseparable
The verb takes an object, but the verb and particle cannot split.

*He **got on** the bus.*

NOT: ~~He got the bus on.~~

4 Three-part
The verb has two particles and doesn't split (transitive, inseparable).

*We're **looking forward to** seeing you.*

NOT: ~~We're looking forward seeing you to.~~

Key vocabulary

Memory
commemorate   homesick   in memory of   memento
memorial   nostalgia   remember   remind us of

Biographies
a difficult start in life   against the odds
from an early age   is best known for
is widely considered to be
one of the greatest ... of all times

Phrasal verbs
call off   carry on   come back   come up with
get over   go on   go through   find out
put up with   split up   turn into   turn up

The senses
feel   hear   hold   listen to   look   look at   see
smell   sound   taste   touch   watch

Listen to the explanations and vocabulary.

ACTIVEBOOK

see Writing bank page 162

145

1 Complete the sentences using the verbs in brackets. You may need to use some extra words.

He has to wash all the dishes. He probably wishes he _____ (have) a dishwasher.

He has to wash all the dishes. He probably wishes he had a dishwasher.

1   I have to read so many books! I wish I _____ (be) such a slow reader.

2   She's so full she can't sleep. She probably wishes she _____ (eat) so much.

3   I loved Disneyland! I wish I _____ (go) there the last time I was in the US.

4   He hates taking trains. He wishes he _____ (have) a car.

5   There are some job vacancies in the Bahamas. Don't you wish you _____ (can/work) there?

6   My favourite film was on TV yesterday, but at 1:00 a.m. I wish they _____ (show) it earlier.

7   Those children have been inside all day. They probably wish they _____ (can/play) outside.

8   It is such beautiful weather! Do you wish you _____ (be) on holiday?

2 Complete the dialogues using the correct form of the verbs in the box.

> not answer   do   listen   not hear

A: I knocked on the door last night but you (1) _____ . What (2) _____ ?

B: Oh, sorry. I (3) _____ to music and I (4) _____ you.

> go   have   stop

A: (5) _____ a good weekend?

B: Yes, we (6) _____ for a picnic.

A: In the rain?

B: No! The rain (7) _____ by the time we got to the park.

> get back   not go   visit

A: Why (8) _____ to the New Year party? We missed you.

B: I was exhausted because I (9) _____ from Australia that morning.

A: Really? What were you doing there?

B: I (10) _____ my cousins.

3 Write sentences in the Past Perfect or Past Continuous using the words in brackets.

We tried to call her. (She/switch off her phone)
She had switched off her phone.

1   I saw a friend after many years. She looked very different.
(She/change/a lot) _____ .

2   The book was completely new to me.
(I/never/read/before) _____ .

3   Tom was in the pool from 6:15 a.m. to 6:45 a.m.
(At 6:30 a.m. he/swim) _____ .

4   Javed didn't break the window at midnight.
(He/sleep/in his room/at midnight) _____ .

5   I couldn't cross the border into Mexico.
(I/lose/my passport) _____ .

6   Lola went to an interview every day.
(She/look for/a job) _____ .

4 Replace the underlined verbs with the correct form of the phrasal verbs in the box.

> call off   carry on   come up with   find out
> go on   put up with   split up   turn up

1   My husband and I separated last year.

2   She arrived nearly an hour late!

3   What's happening?

4   I can't tolerate your behaviour any longer.

5   They cancelled the wedding at the last minute.

6   I'll probably need to continue working until I'm seventy.

7   Don't worry. He won't discover what we did with the money!

8   He thought of a brilliant new idea.

5 Complete the text with the words and phrases in the box.

> against the odds   best known for
> from an early age   is widely considered to be
> of all time   remembered

Luciano Pavarotti came from a very poor family but, (1) _____ , he became rich and famous. He (2) _____ one of the most commercially successful singers (3) _____ . Pavarotti enjoyed singing (4) _____ but originally dreamed of being a football goalkeeper. He is perhaps (5) _____ his version of *Nessun Dorma*, sung for the 1990 World Cup in Italy. He died in 2007 and will be (6) _____ for a long time to come.

Communication activities

Unit 1 Lesson 1.1 Exercise 10a

Student B

Read the text below and answer the questions.

1 How did François behave at the restaurant?
2 What did his parents-in-law think?
3 Why did he behave that way?
4 How did he feel afterwards?

Not in my culture...

The first time they met François, my parents insisted on taking him to the nicest Persian restaurant in Los Angeles. My father ordered some starters, which François ate enthusiastically while questioning my mother about the ingredients:

'Are these Persian cucumbers?'

'Is the cheese made with sheep's milk?'

Once the starters were finished, François selected the biggest dish on the menu, the *sultani*, a combination of lamb, beef, and chicken on an enormous pile of rice. His order arrived, looking as if someone had just cooked an entire zoo. François ate and ate and ate. My father asked me, in Persian, whether he always ate like this. My mother said, in Persian, that she hoped he wasn't going to get sick. Meanwhile, François kept eating.

By the time he was finished, there was not a grain of rice left on his plate. My mother told him how lucky he was that he could eat enough food for three people and not be fat.

Unbelievably, he ordered dessert, explaining that he couldn't possibly not have the rose water and pistachio ice cream. By then, I was just hoping that if he did throw up, it wouldn't happen in my father's car.

Once we arrived at my house, I asked François why he had eaten so much. 'I know that Middle Easterners love to feed people and I wanted to make a good impression on your parents,' he said. 'But now I need to go and lie down.'

Unit 4 Lesson 4.2 Exercise 11b

Words and phrases connected with shopping:

Verbs	Nouns	Adjectives
spend	money	cheap(er)
afford	impulse buy	reduced
buy ... cheaply	the sales	
pay (hundreds of pounds)	(what a) bargain	
shop around	checkout	
get the best deal	shopping list	
	big ticket item	
	price comparison websites	
	an expensive mistake	
	receipt	
	refund	

Unit 4 Lesson 4.3 Exercise 3

Student B

How you are persuaded to spend more by ...

supermarkets.

We spend more time in them than we want to, we buy seventy-five percent of our food from them and we buy a lot of products that we don't even need.

Supermarkets always have good marketing ideas. When shopping baskets were introduced in the 1950s' stores, they were an immediate success. Now shoppers could walk around and pick up items they previously didn't even look at. Soon came trolleys, and the bigger the trolley, the more people buy. Customers think, 'If I buy lots now, I won't need to come back later.'

Supermarkets help us enjoy shopping by making the environment pleasant. They play music to help us relax and blow air from the in-store bakery around the shop.

Some stores have 'greeters' to welcome you. This gives the illusion of community – the notion that shopping in a giant store isn't so different from visiting a village shop.

Warning signs:

- Two-for-one deals: supermarkets usually offer these when a fruit or vegetable is in season, and so there is a lot of it, and it's cheap.
- Music: if the experience is relaxing, you will stay in the shop longer. The longer you stay, the more you buy.
- The influence of smell: as soon as you walk into the shop, you can smell the bread and coffee. Pleasant aromas can make you buy more.

Unit 5 Lesson 5.1 Exercise 13a

Problems

1 Your hotel has been receiving complaints from the customers because the lifts are too slow. They are very old, expensive lifts with material on the walls. The cost of buying new lifts is extremely high, and the hotel doesn't have enough money. Think of a solution.

2 You work in a university hospital. You want to persuade the students to get an injection against tetanus. You have been sending brochures to the students for one year, but only three percent of the students have come for an injection. Another university hospital has been doing the same thing, but twenty-eight percent of their students have had injections. They've been sending out one extra piece of paper with the brochure. What is on this piece of paper?

Communication activities

Unit 5 Lesson 5.1 Exercise 13c

Solutions

1 The hotel manager put mirrors in the lifts. The complaints stopped immediately. When people have something interesting to look at, they don't mind a delay!

2 The piece of paper contained a map of the university area showing exactly where the hospital was, and the times it was open for students to have their injection. The students knew the dangers of tetanus but wanted to know how to 'fit' the injections into their lives.

Unit 5 Vocabulary Exercise 2a

1 surfing
2 curry
3 mud/earth
4 vacuum cleaner/Hoover
5 bookshelves

Unit 6 Lesson 6.1 Exercise 11

Unit 6 Lesson 6.2 Exercise 6

Student A

Situation 1: In a train station:
You work in the ticket office.
Trains from Sydney to Canberra.
Dep. 06:58 – Arr.11:21 (Mon–Sat)
Dep. 12:10 – Arr. 16:29, Tues, Thurs, Sat, Sun.
Dep. 18:15 – Arr. 22:31, Mon, Wed, Fri, Sun
One-way tickets cost:
Economy $57, 1st class $80

Situation 2: In a tourist office:
You would like to see the Dreamers exhibition of aboriginal art at the Art Gallery of New South Wales in Sydney next Wednesday.
Find out ...
• how to get to the art gallery.
• what time it opens/closes.
• how much the exhibition costs.

Unit 6 Lesson 6.3 Exercise 6a

Marco Polo

Marco Polo was born in around 1254 into a wealthy family of merchants in Venice. At the age of sixteen or seventeen he travelled to the court of Kublai Khan in China with his father and uncle. They stayed in China for seventeen years, and Marco travelled round the country on various diplomatic missions for Khan. In 1292 the Polos left China to accompany a Mongol Princess to Iran, from where they finally returned to Venice in 1295. On his return the stories of Marco's travels were turned into a very popular book which was translated into many languages.

Unit 9 Communication Exercise 3a

Student A

Questions 1–4

1 What has been your greatest achievement?
Think of a specific example and explain exactly how you made it happen. If possible, make sure that it is related to the job you are applying for now.

2 How do you deal with stress?
It is important to say that you enjoy working under pressure and give an example of how you handle stress.

3 What is the most difficult situation you have had to face and how did you deal with it?
Think of a specific example and describe what happened and exactly how you dealt with it. This is something you can prepare in advance.

4 What are your ambitions for the next five years?
Don't say that you would like to have your interviewer's job!

Unit 7 Lesson 7.1 Exercise 12a

Student A

Quiz A

1 Who painted *Guernica* in 1937? Picasso.

2 When did Mozart start composing music? When he was four years old. /1760.

3 Who discovered penicillin in 1928? Sir Alexander Fleming.

4 Which of the world's greatest scientists lived from 1879–1955? Albert Einstein.

5 Which famous city is nicknamed *The Big Apple*? New York.

6 What invention is Guglielmo Marconi responsible for? The radio.

7 Which is the largest desert in the world? The Sahara.

8 Who wrote the best-sellers *The Da Vinci Code* and *The Lost Symbol*? Dan Brown.

9 Which country is the oldest surviving republic in the world? San Marino.

10 When did Tom Daley become Britain's youngest ever male Olympics competitor? In 2008 in Beijing.

Unit 7 Lesson 7.3 Exercise 3a

Student B

Buster Martin retired at ninety-seven, but three years later he decided to go back to work because he was getting bored. He was told to take the day off for his 100th birthday, but turned up to work anyway.

Buster, born in 1906, started work at fifteen and has worked hard ever since. Somehow he and his wife also managed to have seventeen children. He doesn't believe in healthy eating and refuses to drink water.

Peter Oakley, born 1927, is perhaps better known as 'geriatric1927', his username on the video-sharing website YouTube™. He has made over 200 videos describing his life and is one of the most popular directors on the site. In some of the videos he talks about his school days and how lucky he was that he was able to stay on at school after the age of fourteen – in those days only the most intelligent were allowed to do this.

He also recently released a pop song, together with other old age pensioners, to raise money for the charity *Age Concern*.

Unit 5 Vocabulary Exercise 5

Student A

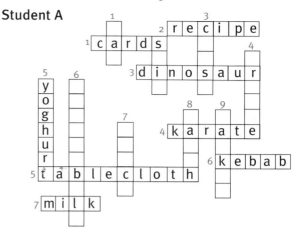

Unit 7 Vocabulary Exercise 3

Student A

1 *Learn by heart* comes from the Ancient Greek belief that the heart was where intelligence and memory were found, not the brain.

2 *A piece of cake* – this means that something is as easy as eating a piece of cake, not making one!

3 *Haven't got a clue* – a clue was originally a ball of string which could be used to mark your path in a maze so you could find your way out safely.

Unit 7 Communication Exercise 4a

The words and phrases to memorise are: correct, manage, exam, mistake, older, every, learn by heart, teacher, children, in at the deep end.

When her husband died in 1970, Mary Wesley found she couldn't survive on her very small pension, so she decided to try and make a living as an author. Her first novel for adults was published when she was seventy-one years old and over the next twenty years before her death, she went on to write ten best-sellers, selling over three million copies. One of her books, *The Camomile Lawn*, was made into a television series and she suddenly found herself rich and even quite famous.

Communication activities

Unit 7 Vocabulary Exercise 3

Student B

1   *Pass with flying colours* – the 'colours' are actually flags, like a fleet of ships sailing into harbour with their flags flying after winning a battle.

2   A *bookworm* is a kind of insect which eats paper, particularly old books, so someone who is a bookworm 'eats up' books.

3   *Teacher's pet* – this meaning of 'pet' actually means 'favourite'. You can also have a 'pet project' – something you particularly like to work on or a 'pet hate' – something you love to hate.

Unit 8 Lesson 8.2 Exercise 13b

1   Asia isn't the biggest continent, but actually it has the most people.

2   Rich countries regularly throw away food, but fifty percent of the world's population don't have enough.

3   Sadly, less than twenty percent of the world's population has running water.

4   Perhaps surprisingly, almost eighty percent of the world's population can read, but only one percent go to university. About five percent of the world's population now owns a computer, up from less than one percent five years ago.

Complete the sentences with your reactions to the facts above.

1   Personally, I was most surprised by the fact that ...

2   Actually, I wasn't surprised by the fact that ... because ...

3   Obviously, ...

4   I was really shocked/surprised/interested to find out that ...

Unit 9 Communication Exercise 3a

Student B

Questions 5–8

5   **Describe a situation where you worked in a team.**
Companies usually want people who work well as part of a team, so this is an important question.

6   **What are your strengths?**
Before the interview think of three key strengths that are relevant to the job and an example for each of them.

7   **What kind of people do you find it difficult to work with?**
You should say that you get on with most people, but sometimes find it hard when other people don't do their job properly.

8   **What are your weaknesses?**
This is a difficult question because you don't really want to tell the interviewer this! Either choose something which is not really a weakness at all – like working too hard – or describe something which used to be a weakness, but that you have now improved.

Unit 8 Communication Exercise 2b

Look at your answers to the quiz on page 116 and write down the letter (LHWP) for each one. Then read your results below.

1	2	3	4
A = H	A = L	A = H	A = L
B = W	B = H	B = P	B = P
C = P	C = W	C = W	C = H
D = L	D = P	D = L	D = W

Mostly L

You love change

You find it difficult to understand why others find change a problem because you really enjoy it. People who love change can be exciting people to be with, but don't forget to explain your ideas to friends, colleagues and family.

Mostly P

You like to plan for change

You think that change is necessary but you like to have a careful plan. This usually works very well, but be careful that you don't miss a good opportunity because you want more time to plan.

Mostly H

You hate change and will do anything to avoid it

Change can be difficult, but we all need to make changes sometimes. If you don't change, then others around you will, and leave you behind. With a little planning and small steps you can feel more comfortable about change.

Mostly W

You worry a lot about change

People who worry about change always think that the outcome will be negative, but it usually isn't. Instead of worrying about what is ahead, think about good change, with positive outcomes.

Unit 10 Lesson 10.2 Exercise 10

Student A

The Stone Angels,

Madison Hall. Date: _____

Second-hand car. _____

In good condition. $_____

As stated in legislation Section 1(d) of the Code of Amsterry Sports Club, 1962, the carrying of firearms is strictly forbidden on these premises.

From   London Terminals
To   Chelmsford
Ticket type   Cheap day rtn

valid on 05/02/11 only

Economic report: _____

• We made a _____ percent profit during the fiscal year of 2010, making that year the most successful in the company's long history.

You can save up to **£1,999** on household furnishings if you buy our **Millennium package.**

SERVICE STATION ____ KILOMETRES

¾ of all accidents take place in the home.
BE CAREFUL!

Unit 4 Lesson 4.3 Exercise 3

Student C

How you are persuaded to spend more by ...

advertising.

Adverts focus either on what products do, or how the products make us feel. Our emotional response to a product is very important. If the advertisement makes us feel good, i.e. it has images which we enjoy and remember, then we start to associate good feelings with the product.

We respond well to adverts which demonstrate a lifestyle we would like to have. Famous people are often used in adverts because of their successful lifestyle. Footballers advertise sports drinks. We buy the drink, and sense the success. A survey of 4,000 adverts found that adverts with celebrities were ten percent more effective than adverts without.

Humour is also used, as funny adverts are remembered for longer. In addition, advertisers appeal to our senses. Unless your mouth waters, a chocolate advert is probably a failure. They want you to want their product.

Warning signs:

• High price: if a product costs a lot of money, it won't necessarily be good quality. It might be just part of its image.
• Famous people: advertisers want you to believe that if you buy their product, you can start to live the lifestyle of the celebrity who advertises it.
• Reward and punishment: 'If you buy this, you will stay young' (the reward), also means 'Unless you buy this, you will look old' (the punishment).

Unit 10 Lesson 10.3 Exercise 2

Student B

How not to spilt up with your partner

OK, so the rich and famous always say 'It was an amicable break-up' or 'We **split up** because of work pressures'. Don't believe a word of it. They may **carry on** smiling for the cameras, but behind the smiles there are some angry people. Here are some examples why.

One famous actress was expecting a baby when her long-term partner, and the father of the child, sent her a fax to inform her that he was leaving her.

But maybe that's not as bad as what one famous actor did. He split up with his celebrity girlfriend on a chat show, live, in front of the US public. How do you **get over** that?!

Or the fiancé of a famous supermodel, who **called off** their wedding by emailing all the guests – before he mentioned it to her.

But if you think they **went through** hell, times were even harder for women a few centuries ago. Take King Henry VIII's wives. Out of his six wives, he divorced two and he had another couple executed. When it's time to say the Big Goodbye, it seems that some unlucky people have always had to **put up with** a lot from their partners.

Communication activities

Unit 5 Vocabulary Exercise 5

Student B

```
      1
      w        2        3
 1    a    x   s        c    h   e   s   s
      x        k             e        4
               3   i         s        f
  5        6    n            s        r
           v                          i
           o        7        8    9   d
           l        b        m    n   g
           l   4    r        a    a   e
           e        i        t    p
  5        y        b   a    l    c   h
           b        i        6    k    i   n
  7        a        c        h    i
           l        k             n
           l
```

Unit 6 Lesson 6.2 Exercise 6

Student B

Situation 1: In a train station:
You would like two one-way tickets to Canberra. Find out …
- what time you can catch the train next Monday.
- how long the journey will take.
- how much the tickets will cost if you travel first class.

Situation 2: In a tourist office:
You work in the tourist office and have the following information about the Art Gallery of New South Wales:
Open every day (except Christmas) 10:00 a.m. – 5:00 p.m.
Late closing Wed at 9:00 p.m.
Free admission.
Nearest train stations are St James and Martin Place, both about 10 minutes walk.
The Gallery is also on the Sydney Explorer bus route – stop 6.

Unit 7 Lesson 7.1 Exercise 12a

Student B

Quiz answers

Quiz B

1 Which islands did Christopher Columbus discover in 1492, before he discovered America? The Bahamas.
2 Who painted the Sistine Chapel? Michelangelo.
3 What song about London was a huge hit for Lily Allen in 2006? *Smile.*
4 Which European country has the smallest area? The Vatican City.
5 Which team bought Cristiano Ronaldo for $163 million? Real Madrid in 2009.
6 Who wrote the song *Imagine* in 1971? John Lennon.
7 What did Laszlo Biro invent? The biro pen.
8 Which is the world's longest river? The Nile.
9 Which famous writer lived from 1564–1616? William Shakespeare.
10 When did Hong Kong become part of China again? 1997.

Unit 10 Lesson 10.2 Exercise 12

Student B

The Stone Angels,

Madison Hall. Date: 15th January 2010

Second-hand car.
In good condition.
$2,500

Economic report:
- We made a 15.6 percent profit during the fiscal year of 2010, making that year the most successful in the company's long history.

As stated in legislation Section 1(d) of the Code of Amsterry Sports Club, 19____, the carrying of firearms is strictly forbidden on these premises.

SERVICE STATION 1½ KILOMETRES

_____ of all accidents take place in the home.
BE CAREFUL!

You can save up to £_____ on household furnishings if you buy our **Millennium package.**

From   London Terminals
To   Chelmsford
Ticket type   Cheap day rtn

valid on _____ /11 only

1 | Informal and semi-formal email

Can do | write a semi-formal email, introduce yourself

A
Hi there,

Great that we're going to be e-pals. Well, what about me? I'm 22, work in an office (boring) and hobbies are snowboarding and skiing. I've attached a photo of me on my last skiing holiday – it was great! Do you get much snow? I LOVE it!!!

Also listen to a lot of music. What bands do you like? I love Lady Gaga. Cool.

Can't wait to find out all about you! :)

Cheers,

Tomas

Tomas

B
Dear Sophie,

My name is Margarita and I will be your teacher this year. I thought that it would be nice if we could get to know each other a little before the term started, so I am emailing everyone.

First, something about me. I live quite near the school with my husband and two children. I've attached a photo of me and the girls in our garden. They are six and eight and I'm sure you can imagine that they keep me quite busy! However, when I do have some spare time, I like walking and cycling. It keeps me fit as well. I also enjoy watching films. What are your hobbies?

It would be great if you could write back and tell me a little about yourself.

Best wishes,

Margarita.

Margarita

1 Read the emails and make notes in the table.

	Tomas	Margarita
Job		
Interests		
Family		

2 Read the emails in exercise 1 again. Which one is informal and which is semi-formal?

3 **a** Look at the features of informal writing in the How to... box. Find one example of each feature in email A.

How to... write informal and semi-formal emails

Informal	Semi-formal
1 Using capitals for emphasis	*Not using capitals except to start a sentence or for a proper noun.*
2 Missing out pronouns	2 _____ pronouns
3 Mostly short sentences	3 Sentences are usually _____
4 Emoticons e.g. :o	4 _____ emoticons
5 Using lots of exclamation marks	5 _____ exclamation marks
6 Greeting with *Hi*, or *Hi there*	6 Greeting with _____
7 Saying goodbye with *Cheers*, *Bye*, *Love*	7 Saying goodbye with _____

b Read email B again. Look at each feature of an informal email in the How to... box and complete the same points for semi-formal emails, noting how they are different.

4 **a** Prepare to write a reply to Margarita. Make notes about your job or studies, your family and your interests.

b Write your reply in a semi-formal style.

Can do write a description of an event

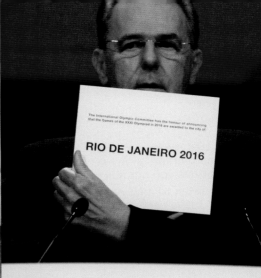

1 **a** Work in pairs and look at the photos. How are they connected?

b Read the article and check your ideas.

> I remember when we heard the news. We had been on the beach all day, waiting to hear. Luckily, it was a sunny day after a week of rain! There were thousands of people on the beach because it was a public holiday and everyone was in a party mood. We just hoped we were going to get what we wanted.
>
> There were two big screens on the beach so we could see the results, and we were also listening to live music. One of my favourite singers was on in the morning and after that there was a samba band and everyone danced.
>
> Suddenly, the news came through on the screens and there was a huge roar from the crowd. Brazil had won the bid to host the 2016 Olympics! A wave of emotion swept over me. Thousands of people were dancing and singing and the sand disappeared under a sea of yellow and green Brazilian flags. There was confetti everywhere. It was unbelievable.
>
> In the end the party went on all night, and it was definitely one of the best days of my life.

2 Look at the How to... box. Tick (✓) the phrases used in each paragraph of the article.

How to... sequence a narrative

1 Setting the scene	I remember when ... This all happened when ... A few years ago ...
2 The main sequence of events	... then ... next ... after that ...
3 The big event (usually something unexpected)	Suddenly ... To my surprise ... However, ...
4 Result	In the end ... ... and I've never forgotten that day. ... we never ... again. It was one of the best/worst days of my life.

3 **a** Prepare to write about an important or interesting event in your own life. Make notes on what to say in each of the paragraphs below.

1 Setting the scene
2 The main sequence of events
3 The big event
4 The result

b Write about your event. Try to use some of the language in the How to... box.

3 | Written complaint

Can do write an email of complaint

Writing bank

1 Work in pairs. Have you ever written to a company to complain about something? Why? What happened? Tell your partner.

2 **a** Read the emails of complaint below. Why is each person complaining?

b Read the emails again and match the topics (1–3) with the paragraphs (A–C) in each email.

1 What has happened since
2 The problem
3 What you want the company to do now

**① **

Dear Sir/Madam,

A On 27th April I emailed you to say that I had not received my latest rental DVD. You responded by saying that you would send out another copy immediately.

B It is now two weeks later and I have still not received this DVD. In the meantime, I have continued to pay my monthly subscription fee.

C I am very disappointed with the service and would like you to refund me this month's subscription and cancel any further payments.

I look forward to your reply,

Joe Clarkson

**② **

Dear Sir/Madam,

A I recently decided to start ordering my groceries online, as it seemed that this would be much more convenient for me. However, my very first delivery this week was nearly three hours late. I was not able to wait this long and, as a result, missed the delivery completely.

B Your company has, however, still charged me for the groceries.

C I consider this to be completely unacceptable and would like an immediate refund.

I hope to hear from you soon,

Emilia Padano

3 Look at the How to... box. Complete the useful phrases from the emails in exercise 2.

How to... complain

Details of the transaction	*I recently purchased ...*
What has happened since	*I have still not _____ this DVD/the item.* *Your company has still _____ me for the groceries/the items.*
How you feel about it	*I am very _____ with the service.* *I consider this to be completely _____ .*
What you want the company to do now	*I would like an immediate _____ .*
Signing off	*I look forward to your _____ .* *I hope to hear from you soon.*

4 **a** Prepare to write an email of complaint. Look at the situation below and make notes to answer each question.

You bought an MP3 player and, after only a few weeks it has stopped working.

1 What did you buy and when?
2 What happened next?
3 How do you feel about it?
4 What do you want the company to do now?

b Write your email of complaint. Use your notes and the phrases in the How to... box to help you.

155

1
a Work in pairs. If you won the lottery, what would you spend the money on?

b Read the report below and compare the findings with your ideas.

> The purpose of this report is to present the findings of a small survey into how people in our class would spend a large lottery win.
>
> Most of the class said that they would share at least some of the money with their friends and family. <u>However</u>, fewer people said that they would give much of the money away to charity. <u>In fact</u>, just one person was willing to do this.
>
> The next most popular choice was to buy a house. Nearly everyone we spoke to would invest their money in property. <u>In addition</u>, several people said that they would buy a boat or a car.
>
> <u>On the other hand</u>, some people would prefer to spend their money on a luxury holiday or a trip round the world.
>
> Relatively few people decided that they would save the money. <u>Nevertheless</u>, a few people claimed they would use some money to pay off existing debts.
>
> <u>In conclusion</u>, it appears that most people would choose to share some money with family and friends. However, our survey also showed that they would spend most of it on themselves.

2
a Look at the How to... box and complete it with the <u>underlined</u> linkers in the report.

How to... use formal linkers

1 Adding an idea	*Moreover,*
	Furthermore,
	_____ ,
2 Making a contrast	*Nevertheless,*
	_____ ,
	_____ ,
	_____ ,
3 Concluding	*Overall,*
	_____ ,

b Choose the correct words in *italics*.

1 Most people would choose to spend their winnings. *Furthermore/In conclusion/Nevertheless*, some people would save most of the money.

2 Nearly everyone we spoke to would buy a house. *However/Moreover/On the other hand*, some people would buy a holiday home as well.

3 A lot of people wanted to go abroad. *However/Furthermore/Overall*, some people wanted to emigrate.

4 Most people would not give much money to charity. *However/Furthermore/In conclusion*, they said they would give some money away to friends and family.

5 *Overall/In addition/Nevertheless*, our survey showed that most people would share some money with their friends and family and spend some on themselves.

3 Read the report again and <u>underline</u> ...
1 a phrase to introduce a report.
2 phrases to say how many people said something.
3 two phrases to conclude a report.

4
a Prepare to write a report. Look at your survey results from exercise 12 on page 55 and decide on the key points you want to present.

b Write a report on your findings using linkers from the How to... box and phrases from exercise 3.

5 | Description

Can do write a detailed description of an object

Family heirlooms

It's a kind of jug, though I'm not sure if it was used for tea or water. It's made of metal and beautifully decorated with blue and red painted flowers. The part of it that is used for pouring is very long and thin, and the handle is long and narrow too. It has a long neck and a rounded body, with an oval decorative panel.

It used to belong to my grandmother. She kept it on a shelf in the sitting room and whenever I visited her I used to admire it. So one day she asked me if I would like to have it for myself. I love it because it's so old and unusual and one day I hope I'll give it to my children.

Do you have a valuable or special object which has been in your family for a long time? Or perhaps you have something which you'd like to leave to your children or grandchildren to remember you by? Tell us about your family heirloom and send a picture. Email www.mymagazine.com

1 Read the extract above from an online article about family heirlooms. Which object (A, B or C) is being described?

2 Read the How to... box and tick (✓) the words and phrases used in the extract.

How to... describe an object

Explaining	*It's a kind of/type of ...*
	It's made of ...
	It's used for ...
	It's something you use to ...
Talking about how it looks	*rectangular/oval/square/curved/ triangular/diamond-shaped*
	tiny/wide/narrow/long/short
	shiny/decorated/modern/ old-fashioned
Giving background information	*It (used to) belong(s) to ...*
	I/we keep it in/on ...
	I'm not sure if ...
	It's been in my family since ...
	I love it because ...

3 **a** Think of a family heirloom you have, or imagine you own one of the other objects on this page. Make notes about the object. Think about ...

- how to describe it.
- how long it has been in your family.
- who it belongs/belonged to and why/how they got it.
- why it is important to you or your family.
- how you feel about it.

b Write about your heirloom for the magazine. Use your notes and language from the How to... box.

Can do write a detailed description of a place

1 Look at the photos and read the competition entry below. Which view (A, B or C) is being described?

A

C

B

2 Complete the competition entry in exercise 1 with suitable adjectives from the box.

> dramatic   lush   relaxing   rocky   sandy
> snow-capped   thick   traditional   tropical

3 Read and complete the How to... box with examples from the competition entry in exercise 1.

Sara Inman is the latest winner in our weekly travel writing competition for her description of the view from her window.

The view from my window is so green and peaceful. It's a beautiful sunny day and the sky is a bright turquoise, with just a few white clouds.

On the left, there is a (1) _____ Swiss church, surrounded by trees. Nearby, there are a few houses, all set in a (2) _____ green valley, with a handful of trees dotted about.

In the distance I can see the (3) _____ mountains and, a little nearer, a mountain covered with trees. A little way off on the right there's a small road, which leads to the village.

The whole scene is so perfect, it almost doesn't look real. It makes me feel glad to be alive.

To enter next month's competition and win £50, email your entry to www.viewfrommywindow.co.uk

How to... write a description of a place

Structure	Language
Introduction: give your general impressions of the place	*The view from my window is* _____ . *It's a* _____ *day.*
Detail: what you can see and where	*On the left there is* _____ . *Nearby there are* _____ . *In the distance I can see* _____ *A little nearer (there is)* _____ . *A little way off on the right there's* _____ .
Conclusion: how it makes you feel/why you like or dislike it	*The whole scene is* _____ . *It makes me feel* _____ .

4 **a** Prepare to write about the view from your window or a place you remember well. Make notes about what you can see.

b Write an entry for the competition in exercise 1 using your notes and the How to... box to help you.

From
London to Bangladesh
by mobile phone

by Sara Chamberlain

A Although I'm American, I've always considered South Asia my home. The minute I get off the plane I relax. I suppose this is because I grew up in India. When I was eighteen, I went back to America, to go to university. Leaving the vibrancy and exoticism of India behind for America was a little bit like going from technicolor to black and white.

B Since then I've always been a bit of a traveller, but I've always been looking for a chance to return to my roots.

C Two years ago I was finally given the opportunity. I was asked if I would like to do some research into the mobile telephone industry in Bangladesh, to help with the planning of an English language teaching project. Two weeks later I was on a plane.

D It was thirty-eight degrees and raining when I arrived in Dhaka. It took more than an hour to navigate through the cycle rickshaws, scooters, trucks and buses to our office in Kawran bazaar.

E Accompanied by a friend from our office, I began trying to gather information about mobile phone use in Bangladesh. My idea was to use basic technology to enable low-income people to access English language lessons using a simple voice call or text.

F What followed were fourteen months of very hard work developing the project. Eventually all six of Bangladesh's mobile phone operators agreed to offer English language lessons to their mobile subscribers at fifty percent less than the standard rate. We are now offering hundreds of three-minute English lessons on mobile phones across the country for less than four pence each.

G In less than two weeks we've already had half a million calls. I suspect Asia might continue to be my home for some time.

1 Read the article and answer the questions.
1. Why was Sara happy to be asked to go to Bangladesh?
2. What idea for using mobile phones did she have?
3. Was her idea a success? How do you know?

2 **a** Read the article again and match the summaries (1–7) with the paragraphs (A–G).
1. The weather and traffic in Dhaka were awful.
2. Sara is planning to stay in Bangladesh for a while longer.
3. Sara's idea was to use mobile phones to offer cheap English lessons.
4. Sara has travelled a lot.
5. Sara agreed to take part in some research in Bangladesh.
6. It took a long time but in the end the project was successful.
7. Sara grew up in India and missed it when she left.

b Decide which three of the paragraph summaries in exercise 2a are not really main points of the article.

3 Read summaries A and B below. Which is the best summary of the whole article. Why?

A

Sara Chamberlain grew up in India and always wanted to return. One day she was asked to take part in an English language teaching project in Bangladesh. Her idea was to use mobile phones to teach English cheaply. Eventually she got all six mobile providers in Bangladesh to agree to offer the service and two weeks later they have had half a million calls.

B

Sara Chamberlain grew up in India until she went back to the United States to go to university. She missed India and always wanted to go back. She has lived in different cities in America and in the UK, but was delighted to be offered the opportunity to go to Bangladesh. In Bangladesh she set up a new project using mobile phones to teach English.

4 Read the How to... box. Choose the correct words in *italics*.

How to... write a summary

1. Find *the main idea/all the ideas* in each paragraph.
2. *Cut out/Add* any ideas which are not essential.
3. Use the main ideas you have found to make a *shorter text/longer text* than the original.

5 Look at the article on page 93. Write a summary of the text using the How to... box to help you.

Can do | write about change

1 Work in pairs and discuss the questions.

1 Look at the photo of Dubai. What do you think it's like to live there?

2 How do you think Dubai might have changed over the past ten years?

3 What changes have happened where you live?

2 **a** Read the emails below and write true (T) or false (F).

1 Keith lives in Dubai. ☐

2 Bradley lives in Dubai. ☐

3 Keith's wife has a new job. ☐

4 Keith and Bradley are old friends. ☐

5 Bradley is unhappy about the new metro system. ☐

b Read Bradley's reply again. What has changed in Dubai over the past ten years? Do you think the changes are positive or negative?

Hi Bradley,

Thanks for your email. Hope you and your family are all well.

I have some exciting news – I'm planning on coming back to live in Dubai! My wife has got a job at the British University, so we're all moving back.

It must be more than 10 years since I left. How has it changed since then? I'd be really interested to hear all about it.

Hope to hear from you soon,

All the best,

Keith.

Dear Keith,

Thanks for your email. We are all well, thanks.

I was really pleased to hear that you're moving back here. It will be great to see you again.

You asked about what has changed in Dubai since you left. Well, there has been a lot of building, including the world's tallest building, the Burj Khalifa. It looks amazing. I suppose it's good that Dubai is expanding but I personally feel that the population is getting a bit too big these days – there are constant problems with parking and traffic! On the plus side, we have a new metro system, which should help a lot with these problems as more lines are opened.

Give my regards to your family. I look forward to meeting up soon.

Best wishes,

Bradley.

---

3 Read the How to... box and complete the examples from the emails in exercise 2.

How to... write a personal email

Beginning the email	_____ your email. _____ all well.
Introducing the topic	_____ exciting news. _____ what has changed in Dubai.
Giving your opinion	_____ it's good that Dubai is expanding. _____ that the population is getting ... _____, we have a new metro system.
Ending the email	_____ from you soon. _____ to your family. _____ meeting up soon/ hearing from you.
Signing off	All the _____/Best _____

4 **a** Imagine that you have received an email from an old friend, asking about changes in the place where you live. Make notes about some changes and your opinion about them.

b Write an email replying to your friend. Use language from the How to... box.

9 Email/letter of application

Can do write a formal email/letter of application

1 Work in pairs. Read the letter of application and discuss the questions.

1 What relevant qualifications, skills and experience does Judith have for the job?

2 Do you think this is a good example of a letter of application? Why?

Dear Sir/Madam,

I would like to apply for the job of Tour Guide, which I saw advertised on your website.

As you can see from my curriculum vitae, I recently graduated with a good degree in Italian and I have visited Italy many times. I would be delighted to have the opportunity to live and work in the country.

I believe that I possess excellent communication skills and I very much enjoy working as part of a team. While at university, I set up a group which raised money for charity through sporting events.

Although I do not have any directly relevant experience, I understand that training would be given and I would come to the job with great enthusiasm and motivation.

I enclose my C.V. and look forward to hearing from you in the near future.

Yours faithfully,

Judith Brown

---

2 **a** Read the letter in exercise 1 again and <u>underline</u> the phrases which have the same meaning as the sentences (1–5) below.

1 I'd like to have a go at getting your tour guide job.

2 I really fancy working in Italy.

3 I'm brilliant at communicating with people.

4 I don't have any experience but you'd train me, wouldn't you?

5 Write back soon.

b What is the difference between the phrases in exercise 2a and those in the letter in exercise 1? Which phrases are more suitable in a formal letter?

3 Complete the How to... box with phrases from the letter in exercise 1.

How to... write a formal email/ letter of application

Addressing the reader ...	
when you know their name.	Dear Mr Brown,
when you don't know their name.	Dear _____ ,
Starting the letter	I would _____
Finishing the letter	I **attach** my C.V. (for an email) and _____ .
	I **enclose** my C.V. ... (for a letter)
Signing off ...	
when you know their name.	Yours sincerely,
when you don't know their name.	Yours _____ ,

---

4 **a** Look at the job advertisements below. Choose one, or think of a different job you'd like to apply for. Make notes about the qualifications, skills and experience needed.

Travel consultant

Do you have a passion for travel?

As a travel consultant you would work in a small, friendly team booking holidays and flights to destinations worldwide.

You should have sales experience and be excellent at customer relations.

Waiter/waitress

Brand new 5* hotel, looking for enthusiastic and experienced waiting staff.

40–50 hours per week, early and late shifts, some weekend work.

Uniform provided.

b Write a formal email/letter of application for the job you chose. Use phrases from the How to... box.

10 | Essay

Can do write a simple essay

1 **a** Work in pairs and discuss the following statement.

Fashion is a waste of money.

b Read the essay below. Does the writer agree or disagree with your opinion?

Some people believe that fashion is a waste of money. However, I would like to argue that there are many positive aspects to fashion.

In the first place, I think that most people would agree that designers are wonderfully creative and that fashion can even be an art form. Designers such as Chanel or Versace are still famous long after their deaths for their beautiful designs.

Secondly, it is well-known that people have been interested in fashion for hundreds of years, perhaps even longer. It is natural for people to want to dress up and look their best. Fashion gives you an opportunity to express your own style.

Finally, fashion can be good for the economy. Italy's fashion industry, for example, is worth more than 60 billion euros a year.

To conclude, I do not believe that fashion can be said to be a waste of money when there are so many clear benefits.

2 **a** Read the essay again and <u>underline</u> the topic sentence (the sentence which has the main idea) in each paragraph.

b Now find a supporting idea or example for each main idea in the essay.

3 Look at the How to... box. Tick (✓) the phrases used in the essay.

> ### How to... write a simple essay
>
> | Introduction | *I completely agree that ...* |
> |---|---|
> | | *In this essay I will set out my reasons.* |
> | | *Some people believe that ... However, I would like to argue that ...* |
> | Organising your points | *In the first place, .../Firstly, ...* |
> | | *Secondly, ...* |
> | | *Next, .../Thirdly, ...* |
> | | *Finally, ...* |
> | Conclusion | *To conclude, ...* |
> | | *In conclusion, ...* |

4 **a** Look at the following statement. Do you agree or disagree?

Celebrities should act as good role models.

b Look at the opinions (1–6). Do they agree or disagree with the statement above?

1 Celebrities are just people and they make mistakes like we all do.
2 The most important thing is that celebrities are good at what they are famous for.
3 Celebrities can be an inspiration to us all.
4 People who are admired by young people should try to set a good example.
5 If newspapers didn't print stories about celebrities' bad behaviour, it wouldn't matter what famous people did.
6 Doctors, teachers and firefighters are more important role models for young people.

c Can you think of any other opinions to either agree or disagree with the statement in exercise 4a?

d Choose at least three opinions from exercise 4b that you agree with. For each one, think of a supporting idea or an example.

5 Write an essay giving your opinion on the statement in exercise 4a. Use language from the How to... box.

Pronunciation bank

English phonemes

Consonants

p	b	t	d	k	g	tʃ	dʒ
park	**b**ath	**t**ie	**d**ie	**c**at	**g**ive	**ch**urch	**j**udge
f	v	θ	ð	s	z	ʃ	ʒ
few	**v**isit	**th**row	**th**ey	**s**ell	**z**oo	fre**sh**	mea**s**ure
h	m	n	ŋ	l	r	j	w
hot	**m**ine	**n**ot	si**ng**	**l**ot	**r**oad	**y**ellow	**w**arm

Vowels and diphthongs

iː	ɪ	e	æ	ɑː	ɒ	ɔː	ʊ	uː	ʌ
f**ee**t	f**i**t	b**e**d	b**a**d	b**a**th	b**o**ttle	b**ou**ght	b**oo**k	b**oo**t	b**u**t
ɜː	ə	eɪ	əʊ	aɪ	aʊ	ɔɪ	ɪə	eə	ʊə
b**ir**d	broth**er**	gr**ey**	g**o**ld	b**y**	br**ow**n	b**oy**	h**ere**	h**air**	t**our**

Sound–spelling correspondences

Sound	Spelling	Examples
/ɪ/	i	this listen
	y	gym typical
	ui	build guitar
	e	pretty
/iː/	ee	green sleep
	ie	niece believe
	ea	read teacher
	e	these complete
	ey	key money
	ei	receipt receive
	i	police
/æ/	a	can pasta
/ɑː/	a	can't dance*
	ar	scarf bargain
	al	half
	au	aunt laugh
	ea	heart
/ʌ/	u	fun husband
	o	some mother
	ou	cousin double
/ɒ/	o	hot pocket
	a	watch want

Sound	Spelling	Examples
/ɔː/	or	short sport
	ou	your bought
	au	daughter taught
	al	small always
	aw	draw jigsaw
	ar	warden warm
	oo	floor indoor
/aɪ/	i	like time
	y	dry cycle
	ie	fries tie
	igh	light high
	ei	height
	ey	eyes
	uy	buy
/eɪ/	a	lake hate
	ai	wait train
	ay	play say
	ey	they grey
	ei	eight weight
	ea	break
/əʊ/	o	home open
	ow	show own
	oa	coat road
	ol	cold told

Weak forms

Word	Strong form	Weak form
a, an	/æ/, /æn/	/ə/, /ən/
at	/æt/	/ət/
and	/ænd/	/ən/
are	/ɑː/	/ə/ (or /ər/ before vowels)
been	/biːn/	/bɪn/
can	/kæn/	/kən/
do	/duː/	/də/
does	/dʌz/	/dəz/
has	/hæz/	/həz/, /əz/
have	/hæv/	/həv/, /əv/
than	/ðæn/	/ðən/
them	/ðem/	/ðəm/
to	/tuː/	/tə/ (before consonants)
was	/wɒz/	/wəz/

* In American English the sound in words like *can't* and *dance* is the shorter /æ/ sound, like *can* and *man*.

Sounds and Spelling

'ea' (Lesson 1.2); 'a' (Lesson 5.2); 'o' (Lesson 8.2)

See the sound-spelling correspondences chart above for the different ways these sounds (and others) can be spelt.

Word stress

Words ending -ee, -eer, -ese and -ette (Lesson 2.3)

Words with two or more syllables and these endings have the stress on the last syllable.

Compound nouns (Lesson 3.3)

With a few exceptions, noun + noun compounds are stressed on the first word and adjective + noun compounds are stressed on the second word.

Prefixes and suffixes (Unit 3 Vocabulary); (Lesson 7.2)

Word stress may change for different parts of speech.

inspire – inspiration

Prefixes are not stressed.

Phrasal verbs (Lesson 10.3)

The stress pattern of phrasal verbs varies depending on what type of phrasal verb it is.

Types A, B and D have two stresses, with the main stress on the particle.

I called him back.

Type C has just one stress on the main verb.

He's going through a difficult time.

Pronunciation bank

Sentence stress

Weak forms (Lesson 5.1); (Lesson 8.3)

The most important words in a sentence (the content words) are stressed. This means that the other words (usually grammar words) are unstressed and reduced to their weak forms.

I've never been to Paris.
/əv/   /bɪn/

If I'd gone to bed earlier, I wouldn't have been so tired.
        /tə/   /wʊdntəvbɪn/

Using sentence stress to correct (Lesson 6.3)

When we hear a mistake and we correct it, we give particular stress to the part of the sentence which is wrong.

A: Is that your son?
B: No, he's my husband!

Connected speech

(Lesson 4.2); (Lesson 7.3)

To help reduce unstressed words and make the sentence 'flow' there are certain ways that words are linked together.

A consonant at the end of one word links to a vowel at the beginning of another.

What are you doing?

If /t/ and /d/ are next to each other they can become one sound.

Can you start doing it now?

/t/ and /d/ are often not sounded when they are between two other consonants.

I mustn't forget

In many English accents the final 'r' in a word is not pronounced. But when a vowel comes next it is, to make the link easier.

Intonation

Echo questions (Lesson 1.1)

To use echo questions to show interest, our voice goes down and then up.

A: I grew up in Peru.
B: Did you?

Question tags (Lesson 4.1)

To ask a real question the intonation of the question tag is:

When we expect the other person to agree with us, the intonation of the question tag is:

Questions: Yes/No, Wh- and indirect (Lesson 6.2)

Question intonation varies, depending on the type of question:

A Yes/No questions: Is there a bank near here?

B Wh- questions: What time does the museum open?

C Indirect questions: Could you tell me what time the train leaves?

Pausing (Lesson 9.1)

When pausing for emphasis the intonation should go up before the pause when you have not yet finished, and down when you have.

We'll allow the chefs to choose the dishes and the menu will be very big, with something for everybody.

Further pronunciation areas

UK and US English (Unit 9 Vocabulary)

Both British and American accents vary, but some common differences are:

1 Words where the sound /uː/ follows /t/ /d/ or /n/ we have an extra sound, /j/, in UK English.
   tune /tjuːn/ (UK)   /tuːn/ (US)

2 Words with /ɑː/ in standard UK English can have /æ/ in US English.
   grass bath laugh

3 Many words pronounced /ɔː/ in the UK are pronounced /ɑː/ in the US.
   caught   saw   bought   talk

4 't' or 'tt' in the middle of a word tends to be pronounced /d/ in US English, or even disappear.
   Butter sounds like budder and twenty like twenny.

Pronouncing numbers (Lesson 10.2)

Years up until this century are said in two sections:

1979 – nineteen seventy-nine

1802 – eighteen 'oh' two

For the years 2000–2009 we say:

2000 – two thousand

2002 – two thousand and two

However we can say the year 2010 and over in two ways:

2012 – two thousand and twelve or twenty twelve

Irregular verbs

Verb	Past Simple	Past Participle	Verb	Past Simple	Past Participle
be	was/were	been	leave	left	left
beat	beat	beaten	lend	lent	lent
become	became	become	let	let	let
begin	began	begun	lie	lay	lain
bend	bent	bent	light	lit	lit
bite	bit	bitten	lose	lost	lost
blow	blew	blown	make	made	made
break	broke	broken	mean	meant	meant
bring	brought	brought	meet	met	met
build	built	built	must	had to	had to
burn	burned/burnt	burned/burnt	pay	paid	paid
burst	burst	burst	put	put	put
buy	bought	bought	read/ri:d/	read/red/	read/red/
can	could	been able	ride	rode	ridden
catch	caught	caught	ring	rang	rung
choose	chose	chosen	rise	rose	risen
come	came	come	run	ran	run
cost	cost	cost	say	said	said
cut	cut	cut	see	saw	seen
dig	dug	dug	sell	sold	sold
do	did	done	send	sent	sent
draw	drew	drawn	set	set	set
dream	dreamed/dreamt	dreamed/dreamt	shake	shook	shaken
drink	drank	drunk	shine	shone	shone
drive	drove	driven	shoot	shot	shot
eat	ate	eaten	show	showed	shown
fall	fell	fallen	shut	shut	shut
feed	fed	fed	sing	sang	sung
feel	felt	felt	sink	sank	sunk
fight	fought	fought	sit	sat	sat
find	found	found	sleep	slept	slept
fly	flew	flown	slide	slid	slid
forget	forgot	forgotten	smell	smelled/smelt	smelled/smelt
forgive	forgave	forgiven	speak	spoke	spoken
freeze	froze	frozen	spend	spent	spent
get	got	got	spill	spilled/spilt	spilled/spilt
give	gave	given	spoil	spoiled/spoilt	spoiled/spoilt
go	went	gone/been	stand	stood	stood
grow	grew	grown	steal	stole	stolen
hang	hung	hanged/hung	stick	stuck	stuck
have	had	had	swim	swam	swum
hear	heard	heard	take	took	taken
hide	hid	hidden	teach	taught	taught
hit	hit	hit	tear	tore	torn
hold	held	held	tell	told	told
hurt	hurt	hurt	think	thought	thought
keep	kept	kept	throw	threw	thrown
kneel	knelt	knelt	understand	understood	understood
know	knew	known	wake	woke	woken
lay	laid	laid	wear	wore	worn
lead	led	led	win	won	won
learn	learned/learnt	learned/learnt	write	wrote	written

Audioscripts

Track 1.2

Dialogue 1

M = Man, W = Woman

M: What activities and hobbies are you good at?

W: I'm quite good at juggling … .

M: Are you? How did you learn to do that?

W: Well, I started off just throwing and catching one ball, then two and now I can juggle with five balls at once.

M: Can you juggle with plates?

W: No! I don't think I could do that!

Dialogue 2

M = Man, W = Woman

W: What clubs do you belong to?

M: I don't belong to any, but my daughter is a member of an astronomy club.

W: Is she? Can she tell you what will happen in the future, then?

M: No, astronomy, not astrology! She studies the stars and planets.

W: Oh, whoops. I always get those two mixed up … Does she have a telescope then?

M: Yes, it was expensive, I can tell you … .

Dialogue 3

W = Woman, T = Teenager

W: What types of exercise are you keen on?

T: I'm keen on snowkiting.

W: Really? What's that?

T: It's like snowboarding, you know, going down a mountain on a board, but you have a kite attached too, so you go even faster.

W: I haven't even been skiing! Isn't it terrifying?

T: Yes, it is. That's the whole point!

W: Do you do it regularly?

T: No, I don't. About once a year.

Dialogue 4

M = Man, W = Woman

W: What cultures are you interested in?

M: I'm really interested in Chinese culture.

W: Have you been there?

M: Yes, I have. I went there on holiday a few years ago and just found it fascinating. I'm trying to learn Mandarin now, oh, and I've started t'ai chi classes as well.

W: Have you? Isn't that a kind of martial art?

M: Well, yes, but it doesn't involve any fighting. It's a series of slow movements, almost like a slow dance. It's really relaxing.

Dialogue 5

M = Man, W = Woman

M: What do you spend too much time on?

W: Oh, that's easy! Sudoku.

M: What's that?

W: Sudoku? It's a kind of number puzzle invented in Japan. You have to complete a grid so that all the lines and boxes contain all of the numbers from one to nine.

M: I haven't tried that.

Track 1.5

Right, well let me tell you a little bit about Rob. Um he's my best friend, um, which many people find difficult to believe. Um, many people don't have, er a best friend who is eighteen years older than them, so I suppose this is quite an unusual friendship. Um, we met, er, about three years ago. We were working in the same school and, um at first I found Rob to be quite an eccentric character, um, with lots of gestures and animations um but he – he also seemed a lot younger than he actually was, which is what I liked about him. … Um he's also – he's a very sincere, er funny, kind um person as well, which is also what I like about him too. Um, we share the same interests as well. We like the same books, we enjoy the same films and we have the same

sort of sense of humour. Er, the only real difference between us is that he – he loves cricket, but I absolutely hate it. Um, but we're still very good friends.

Track 1.8

Speaker 1:

My father has been a big influence on me. I really respect him. Um … partly because of what he does – we do the same job – but I think also his character.

We're quite similar in many ways. Um … he's sort of very calm. The only time he got angry was once, about twenty years ago when I was fifteen. I came home at five in the morning and I didn't call to say I'd be late. We had a big argument and didn't speak to each other for a week. But apart from that, I've never seen him lose his temper and he has always been very kind to me.

Speaker 2:

So, I want to speak about Romina. She was my best friend for about twelve years. Before meeting her most of my friends were boys and I didn't have many good girlfriends. We met at university and began studying together and going out in the evenings together, and we developed this method of studying before exams. We basically spent the whole night drinking coffee and testing each other. It was terrible for our health but good for our friendship. Unfortunately, we're not in touch any more. We fell out over money while we were on holiday last year, and we haven't seen each other since then. I miss her.

Speaker 3:

I work in a supermarket and I've been there for about two years. When I started, I got on really well with all my colleagues. They were all really nice, except one. This one girl – I think her name was Sarah – she was always unfriendly to me. I don't know why. Then I found out that she was saying bad things about me. She said I was lazy and a bad worker, that kind of thing. I really saw red and we had a huge row. I still don't know what it was really about though … Anyway, Sarah stopped working at the supermarket about a year ago. I don't know what she's doing now.

Track 1.9

Online dating is becoming the twenty-first century way to find a partner. In the UK last year more than seven million people used a dating website. Far from being unusual, it now seems that everyone's using the Internet as a way to meet people. There are special websites for readers of particular newspapers, for animal lovers, for classical music fans and one which allows only beautiful people to join! For many people though, the idea of having to write a profile, a description of themselves, is very off-putting. Canlintroduceyou.com has a clever way to get round that problem. Rather than writing your own profile, a friend describes you, which makes the whole process much less embarrassing. It seems that there really is a dating website to suit everyone.

Track 1.10

B = Ben, S = Sue, E = Ekaterina

B: Do you prefer watching foreign films with subtitles, or dubbing, Sue?

S: Um, well, I lived in Spain for a while and most of their films and their cinemas actually have dubbing, you know, when they have different actors doing the voices, so I used to try and go to cinemas where there were original version films because

I prefer to read the subtitles than – than listen to actors' voices pretending to be different actors. I just hate watching a film with a famous actor, like, say Al Pacino, and hear a different voice coming out. He has such a distinctive voice. It's really odd.

B: And what do you think, Ekaterina?

E: I agree actually, because I think that subtitles allow you to hear the original actors' voices and all their emotions and so I think it's more kind of realistic I'd say, yeah.

B: But you lose so much of the meaning because you can't put all of those spoken words onto a short subtitle.

E: And sometimes the translations are really poor, so that you miss the whole point of what they're trying to say.

S: Well, that's true, but that can happen with dubbing as well, can't it? If the translation isn't good quality.

B: Well, I just think it's really hard to watch the film and read the subtitles at the same time. And it's particularly hard for children, isn't it?

E: Yes, that's why in my country children's films are usually dubbed.

S: That makes sense. And anyway, for cartoons it wouldn't really matter, would it?

B: No.

E: But you know, we have another way of translating foreign films. Sometimes, especially on TV, we have one person translating all the voices, it's called the lektor.

B: One voice for the characters?

S: Isn't that confusing? How do you know when it changes from a female character to a male character for example?

E: Well, if it's done professionally, it's fine. I don't know, I guess it's what you're used to. But a lot of people like it and, of course, it's pretty cheap to translate films in this way.

S: Can you still hear the original film underneath?

E: Yes, usually you can, but at a lower volume. So it's actually quite good if you do speak some of the language the film is in … .

Track 1.11

1 Going to the cinema is too expensive these days.

2 Films are becoming too violent.

3 The use of computerised special effects has made films more exciting.

4 Big film stars deserve to earn millions of dollars.

5 Watching films in English is a great way to learn.

Track 1.12

P = Presenter, Ju = Julian, A = Anna, C = Chris, Jo = Joe

P: And in today's programme we hear from our panel of testers. This week they've been trying out some of the hottest new eco-gadgets. What did they think of the products, and are they actually any better for the environment? Julian, what was your gadget?

Ju: Mine was the weird looking thing with the propeller and the glove. It's actually a device you can wear while riding a bicycle that makes you go fast- much faster in fact! The glove controls the speed, and you can do up to 130 km an hour. I can't say I tried going that fast myself, but it was certainly a lot faster and easier than cycling normally. It's powered by petrol, which is really what I didn't like about it. Basically, it's made a completely eco-friendly means of transport, a bike, use fuel. That said, it does apparently use a lot less petrol than needed by a car, so I guess it could be a better choice.

P: And Anna, what did you take home?

A: I took home the two cardboard boxes. They're actually speakers for plugging into your MP3 player. I wasn't expecting much, to be honest, but I was pleasantly surprised. The sound they produced was actually very clear. They're cheap, but to be honest, I still don't think they look very good.

P: Chris, how did you get on with your gadget?

C: Well, mine looks like a soft toy, and it's a kind of octopus shape. In fact, it's a webcam – you know, a kind of camera for seeing and talking to people over the Internet. It worked really well and it looked a lot nicer than a plastic one … .

P: But is it more eco-friendly?

C: Yes, I think so; most of the material used to make it has been recycled. Of course, it doesn't exactly look professional if you wanted to use it at work.

P: And, finally, Joe, what was your gadget?

Jo: It was a rather clever kind of radio. It's quite small and square and it has a handle which you can wind up to get energy to make the radio work, or you can use the solar panel on the top. It was easy to wind up, and I got about twenty minutes of playtime out of winding it up for one minute. The solar panel was less successful – but perhaps that's because it just isn't sunny enough in this country … .

Track 1.16

R = Rachel, E = Eben

R: Do you believe everything you read in the news normally?

E: No, not really. Um, I read lots of different papers and I find that they all report the same story differently. The interesting trick they play is that each newspaper seems to tell a different part of the story, so they withhold the information.

R: Yeah they seem to decide differently as to what they think is going to be worthy of a story for somebody to read and they do reflect on it completely differently sometimes. It's difficult to know what's important and what's not.

E: Yes, and as I said, it's strange that – it seems that sometimes they will hold back information so that the story sounds worse than it actually is and it almost comes across as if the newspaper wants you to get angry.

R: Or sometimes they'll express something that's supposed to be so exciting, and you're not quite sure whether you really agree with it being that exciting, or that interesting, as it actually is … .

E: Which is – yes, I suppose that raises the other point, writing news is a business, it's an industry. They have to come up with stories every day, all day, and so they have to almost write a little bit like fiction as a, you know, to make it exciting.

R: Well yeah, and they have to – they have to sell newspapers, they have to make money. So sometimes you think that that's the only reason that they may be writing a story.

Track 1.18

It's a horror film, set in Spain. It's about a woman who buys the house where she used to live as a child. Her son starts to see the ghosts of children in the house and then he suddenly disappears. The main characters are the woman and her husband. There is also a rather spooky old woman.

Track 1.19

The house that the woman, Laura, buys, used to be an orphanage and the ghosts are of children who lived there. When Simón, her son disappears, the police think that he may have been taken by the spooky old woman, Benigna, who, it turns out used to work at the orphanage. However, Laura becomes more and more sure that he has been taken by the ghosts. In the end Laura finds Simón, but I won't spoil the ending by telling you how!

Track 1.20

1 The Dos Santos family

I = Interviewer, M = Miriam, C = Carlos

I: So how do you feel about the house swap?

M: Oh, I can't wait. I can hardly believe we're spending more than one month in London. We've never been there before.

I: I'm sure you'll love it.

M: Yes, I'm sure we will.

I: What are you going to do while you're there, Carlos?

C: We're going to see all the sights and the museums … .

M: And I'm going to do lots and lots of shopping.

I: Great. There are some wonderful shops in London. I'll give you the address of a great shoe shop.

M: I'm going to spend lots of money, and buy beautiful clothes and souvenirs for my family … .

C: And we're visiting some friends in Oxford on 3rd June.

M: I think they'll have nice shops there too and of course … .

2 The Armitage family

I = Interviewer, J = Jeremy, S = Sarah

I: So, are you ready for Spain?

J: Yes, I think so. We've always wanted to visit Spain. It has such a rich culture. I want the girls to experience that while they are young, even though they're not very keen. We're going to see the cathedrals …

S: And we love Spanish food, so we're going to try all the local dishes, particularly the seafood. Of course the girls will probably want to go to MacDonalds …

J: Yes, but we won't go to McDonald's. Forget it!

S: Oh, and we're also going to go to the beach.

J: Yes, we're looking forward to that. I really hope this'll be the holiday of a lifetime for us all.

Track 1.21

Miriam Dos Santos

I = Interviewer, M = Miriam

I: Hi Miriam. So how was London?

M: Well London was fantastic, but the house was a disaster.

I: Oh dear. Why was that?

M: First of all, it was in the middle of nowhere. It was a long way from the centre, and very difficult to find. We got completely lost looking for it. In the end we had to ask a taxi driver to take us there, which was very expensive. And when we went inside, my goodness, it was so old, and dark. I don't think they had changed anything in that house for thirty years. It was like something out of a film. Nothing worked properly. Even the heating didn't work, so there was no hot water, and the shower didn't work either. Anyway, I was really disappointed, and so we're going to complain to the company. We'll ask them about the central heating and why the information on the website was wrong and we'll also ask them … .

Jeremy Armitage

I = Interviewer, J = Jeremy

I: How was Spain?

J: I have to be honest with you. It wasn't good.

I: Oh dear. Why was that?

J: Well, the main problem was the flat. It was too small. The girls had to stay in the single room together, but it was more like a cupboard than a room. It was tiny! And the other rooms weren't much bigger! And it was so hot, and there was no fan, so we had big arguments. Also, the mosquitoes were terrible, so it was very difficult to sleep at night. And downstairs there was a bar, which played loud music until four in the morning. I think the only reason the area was quiet during the day is because everyone was sleeping after being awake all night!
Anyway, the girls refused to do the things I wanted to do. All they wanted to do was try and get a suntan. They don't care about culture, and didn't want to eat the delicious food. They just wanted chips! At the end of the month, I was so pleased to get home. I am never going to do a home swap again!

Track 1.22

R = Representative, M = Miriam

R: Hello, yourhome-myhome. How can I help you?

M: Hello, my name is Miriam dos Santos. I recently did a house swap with one of the properties on your website and I'm afraid I wasn't at all happy with the experience.

R: Oh, I'm sorry to hear that. Can you just give me some details? What was the reference number of the house?

M: 742778.

R: OK, I'm just getting the details … Yes, right, what was the problem exactly?

M: Well, I don't like to complain but there really were a lot of problems. For starters, we couldn't find the place. It was in the middle of nowhere. The information on the website said that it would be easy to get into the city centre, but in fact it took over two hours to get there … .

R: Well, of course, it does depend on the time of day. Rush hour can be a problem.

M: No, I'm sorry, but it was just a long way from the centre. And when we got there the house was in a terrible mess. There were dirty dishes and cups everywhere; the bathroom was disgusting and far too small.

R: Oh dear, yes, there was supposed to be a cleaner coming in before you arrived but she was ill, so it didn't happen. We must apologise about that.

M: Oh, well, that wasn't the only problem, actually. There weren't any clean sheets or towels, so we had to go out and buy some more and the central heating wasn't working, so the house was freezing and there was no hot water.

R: Ah, actually, the heating was working but it was switched off. You needed to switch it on.

M: Well, in that case, why didn't the man I spoke to at your office explain that at the time? I'm sorry, but it just isn't good enough.

R: No, I do apologise for the inconvenience.

M: Well, actually, I'd like you to give me a full refund of the fee we paid to yourhome-myhome.

R: Well, it isn't company policy to give a refund. Perhaps we could give you a goodwill payment of, say, £100 to pay for the sheets and towels you had to buy? How would that be?

M: Well, I think you should give me a refund, but I suppose that's something.

R: And I do apologise again … .

Track 1.25

I loved living in Japan. I lived there for two years, um, and I had a really great time. I went – I lived in Kyoto, which is a really, really beautiful city, it's got, um, it's got amazing – lots of old architecture, um it's very beautiful and it's a very lively bustling city. There's lots to do there, um it's got really good um restaurants with traditional Japanese food and it's got restaurants with um food from all over the world as well.

And it's got great shops and very good night life and it's – the thing I liked about Japan is, although it's very crowded and bustling and you've got lots of people on the streets and lots of bikes um you can sort of step off the streets and go into the er the older traditional temples, um, and when you go in those areas its – it's really quiet and calm and it's – it's nice, it's very peaceful in those places.

Um, the only thing I suppose that was a disadvantage in – in – in Kyoto was the –the heat. In the summer it gets very hot, there's a lot of humidity, um, so actually it's quite a relief to go into some of the more modern shopping areas so you can have the, er, the air-conditioning on, which is – which is really nice because actually in my apartment in Kyoto I didn't have any air-conditioning so it was – it was very uncomfortable in the summer and sleeping at night was a real problem.

So yeah, sometimes at weekends to escape I used to just walk around the, um, the shopping areas and go in the shops so I could enjoy the air-conditioning, which was really nice as well. The people were very, very friendly um in Kyoto and that was one thing I liked, even not speaking the language very well and not knowing the area very well you could go out and feel that you were quite in good hands really because the Japanese people would always look after you.

Track 1.26

T = Tracy, S = Stig

T: I don't think there's any doubt that the way we live now we have – we have to change somehow, um, you know. We're gonna end up with – with no water, with no heating, with – with nothing if we don't change the way that we all live, so I think the point that he's making about um homes being smaller um so that we can afford to heat them and to have water for them and, you know, different furniture and things like that is a really great idea.

S: I'm not sure I agree with that. I think rich people will always be able to buy big houses. It'll only be the poor people perhaps who get smaller and smaller houses as we run out of space.

T: You think – you think rich people won't give up their swimming pools for anything?

S: Well, not necessarily their swimming pools, but there'll always be rich footballers who can afford to buy massive houses. I don't think that's gonna change.

T: I think maybe, maybe, having lived in Hong Kong and places that don't have as much space is that you realise suddenly how little space you really do need and that, you know, things like table tops being used as computer screens as well, um, isn't so out of the realms of possibility.

S: No, I think that's – that's true, I mean countries that don't have much space certainly will need to think about how they use that space and might – might need to build smaller and smaller homes but I think the people who have the money for the homes will definitely continue to buy massive houses.

T: Yeah, that's true. I mean I can't imagine that, um, anyone will ever give up their cars. I can't see a future where there's definitely fewer cars or definitely, er, fewer people moving around like that. I can't ever imagine that happening, can you?

S: No, I can't really. I think people will just have to develop new fuels, for example hydrogen's being used to run cars. Er, you've got an increase in the number of electric cars and I think governments will just have to develop, you know, filling stations for electricity instead of petrol.

T: Yeah, these things don't tend to happen unless you're kind of forced into them. You know, if you're given the choice between a flashy car or an electric car, you're never going to choose the – the cheap option. You're always gonna go for the – for the nice one.

S: Yeah, this idea about fish tanks that – that will provide fish to eat and produce fresh vegetables … I can't see this happening at all. I mean people will keep fish as pets but I can't see them growing quickly enough to keep in your kitchen and then have for dinner.

T: It's hard to imagine a load of tropical fish in your kitchen that you then – your kids pick out and eat.

S: Yeah, I agree.

T: Um but they, I mean they are things that are around already, like um fridges that you can send messages to from your mobile phone to um … .

S: Can you?

T: Yeah, that you can tell them what you want them to – to order from online supermarkets and things like that, you know, it knows when you're running low on things.

S: Cool.

T: Um, I haven't heard of it being able to tell you when it's about to go out of date but sounds like a good idea to me.

S: Yeah I think, you know, the thing about robots being er more common in the future: I think that's probably right. I mean, you know, they already have the little vacuum cleaners that run round your living room cleaning it for you. So I think they'll be developed further.

T: It seems hard to imagine but I don't think any of us anticipated what kind of things we'd already all have in our homes, you know, having a computer in every home was unimaginable at one point. So – so you never know where we're gonna end up.

S: No, you don't.

Track 1.28

Speaker 1:

I live in the suburbs of the city. I'd say my lifestyle was very busy and stressful. I wear a suit every day. I work sixty hours a week and it takes me more than an hour to commute into the centre to get to work. I hate it! So I need a change, and I'd like to move to the country. I hope to become completely self-sufficient, grow my own food and have some chickens. I'm going to take a course in farming at the local college and I'll probably get some bees as well. I love honey! I might even get rid of the television, do some reading in the evenings instead, but I'll probably keep my computer.

Speaker 2:

I'm from a very small town. It's the most boring place you can imagine. It's for people who want a quiet life. There's one school, one post office and only a few shops and that's all. I guess it's quite healthy, no pollution or anything, but it's also very dull. So, I want to experience city life. My dream is to live right in the middle of a big city where there's loads going on. So, what am I going to do there? I'm going to find a job, of course, because I know the city is expensive. In my free time, I'll definitely go clubbing a lot to try and meet people and make friends. I imagine there'll be people from lots of different countries and cultures. I could also do a course, learn another language … .

Track 1.29

Frank Abagnale, a good-looking English boy, pretended to be first a pilot, then a doctor and then a lawyer. For five years he travelled the world for free, stayed in expensive hotels and had relationships with beautiful women. Furthermore, by the age of twenty-one he had tricked and cheated his way to $250 million. In the golden age of James Bond, Abagnale really was an international man of mystery. He was wanted by the FBI and Interpol (International Police) in twenty-six cities. Abagnale's charm was his most important tool. He dressed well and everybody believed everything he said. Leonardo DiCaprio, who plays Frank Abagnale in the film *Catch me if you can* said, 'Frank Abagnale is one of the greatest actors who has walked the Earth.' Abagnale was a lonely child. When his German mother divorced his father, Abagnale had to choose which parent to live with. Instead, he ran away from home and began his life as an international trickster. He got a Pan Am pilot's uniform by saying that his was stolen and that he had an urgent flight. This allowed him to stay in any hotel he wanted: Pan Am always paid the bill. What's more, he even pretended to be a footballer and played for a professional team for a year.

He broke the law constantly but he never went to prison until he was finally caught in the USA. Despite his crimes, Abagnale never had any enemies.

These days Abagnale doesn't need to trick anybody: he is a successful consultant. He advises companies on how to cheat their customers, and he also lectures at the FBI Academy. He wrote his autobiography in the 1970s and sold the film rights for $250,000.

Track 1.30

A: OK, so which of these do you think is the most dishonest thing to do?

B: Right, well, I think it would have to be copying work from the Internet, don't you?

A: Mmm, I guess so. What about copying a CD from a friend? I do that a lot, don't you?

B: Er, yes, I suppose I shouldn't really, should I? What about taking stationery home from work?

A: I think that depends what it is. I don't think the odd pen is a problem, is it?

B: No, but you haven't taken anything bigger, have you?

A: No, of course not! I do know someone who took a whole box of pens though. That's a bit different, isn't it?

B: Definitely. Now, have you ever lied about your age on an Internet dating site?

A: If I had, I wouldn't tell you, would I? I think that's pretty dishonest, actually, but people do it all the time, don't they?

B: Yes, and not just about their age … .

A: Hmm. What about switching price labels in a shop? I wouldn't do that, would you?

B: No, definitely not. That's just stealing, plain and simple. And I wouldn't buy something, wear it and then return it either.

A: No, neither would I. So, which is worst? I think switching price labels, actually.

B: Yes, and then, maybe … .

Track 1.32

1 Right, well, I think it would have to be copying work from the Internet, don't you?
2 I guess so. What about copying a CD from a friend? I do that a lot, don't you?
3 I don't think the odd pen is a problem, is it?
4 No, but you haven't taken anything bigger, have you?
5 That's a bit different, isn't it?
6 If I had, I wouldn't tell you, would I?
7 I think that's pretty dishonest, actually, but people do it all the time, don't they?

Track 1.33

Thank you for coming. It's good to see so many young entrepreneurs here. Today I'm going to talk about how to get rich. The American writer Scott Fitzgerald once said, 'Let me tell you about the rich. They are very different from you and me'. He's right. The super-rich have a number of personal qualities that make them different. But they aren't all good qualities. Here are some ideas for you entrepreneurs who want to get rich.

Track 1.34

Here are some ideas for you entrepreneurs who want to get rich. The first thing is, you sometimes have to be a bit mean. You shouldn't be too generous. John Paul Getty, one of the richest men in history, put payphones in the bedrooms of his house so that his friends couldn't make free phone calls. Number two: you should start early. Really rich people know they want to be rich even when they are children. Matthew Freud sold mice to his school friends. He said he would be a millionaire by the time he was twenty-five years old. He was right. Number three: don't be too extravagant. You mustn't waste your money on stupid things. Bill Gates doesn't wear a suit. He doesn't care about looking good because he doesn't have to look good. If you spend all your money on expensive holidays and presents, you will probably never be rich. Number four: be confident. You must believe in yourself. Everyone has great ideas but 99.9 percent of us never do anything about them. Anita Roddick, the boss of Body Shop, said 'It's all about having a good idea and having the confidence to sell it to the public.' Number five: you have to work hard. Work long hours. This is the most important thing. No one ever got rich by sleeping half the day. Rupert Murdoch goes to five o'clock

meetings. That's 5.00 in the morning. Bernie Ecclestone, the Formula One billionaire, went to his office at 6.00 in the morning. Every day. Even when he reached the age of seventy.

Number six: think big. Be ambitious. You shouldn't think about the limits of your business. Sell yourself to the world, not only your home town. Of course there are lots of other … .

Track 1.36

P = Presenter, M = Maria

P: In the old days, before TV remote controls were invented, when the adverts came on TV, you had to actually stand up, go over to the telly and turn down the volume or turn the TV off to avoid seeing them. Nowadays, not only can we switch the sound off instantly, but we also often record programmes and just skip the adverts. Similarly, with the Internet, most people now choose to turn pop-up windows, those annoying little adverts that appear on your webpage, off, so we never even see them.

But advertisers have a new weapon in the fight to get our attention – behavioural advertising. Here with us today to talk about it, is Maria Schulz, author of a new book on advertising in the Internet age. Maria, hi, can I start by asking you, what exactly is behavioural advertising?

M: Hi. Well, behavioural advertising is basically advertising which sends adverts to specific people based on what they are actually interested in.

P: Sorry, I'm not with you. How do they know what people are interested in?

M: By monitoring their web habits, or the websites that they visit. So, if you have recently visited a site to find out about flights to Paris, you may be sent advertisements for hotels in Paris and so on.

P: Are you saying that advertisers will be watching which Internet sites we visit? I have to say that makes me feel pretty uncomfortable. I really don't like the idea that a company has that kind of information about me.

M: Well, they have the information, but they don't actually know who you are – they won't have an address or a name or anything. But you're not alone in feeling uncomfortable about this. In a recent poll, 95 percent of people asked were against the idea.

P: I'm not surprised. It's a terrible idea.

M: But would you rather have adverts which you have no interest in at all?

P: I'd rather not have any adverts, I suppose.

M: Even if that meant you could no longer watch, say, a TV programme you've missed for free? In the same survey, 60 percent of people asked said that they would rather have adverts than pay to watch TV programmes online.

P: I suppose that's a good point … .

Track 1.37

J = Jonathon, P = Polly

J: What do you think of a hundred and forty million dollars being spent for a single painting?

P: Oh you mean the Jackson Pollock painting? Um, I don't think it's that much of a waste of money there's only, um, one of those paintings so it's a, it's a piece of history and if you get to own that then that's quite cool, wouldn't – wouldn't you like to have that hanging on your wall?

J: I would for the – for the worth of it that's true, and it's attractive to look at, but I just feel for instance a Picasso is, you can see the skill in the paint work but I just feel it's a – it's a dribble that a child could produce.

P: Oh really?

J: Mmm, oh well.

P: Yeah. Well, um, compared to say spending money on sending a man to the moon, it's not as worthwhile as – not as worthwhile as that, I think sending a – a man to the moon and spending two point two billion dollars on it would be a … .

J: Yes I can see, I can see that that has got some meaning for man and with the problems we have on this planet such as starvation and shortages of water and mounting debt we have to look at alternative ways of housing all the people, so I can see the justification of that compared to spending so much for a single painting. From that point of view it's worth it.

P: Oh OK. Um, well sticking with science, what about the Hadron Collider?

J: Ah yes, well with that one I think there's, it's looking like the world's biggest waste of money don't you agree, because there's, ah …

P: Mmm, I do agree there yeah.

J: … there's still, there's still big questions and there's been so much go wrong with it and it's such a, four to six billion is such a vast amount and – is it four to six billion?

P: Ah, four point six billion.

J: Ah, it's such a – a vast amount of money and no – and what would we do if we did find out how the Earth actually came into being?

P: Yeah I think there's too much risk that it's, um, not going to work at all.

J: Mmm. What have you, um – have you ever tasted a – an expensive sandwich made with Wagyu … Wagyu beef?

P: Um, no I think that's crazy, um, I think that five pounds for a sandwich is too much and eighty-five dollars is, um, just ridiculous the … .

J: Yeah.

P: … the relationship between the taste and the cost can't, ah … .

J: Mmm. Did you realise that every day they fly it from Chile to Heathrow at five thirty in the morning, what an expense to the carbon footprint?

P: Oh yeah that's a waste of money and of, um, and of carbon.

J: And it's also full of fat apparently it's, ur, I can't see how people would want to spend that amount of money and it's just like caviar, it's just a food for the rich and there's so many people going short of food it just seems almost unjustifiable. I don't know how people could pay that amount.

P: Yeah, I think it's crazy.

J: Mmm.

Track 1.39

J = Jon, M = Maddy, S = Sara

J: So what do you think about that one?

M: I'm not sure if I like it or not. It makes me feel really sad. I do like the way the artist has done so much with just a few colours though. It reminds me of an old sepia photograph. Do you think they're homeless?

S: I'm not sure, but I agree it's a bit depressing. I really like this one. The colours are really vivid, aren't they? The

Audioscripts

way the different women are sitting at different angles. It's really striking. Oh, and I like the way you can see how hot the sun is.

J: This is my favourite one. It's just so unusual…

M: Really? I think it's horrible, really quite disturbing. It looks as if someone has been covered in dead fish! Eurgh. This one is more my kind of thing.

S: Yes, I like that one too. It tells a story. Why is she looking out of the window? Is she just bored, or is there something really interesting going on out there? It's really intriguing, isn't it?

Track 1.40

Mike:
I've been taking classes in origami for three months. Basically, you learn how to make beautiful objects using paper. It's an ancient Japanese art and I really love it. It's very creative because you actually make very beautiful things, birds, animals … and you can keep them forever. I've given some away as birthday presents and people love them!

Tom:
Well, my hobby is cooking. I think it's actually quite creative because I've made up lots of my own recipes. It isn't really creative if you just follow a recipe book. People say I'm a good cook. I've been trying to open my own restaurant for ages but I don't have the money yet. But it's something I'll definitely do in the future.

Ruth:
I think you have to be creative to look after children. It's important to really let them develop their own ideas and imagination. I've been playing with my three children this morning and the room is a complete mess because we've been pretending it's a zoo. But letting them be creative is much more important than being tidy!

Track 1.42

I = Interviewer, H = Hannah
I: Hannah, did it surprise you how you spend your free time?

H: Yeah, I didn't expect to see these results at all. Um … I'm a film-maker so I think it's normal to spend a lot of time watching films at the cinema and on DVD, but a lot of other things surprised me.

I: For example?

H: For example, I spend eight percent of my free time shopping. Well, I can't stand shopping. It drives me mad.

I: Really?

H: Yeah, and the housework – I don't mind doing the housework, but it's not very interesting and I'd prefer to do less of that kind of thing. Also, I noticed that I spend fifteen percent of my time watching TV and only ten percent reading, which surprises me because I enjoy reading and I always look forward to starting a new book.

I: You don't like TV so much?

H: Well, most TV is like junk food for the brain and I should watch less. Other things … um … I love cooking, and I try to cook a proper meal at least four nights a week. And I often invite friends over to have dinner so it doesn't surprise me that I spend seven percent of my time cooking and eating.

I: Is there anything you'd really like to change?

H: Um … I never manage to do much exercise. I'd really like to go running every day just for half an hour but I never seem to find the time. So that's one thing I'd like to change.

Track 1.44

I = Interviewer, J = Julia
I: So, can you tell me a bit about some typical Argentinian dishes?

J: Well, the first thing to say is that everyone eats quite a lot of meat. They love grilled meat on the *asado*, or barbecue. The meat is sometimes marinated first – they put it in a sauce overnight to soak up the flavour before it's cooked. A popular marinade is *chimichurri*, which is made with garlic, oil and herbs. Another favourite type of food is *empanadas*. These are a kind of little pie, baked in the oven and stuffed with different fillings – meat, again, cheese and vegetables. These can be served hot or cold.

I: And what about dessert?

J: The most famous sweet has to be *dulce de leche*. It's made by boiling milk and sugar together. It's usually served with cake or biscuits.

Track 1.45

Last summer I went to a wonderful restaurant in Bruges in Belgium – it was for my boyfriend's birthday and we decided to go to Bruges for the weekend. We went to a lovely restaurant in the centre of Bruges which used to be a cathedral so the inside of the building was very, very old. It was summertime so we could sit outside, and the atmosphere was – was very peaceful and relaxing.
It was quite, um, a nice evening so we sat outside and enjoyed the sunshine. The restaurant's quite expensive, but we decided to treat ourselves and I had vegetarian lasagne and my boyfriend had steak. The restaurant serves quite a lot of different types of food but it's famous for, um, fish and meat. Probably the worst thing about the restaurant is the service, the service is quite slow, but it didn't matter, we still had a nice time.

Track 1.46

1   It's a type of sport which you do in the sea. You need a board and big waves. It can be dangerous, but it's really exciting.
2   It's a kind of meal you get in Indian restaurants. It's hot and spicy and usually has meat in it. You eat it with rice.
3   It's the stuff you find under the grass. It's brown. You see it when it rains.
4   It's something you use for cleaning the house. It's a machine that picks up dust and small pieces of dirt.
5   They're usually made of wood. They're a useful thing to have in the house, because you can put your books on them.

Track 1.47

A computer screen is rectangular. An egg is oval. A plate is round. A floppy disk is square. An elephant is heavy. A mouse is light. The Grand Canyon is enormous. Buckingham Palace is huge. An ant is tiny. The main road is wide. The back streets are narrow. Soap is smooth. A beard is rough. Toffee is sticky. Ice cream is soft. A stone is hard.

Track 1.49

I'm going to tell you about capoeira. Capoeira is a kind of martial art, which is also like a dance. It originated in Brazil, where it was started by the African slaves. The story goes that the slaves were forbidden from fighting, so they developed a kind of fighting which, to the slave owners, just looked like a dance.

The music is very important as the songs are sung while a game is being played to tell the story of capoeira and the slaves' struggle. The most important instrument is the *berimbau*, a kind of guitar with just one string.
You need to be very fit and strong, particularly your arms, as you often have to use your hands to balance. Every movement needs to be done perfectly, so you should have good control of your body. Everyone sits around in a circle, singing and playing music, and two people fight in the centre. To fight the other person you kick with your feet, but … er … nowadays, there's no contact. As soon as you see the other person's hand or foot coming towards you, you have to move away quickly. You must be careful the other person doesn't kick you. If the other person kicks you, then you lose.
People who play capoeira are called *capoeiristas*. Capoeiristas usually wear white clothes. If the white costume is still clean at the end of the game, that shows how skilful you are because it means you haven't been kicked or knocked to the floor.
Afterwards, you can … er … relax and talk about the fight. And … er … we often spend the evening together, listening to music. I've been doing capoeira for three years. I've improved a lot since I first started, and now I wear a green belt. In the future, I would like to become a trainer, called a Master, and teach other people about this beautiful sport.

Track 2.1

Helen:
This is a photo that I took um in Thailand on the island of Ko Samui. Um, I took it about lunchtime. It was a very, very hot day and it was monsoon season, so sometimes it was very, very hot and clear and then sometimes it would just suddenly rain. But at this time it was – it was very hot.
In the photo there's a big fishing boat, which was just on the beach and then behind the – the boat you can see the sea and some islands. It was a very peaceful day and very quiet and we had a bit of breakfast on the beach and after that we sat on the beach reading books and not doing very much, so it was a very relaxing and a very nice day.

Matthew:
This photo was taken last summer while I was on holiday with my wife. Um we were in Kent and this is a – a photo of a place called Scotney Castle. We'd been walking around in the countryside and we suddenly stumbled upon this place and it was so beautiful.
So in the photograph you can see in the foreground a castle reflected in a lake. Um I took the photo and then for the rest of the day I had to do um other things because it suddenly started pouring with rain.
Um but it was so lovely just to have found such a beautiful place, um just – just by exploring the countryside.

Tracy:
This is a photo of the centre of Hong Kong Island. It's kind of a long er road that – that travels kind of the whole length of the island and um I'm actually on a tram looking down at um all the people, much like the one in the centre of the photo. Um, in the foreground you can see all the people crossing the road there.
… Um, it's a really, really busy part of the road, a really busy junction, um and then on the left-hand side you can see all the shops and um there's a little market just down the – the

side road there. Um, it was taken in November so the weather was really, really nice, um not too hot but um not getting really cold yet, so it was beautiful for taking photos.

… We had a really amazing day, um we spent a lot of time walking around that day and just hopping on and off the tram to try and find nice places to visit and it was a – a really lovely trip.

Track 2.2

Dialogue 1
M = Mark, W = Woman
M: I'd like two tickets from Melbourne to Adelaide, please, leaving tomorrow morning.
W: Standard class or premium?
M: Standard, please.
W: That's a hundred and eighty dollars, please.
M: Thank you. Could you tell me what time the train gets into Adelaide?
W: 17.45. But we are expecting some delays to the service. You need to listen to the announcements.
M: Oh! Thanks.

Dialogue 2
K = Kate, M = Man
K: Excuse me. How do we get to the National Railway Museum?
M: Um … right. The quickest thing to do is to take the Outer Harbor train to Port Adelaide Station.
K: Is it far?
M: No, the station you need is just a short walk from here, and then it takes about ten minutes.
K: OK. Thank you.
M: But the museum is closed at the moment.
K: Oh! Thank you anyway.

Dialogue 3
M = Mark, W = Woman
M: Excuse me. Is there a post office near here?
W: Yes, there's one just down the road. Just go straight on and it's on your left.
M: Thank you.
W: But it's closed now. You need to go before 5 o'clock.
M: Oh no! Thank you.

Dialogue 4
M = Mark, W = Woman
M: Excuse me. Does this bus go to Werribee Park?
W: No, this one's for the airport. You need the shuttlebus. Look, it's just over there.
M: OK, thanks.
W: But you need to buy a ticket in advance.
M: Oh, OK … Thanks for your help.

Dialogue 5
K = Kate, M = Man
K: Two student tickets, please.
M: Have you got a student card?
K: Yes. One moment. Oh. I can't find it. I think I've left it at the hotel.
M: Then I'm afraid you'll have to pay the full price. That'll be forty-two dollars please.
K: Forty-two dollars! OK. Thanks.

Track 2.5

P = Presenter, J = Joanne
P: And with us in the studio today we have Joanne Bright, author of a new book about women travellers in the eighteenth and nineteenth centuries. Joanne, it can't have been easy to travel the world then, especially as a woman. These women must have been terribly brave and adventurous.

J: Well, some of them certainly were, but we mustn't forget that probably most women travellers didn't actually choose to make their journeys in the first place. Their husbands decided to go abroad, or were sent abroad, and the women followed. That was certainly the case with Lady Mary Wortley Montagu, whose husband was sent as ambassador to Istanbul in Turkey, in 1716.
P: Didn't she want to go?
J: Well, we don't know for sure, but she certainly seemed to enjoy herself when she got there! She wrote a series of letters back to her friends and family, which were published after her death. The unusual thing about Lady Mary is how open she was to the new culture. In fact, in many ways, she decided that it was much better than her own. She commented on how polite the Turkish ladies were about her European dress, pointing out that English ladies would probably have laughed at someone dressed as differently as she was. In fact, she started wearing Turkish dress herself. And she noticed the Turkish women protecting their children against the disease of small pox by using inoculation, where a small dose of the disease was given to prevent them catching the disease badly later. Lady Mary had recently caught smallpox herself and her face was very badly damaged as a result, so she very much wanted to protect her children from it. She had her son inoculated in Turkey, the first English person to be protected in this way, and, when she returned home to England, she helped to persuade the English doctors to develop a similar technique.
P: Goodness, she really achieved something through her visit then … .

Track 2.7

K = Kate, H = Heather, E = Ekaterina
K: OK. So we need to plan this day in London. I think because there's gonna be so much to do, it would be good to get it planned before we get there.
H: Yeah, there's a lot of choice, isn't there?
E: Yeah, sure.
H: What do you guys want to do?
K: Well I like the idea of the show in the evening. Um … .
H Oh yeah, it says here that um Les Mis is playing, um oh yeah, but tickets are forty pounds. Are you guys OK with paying forty pounds for the show?
K: I'm happy with that.
E: It sounds quite expensive but probably it's worth it.
H: Yeah, I think so.
E: It's one of the most famous ones in London. So … .
H: Cool. OK, let's do that then. What about the daytime?
K: Um I quite like the sound of the London Walks. They're quite cheap and it's not gonna take up all day. Yeah, you guys OK with that too?
E: Yeah, I think so.
H: Yeah, we'd probably see quite a bit going around … walking.
K: Yeah. Yeah, I think we should.
H: Alright, cool. Oh, oh, oh, can we go to Camden Market too? I heard it's really good there.
K: Yeah, I heard that too.
H: There's loads to see and, you know, you can eat good food and …

E: … visit different shops and …
H: Yeah.
E: … buy something.
K: Absolutely.
E: … artistic.
H: Oh but what if it rains? Hang on a minute.
K: Mmm, that's true.
E: We have a couple of museums here so we can probably pick one.
H: Which one were you looking at?
E: Um, how about the British Museum?
H: Oh and it's free.
E: Yeah, wow.
K: I like the sound of that.
H: Yeah, me too. Looks like we've um chosen a few things.
K: Yeah, and I think we can hopefully dodge the rain.
H: Alright, as long as we're there on time for the show then we'll be OK with the day.
K: OK.
H: I look forward to it.

Track 2.8

Natalie:
When I was a child I used to do music exams and for every music exam I had to learn a piece of music. Now I used to play the drums. I started when I was five and I did, er, seven different music exams, seven grades, and for every exam I had to learn a piece of music. … At the beginning it was only ten bars or something but it was really hard and I used to practise them over and over again and I used to drive my parents crazy because um obviously I was playing the drums at home. At the beginning I used to play just on books and so it was quite quiet. But then when I was seven I got my first drum kit and I, um, played constantly and the same pieces over and over again. That was one thing that I had to learn by heart.

Track 2.9

Phil:
About a year and a half ago I took an interest in the language Yiddish, which is the language that my family spoke when they came to this country about a hundred years ago. Um, it's quite a – a beautiful language, or I think so anyway, and it's about a thousand years old. Although I knew a few words of Yiddish from my family and from TV shows, you hear them on American TV shows all the time, um I didn't realise it was related to German and er I was amazed how quickly I started picking it up. … I did German at school you see. I'm now at about GCSE level, having found myself er, a weekly class, and um, I did a week intensive course last summer and er it's opened up a whole new culture, as well as a language, including sort of poetry and music and the way that my ancestors lived, and so hopefully I'm going to attend the summer course again this year and, er, impress them with how much I've learnt since last year.

Track 2.10

Rachel:
Um, an occasion where I had a really steep learning curve was when I um got the job to go and work in a kids' camp in America and I really didn't know what to expect and when I got there it completely surprised me. … I was just thrown into everything, my whole day was taken up either looking after children or running a class or taking them to and from somewhere and I had no time to myself, and I think it was the closest thing ever to being a parent, where you were just –

your – your time is just completely consumed by lots of other people and I had no time to myself at all really.

Track 2.11

Sean:

For my eighteenth birthday my parents asked me what I wanted as a present and I can't remember why I asked for a parachute jump. And so, about a month later, I took a one-day crash course in parachuting and it took place at a local airfield and there must have been about seven or eight other students there and there was already a great atmosphere. Everyone was really excited to be there. And in the morning we looked at how parachutes work, how to put them on properly and how to do a safety check and also how to steer the parachute back to the airfield. And then after lunch we covered what to do if the parachute didn't open properly and how to use the emergency chute and we spent – spent a lot of time on how to land safely.
… And of course at the end of the day we went up in the aeroplane to do the jump and I remember really trembling and I don't really know why, whether I was scared or just very, very cold. Doing the jump was fantastic, I mean really thrilling. It really made you feel alive. Um but it was all over too soon, although I'm not sure I'd want to do it again.

Track 2.12

Yvette:

Um, the time I was most thrown in at the deep end um was when I took a job in Indonesia, um, about six years ago. Um it was the first time that I'd been to Asia so um firstly there was the culture shock of living in a – a completely different country, with lots of different customs. Um, secondly, I took a job, er, where I was managing four teachers, so I had a lot of responsibility; um, I had to work very hard.
… Um, er on top of managing the teachers I had to teach classes and organise exams as well so I was working quite long hours. It was – it was a great experience, even though it was hard work. Um, I met some fantastic people, I learnt a very small amount of the language, um, but I had a really good time.

Track 2.13

A: Hey, do you remember Mr Halsworth, you know, the History teacher?
B: Oh yeah, I think so. Yes. He was that short man, with those terrible glasses. Oof, he was really boring, wasn't he? … And we were always so naughty in his classes. We'd throw paper at him and one time some of the boys actually climbed out of the window while his back was turned … !
A: Poor man. He used to shout so much he'd go bright red in the face … .
B: What about Miss Matthews – the Music teacher? Do you remember her? Oh, she was lovely. She used to play us Mozart, and teach us songs from Africa. I think she used to live in Zimbabwe. I really liked her lessons: they were so relaxing and enjoyable. And she was inspiring. I wasn't particularly musical, but she got me listening to music.
A: Yes, she was lovely. And so patient. Not like Mrs Sharp, eh? You remember, the Physics teacher? She was frightening! I didn't use to like her lessons at all. She used to make me sit at the front of the class, right under her nose, and ask me all the most difficult questions. And if you failed a test, or forgot to do your

homework, she would punish you. Oh, and, what about, do you remember Mr Ford, the Religious Studies teacher?
B: Oh yes. He was great!
A: He was so clever, wasn't he? He used to teach us all about different religions of the world, like Rastafarianism, and he was also interested in astronomy, so we'd learn about the stars too. He was very knowledgeable. Wasted on us, really … .
B: Yes, and he never lost his temper, not even when we used to … .

Track 2.16

P = Presenter, B = Brenda

P: In the late 1960s a university was set up in France, which now has more than 3,000 branches worldwide and 200,000 students in the UK alone. But you can't get a degree at this university; in fact it has never set a single exam. Brenda Johns is here to talk to us today about this university; the university of the third age, or U3A for short. Brenda, what does 'third age' mean?
B: Well, the first age is childhood, the second age, your working life, and the third age is after retirement. Our members are usually over fifty-five and not working full time.
P: And why no exams?
B: Well, it's a university in the very widest sense, a learning organisation for people who want to learn and share their knowledge. Some of the branches are very academic, with courses in subjects like Philosophy, Mandarin Chinese or Latin; others are more relaxed, with groups learning to paint or do yoga. But none of them have any formal assessment. Every U3A has a study group coordinator who finds out what people want to learn and brings them together. Anyone can suggest starting a course in any subject and if enough other people like the idea, the course goes ahead.
P: Obviously, the idea is pretty popular. What's the attraction, do you think, of studying when you're retired? Surely that's the time to take things easy?
B: A lot of people feel that it keeps their brains active, and, for some people, it's the first time they've had a chance to spend some time on what really interests them. And it's very much a social thing too. When you retire you suddenly find yourself spending a lot of time at home on your own.
P: I had no idea it was so popular worldwide.
B: Oh yes, there are branches all over the world, all doing things in their own way. Last year members of the Cape Town branch, in South Africa, went on a twenty-one-day study tour of Central Europe and the Prague branch then made a return visit a couple of months later. In Valencia, Spain, they do things slightly differently from here in the UK: there the U3A students go to lectures and seminars alongside the regular university students. Oh, and in Montreal, Canada, the U3Aers spend some of their time doing community work, such as teaching English to speakers of other languages.
P: And can't you study online now?
B: Yes, the Virtual U3A was launched in 2009 for distance learning. It's great if people can't get to local meetings for whatever reason. Some of the courses are free, or there's a small charge if there's a tutor to mark work and so on … .

Track 2.17

P = Polly, E = Eben

P: And so Eben, at what age do you think um someone is old?
E: That's an interesting question, isn't it, because thirty or fifty years ago I think, when you were in your fifties or sixties you were considered old, and these days, that's when your second life starts and I don't think you're old until you hit seventies or eighties and maybe it also depends on your physical health, how healthy are you.
P: Yeah, and your mind as well.
E: Yes and I think a lot of people are younger these days; they're closer to their kids for example. There isn't much of a generation gap. So do you know any very active old people then?
P: Um, yes, one in particular: er my friend's granddad, um he's about seventy-five and he lives, er, on the coast and when he comes to visit my friend um it's an eighty-mile journey but he still comes on his bike, even though he's, um, he's seventy-five, and I just think that's amazing that someone who's seventy-five can, er, cycle that really long journey.
E: I suppose that proves the point. Seventy-five is old under any definition but if you're physically fit, you act young.
P: He is so fit, he's always going out on his bike and doing all these really long – really long journeys. Um, so the people in the text, are you inspired by – by any of them?
E: Actually by most of them. It's incredible to think that you could be past fifty and start a new career and succeed at it. I was particularly impressed by Mary Wesley, who started writing, who – when she was in her seventies because I think her husband had died and the text says she was almost destitute so she had to make a living and she'd had a very interesting life by anybody's standards, she starts writing about it.
… She turns out to be a brilliant writer, makes a huge success, writes another ten books before she turns ninety and is now admired and well-known across the country.
P: Oh that is impressive. Yeah, yeah.
E: So what do you reckon you'll be doing when you're old, whatever that means?
P: Well um I would like to be a – a grandma with lots of grandchildren, so I'd like to see myself looking after my large brood of er, er of grandchildren and being a – a cool grandma.
E: So you won't be writing novels or climbing mountains or doing outrageous things. You'll be a grandma.
P: I hope so. Er, well, if I don't have enough grandchildren I'll have to find something else, but the grandchildren would be ideal, yeah.
E: Sounds good.

Track 2.20

I = Interviewer, J = Jake

I: Would you mind telling me a bit about your abilities? Is there something unusual that you can do?
J: Oh, er, I don't know really. Er, Oh, I can knit, actually. That isn't something that boys tend to do, but my granny taught me.
I: That could be useful! And can you give me an example of something that you can do now that you couldn't do ten years ago?
J: Lots of things, I expect. Well, I can drive. When I was a student I didn't use to have

a car so it wasn't really worth learning, but I passed my test last year, after I graduated. Oh, and I can cook now.

I: So why did you learn to do that?

J: Well, when I moved away from home I kind of had to learn!

I: Right, now, would you mind telling me about something you could do when you were a child that you can't now.

J: Oh, yes, that's easy. I used to be able to sing really nicely, but then my voice broke and now my singing voice is pretty awful.

I: That's a shame. Right, finally, could you tell me about something difficult you managed to do recently?

J: Yes, I managed to climb the three peaks. That's where you climb the three biggest mountains in Britain all on the same day. It was pretty hard work, I can tell you!

I: I bet it was. I'd love to hear a bit more about that … .

Track 2.21

S = Stig, C = Carol

S: So tell me about the time you changed your mind.

C: Well, when I first got married I thought I was going to change my last name, because my husband's name was much easier to spell and much easier to pronounce, but then, because we were living in China, it was very complicated to change my passport and all of my details so I decided against it.
But now that we're in the UK I'm thinking that I might actually change it anyhow. How about you, have you ever had an experience like that?

S: Er ah, a few years ago actually, when I was er living in Japan, I – I got a new job and because the apartment I was living in was tied to my old job, I had to move as well, so I changed city, changed job, changed apartment and it was almost like I took over someone else's life because not only did I take this woman's job, I took her apartment, I took her furniture, I was almost kind of expecting to have her friends as well, but that – it didn't work like that.
But anyway, I moved into this new apartment and I didn't really like it actually, it was dark and cold and it was near a main road so when the – the lorries used to go by I'd actually wake up from my whole apartment shaking from the lorries going by so … Fortunately I only lived there a year and then I moved again, into a much nicer place.

C: That's good.

Track 2.22

Emma:

Well, I live in Madrid, er, I've been here for about nine years and I really love living in – in a big city, um it's really vibrant, it has lots of things going on, um I go out quite a lot with my friends, um well I think the nightlife here is quite famous and we, er, we always have a good time. Um, there are just a few things that maybe I'd like to change.
Um it's quite a noisy city, um lots of traffic, er, cars making noise, horns honking etc, and also there always seems to be a lot of congestion um building work going on, um lots of construction, er, roads being blocked and things like that.
Um and in the summer, as well, it can be really polluted, so there's lots of congestion problems. But generally I'm really happy here and er, I think it's quite um a good city to live in, good experience, and if you like um city life I'd really recommend Madrid.

Kirsten:

Well I love Edinburgh. It's a beautiful city, it's historical, it's interesting, it's one of the most pleasant places I've ever lived. There's not very much I'd change about it. I suppose I'd like to change the weather because it's terribly cold, but there's not much I can do about that.
Other things I'd like to change perhaps, there's a lot of congestion at the moment. Er, the city council decided to build a tram system, which will probably be really good one day er and is certainly environmentally friendly, but it's taking years to build and meanwhile there's a lot of traffic jams and people complain an awful lot about it, which isn't very pleasant.
Um, there are a lot of very beautiful buildings in the centre of Edinburgh, but if you go to the outskirts there are a lot of quite ugly tower blocks, which kind of gives you a feeling of two cities. So it would be nicer perhaps if more money was spent on making the outskirts of the city as beautiful as the centre. But apart from that, I love Edinburgh and I don't think I'd want to live anywhere else.

Track 2.25

W = Woman, M = Man

W: The biggest change? I think it's probably been medical progress. The situation has really improved. Luckily, doctors and surgeons can cure so many diseases now that were just impossible when I was younger.

M: Well, that's certainly true.

W: Life-saving cures and operations have become more and more common. In the future, disease probably won't be such a big problem, because we'll discover cures for most of the really bad diseases.

M: I don't know about that. There are still no cures for some of the most common diseases, like flu. And in developing countries, there isn't enough money to pay for some of the cures, so the situation hasn't changed.

W: Yes, you have a point there, but … .

M: No, I think that the biggest change has been the change in our awareness of the environment. Unfortunately, although we're more aware, the situation is getting worse and worse.

W: Well, that's your opinion.

M: And the number of cars on the roads is growing quickly, so not surprisingly the amount of pollution just grows and grows. And it's starting to affect the climate. We're seeing more extreme weather and more natural disasters … .

W: Oh, come on. I think you're over-reacting a bit … .

Track 2.26

Roger:

I stopped work a year ago, when we discovered Jack, our three-year-old son, had a kidney problem. Before that, I just worked all the time. All I thought about was making money for my family. But when we discovered Jack was seriously ill, it changed our world completely. I decided to give up my job, so that I could spend time with him. Now I pick up the children from school every day, and we walk home through the park. It's been great to be with Jack, and now he has had an operation, which hopefully will mean that his life will go back to normal. As for me? Well, I won't be able to go back to my old job, so maybe I'll change career and start my own business. But for me it was the right decision. If I'd stayed at work, I wouldn't have spent time with Jack when he really needed me.

Tunde:

My family wanted me to work in the family business, like my brothers did, but I was never interested in that. I had always dreamed of going to study in another country, to study Art. So when I finished school, I applied, and I was offered a place at the university in Paris. It was a big decision to come here, leaving my family and friends, and … er … coming to this country. Everything is so different here and I don't even speak the language, but it has worked out very well. I met my fiancée, Nancy, here, and we are planning to get married when I finish my degree. So I'm happy I came here. If I hadn't come to France, I wouldn't have met Nancy!

Sarah:

My boyfriend was working nights as a lorry driver. We weren't very happy because we didn't really see each other. Then we went on holiday to Italy, and while we were there, we saw this old olive farm for sale. It needed lots of work doing to it, but it was beautiful, and we just fell in love with the house the moment we saw it. We came back to England, sold our house, left our jobs, and said goodbye to our friends. Two months later, we drove down to Italy to start our new life growing olives to make olive oil. It was very hard for the first year and we nearly changed our minds. We didn't have much money, and we knew nothing about farming olives or how to run our own business. But now things are much better, and we enjoy working together. I am glad we didn't have a change of heart. If we'd gone back to England, we wouldn't have been happy.

Track 2.29

A

Yes, definitely. I work on a cruise ship and when we have stopovers we get to see a bit of the country. Just for a day or two, but it's enough to get a taste of what it's like. I've been all over the world … to some really interesting places … South America, the Caribbean and so on. You get to meet some interesting people too. I was talking to a passenger recently who turned out to be a doctor, some sort of famous doctor, who'd treated some really important people. So, yes, my job can be very interesting.

B

I joined the gym about three months ago and it's made a real difference to my life. It was difficult at first … you know there were times when I just wanted to go home and watch TV … but it quickly became part of my daily routine. I feel so much better now. I've got so much more energy … and I've made a lots of new friends too.

C

My wife and I are going to open a restaurant near where we live. It'll be an Italian restaurant as she's from Italy. We're a bit worried about it, of course, but it's something we've always wanted to do and it's now or never. Um … at the moment, we're doing all the financial calculations, but I'm planning to leave my job next month. It'll be a major change for both of us but we're really looking forward to it.

Audioscripts

D

Well, I don't want to stay in my present job for too long, that's for sure. And I certainly don't want to settle down at the moment either. I'm always looking for new experiences ... new places to go ... new people to meet ... so yes, I think it's true to say that I like change!

E

I think it depends really. Some people need a routine. Babies, older people ... perhaps. They like to do everything in the same way, in the same order. I don't know. I think life is probably a bit boring if you always do that, but it depends. My granddad had a very strict routine. He always ate at the same time and went to bed at the same time, and it worked for him, but it's not for everybody, is it?

Track 2.30

I = Interviewer, W = Woman

I: When you apply for a job, do you normally send a CV? Do you need to include references?

W: It's usually better to fill in an application form, that way you can really show how your experience and qualifications really fit this job. And I don't usually give references until they ask me for them, but I know who I can ask to give me a good reference.

I: How do you hear about job vacancies in your profession?

W: In the newspapers or specialist magazines.

I: Are you employed or self–employed?

W: Employed, I work for a big manufacturing firm.

I: Do you do a nine to five job, then?

W: Pretty much. There isn't much flexibility.

I: Would you like to work flexitime?

W: It would be useful, so I could drop the children off at school, for example.

I: How often do you work overtime?

W: I sometimes do overtime in the evenings or at weekends.

I: Would you like to be self-employed or work freelance?

W: Yes, I'd love to be my own boss or at least be able to choose who I work for and when.

I: How often do you expect to get a pay rise in your job? Is it easy to get promoted?

W: I usually get a small pay rise every year as prices go up. I've been in the same job for ten years though, so it obviously isn't that easy to get promoted!

I: And what are the perks of your job?

W: There are a few perks, like a company car and the occasional nice meal out with clients.

Track 2.31

C = Carol, V = Verity, J = James

C: People who work sitting down get paid more than people who work standing up. What do you think about that?

V: I think it's probably true. If I think about teachers, construction workers, nurses, they all work standing up and they don't tend to get paid, at least in the UK, that much.

J: No, certainly not as much as people who work in finance, people who work in the city, who are sitting or are – people who generally work in, er, the financial sector who work in front of computers I think get paid more, don't they?

V: Possibly. Um, how about the next one, the longer the title, the less important the job?

J: I was sent an article recently which was related to this, which said that as companies are, um, not raising people's wages er very much at the moment, they're trying to boost their employees' morale by giving them um interesting job titles, longer job titles, er which makes them sound more important.

V: Oh gosh. That seems quite cynical to me. Um it's just a way of paying people less, isn't it? There are different ways of making people feel important I suppose. What do you think Carol?

C: Um, I think it's um it's all very relative, I suppose. Um, you've got lots of people with long titles who do have, you know, um an important job. You know, we've got the Work Flow and Research Manager here at our place and that's quite an important job, but then again um you know, 'President' ...

V: ... is quite short ...

C: ... is quite short and that's obviously a very important job.
... What about the next one? Most work places have too many rules. Employees aren't children and the office isn't a junior school. What do you think?

J: I think some places have many rules. I don't think people create rules just for the sake of creating rules though. I think larger places in particular, rules are built up, learning from things that have happened in the past, um, and it's the easy way for management to go to create lots of rules I think. Er um ...

V: I agree with you, but the trouble is, if one, person abuses the rules, for example, they look at something on the Internet that they shouldn't be looking at and then the management uses this to punish almost the rest of the workforce who are completely innocent, I don't think that's fair.

C: Let's look at the next one. Most managers spend their time making it difficult for workers to work. I think that – that could be true, um, in some cases. Um you know, and again, kind of going back to the last one, with kind of having too many rules for their employees and – and by having too many rules, not actually being able to do the job that they need to do. Dunno.

V: I suppose often the person who does the job knows, you know, knows it best and should perhaps be in more control of what they do than their line manager, in a way. It seems to make more sense.

J: Mmm, I'm not sure that managers spend time making it difficult for people though. I think they've got better things to do than make it difficult for people usually.

Track 2.32

Good afternoon everybody. Today I'd like to tell you about our idea for a new business. We want to open a restaurant that serves food from all over the world. Our main idea is that the chefs cook food from fifty or sixty countries. The most important thing for us is that the food is great. We'll allow the chefs to choose the dishes and the menu will be very big, with something for everybody. We'll employ three chefs and six waiters. We won't make the waiters wear a uniform, and they will have one special perk: we'll let them eat free at our restaurant. To sum up, our restaurant will be small and friendly but with a great international menu. The name of the restaurant is World Food! Thank you for listening. Are there are any questions?

Track 2.33

A1 = Audience 1, A2 = Audience 2, A3 = Audience 3, S = Speaker

A1: Thank you, that was very interesting. What I'd like to know is will the food be fresh? If so, how can you have such a big menu?

S: Well, I'm not really sure ... I suppose we will need to have some pre-prepared food.

A2: I like the idea of letting the chefs choose the menu. How will you choose the chefs?

S: That's a very interesting question ... . Er, I'm not really sure.

A3: Could you tell me a bit more about the name of the restaurant? How did you choose it?

S: I'll have to get back to you on that one. It was my wife's idea you see.

Track 2.35

1

An *autocratic* style of leadership? Well, that's when the manager makes their decision on their own, without asking their staff. They just tell the staff to do whatever it is that they have decided. Personally, I find that style of management a bit annoying, but it's OK if it's a question of keeping people safe.

2

A *democratic* style of management is when everyone has an opportunity to contribute ideas or say what they think, and then the manager makes the final decision. I like working this way; I find I'm much more motivated than when I'm being told what do. Having said that, it can sometimes mean that it takes a long time for decisions to get made.

3

A *laissez faire* style of management ... well, laissez faire is French, it means 'leave alone', so this is what happens when the manager leaves the workers alone to make their own decisions. If workers have to make a lot of decisions every day, this style works well because they can't keep ringing the boss to ask what to do. But it obviously won't work if the workers haven't had enough training.

Track 2.36

I = Interviewer, W = Mr Wilkins

I: Can I start off by asking you, er, Mr Wilkins, why do you want this job?

W: Well, I have just graduated from the University of Brighton, with a degree in Business with Marketing, so obviously it's an area I'm very interested in.

I: Do you have any work experience in this area?

W: Well, not yet, but I'm very keen to get some.

I: OK. Well, are you good at communicating with people?

W: Oh yes, I think that's a real strength of mine. When I was at university I ran a tennis club, so I had to be able to manage meetings, send out emails and so on. It was good management experience really.

I: And what is your biggest weakness?

W: Oh, er, well I guess I do work too hard sometimes ... .

I = Interviewer, S = Miss Southall

I: Miss Southall, why do you want this job?

S: Well, I think it fits very well with my skills and experience. I've worked in marketing for a couple of years now and I think I'm ready to move on to a more challenging job.

I: What skills do you have that are relevant to this job?

S: Well, I'm very organised and I can work very well on my own.
I: Do you work well with others?
S: Oh yes, but if I'm honest, I do prefer working on my own. I just get more done.
I: And what qualifications do you have?
S: I've got a degree in English and Art. It isn't directly relevant to marketing, I know, but I like to think I'm pretty creative.

Track 2.37

N = Nicky, J = Jonathan
N: Jonathan, tell me about your job.
J: Well my job title is Senior Designer and Buyer at a book publisher's, so what it really means is that I design the layouts for the insides of a book mostly.
N: What abilities would you say you need to have for this job?
J: Well apart from the creative abilities you do need to be organised and be able to control budgets and set schedules and keep to them really well so there is a – what I like about it there is a bit of er, being methodical as well as, um, having to be creative so it's a mixture of the two abilities really.
N: And you have to work as a member of a team as well, don't you?
J: Yes, that's – that's very important because you – you might be working on a project for six months or two years together so you have to support each – each other and cooperate um and just create some harmony within the team. So that's – that's true.

Track 2.38

N = Nicky, P = Polly
N: Polly, tell me about your previous job.
P: Um, I used to be a teacher. Teaching English to um foreign students.
N: Yeah. And what abilities, would you say, a teacher has to have?
P: Um, you have to be, er, able to explain things very clearly and, er, logically and er, if someone doesn't understand the first time, to think of a different way of explaining it and to, er, always be very positive and try and encourage students, even if they're not doing er, even if they're not doing very well.
Um, and you have to be very, er, organised to make sure you're never late for class and that you have your marking done when you said you will and that you've prepared all your lessons and your photocopying in advance. You're not photocopying about ten seconds before the class is about to start, which does sometimes happen.
N: Thank you very much.
P: OK.

Track 2.39

N = Nicky, R = Rachel
N: Tell me about your previous job.
R: Um, I was a professional actress and um, one of my first jobs was playing Peter Pan in a travelling pantomime, just the three of us.
N: Fascinating. Was it hard work?
R: It was incredibly hard work because we were doing three shows a day, six days a week, um, and we were travelling to and from those performances, setting up the performances and actually then performing as well.
N: And what qualifications did you have to have to become an actress in the first place?
R: Um, I didn't actually have any formal qualifications but I had a huge theatrical background, um, I'd done a lot of amateur work growing up and then to actually get the job though I did, um, audition for an agent and then he got me this first job when he took me on, so … .
N: Wonderful. And what skills would you say an actress or an actor has to have?
R: Huge passion and drive for what you're doing. I don't think you could do it without the passion and wanting to perform and act for people. You also need a lot of stamina, um, for the amount of performances that you're doing and you need to keep your training up um and just yeah, just keep very fit.
And you also need to be really flexible. Um, your performances, you know, you could be performing at any kind of venue, um, your shows might need to adapt to your audiences, so yeah, you need to be willing to be flexible all the time.

Track 2.40

Well, when I came to work in the UK, I thought it would be quite easy. After all, we speak the same language, don't we? Well, kind of … but there are a lot of differences in vocabulary. For example a car park is what we call a parking lot. And I got quite confused when I was given directions to my office because I didn't know what a lift was – it's an elevator in the US. Then at lunchtime the confusion continued. In the US we use the word 'chips' for the thin slices of fried potato which come in a packet. So I was very surprised when I asked for chips with my sandwich and they gave me French fries! Apparently I should have asked for 'crisps'. But it isn't just different vocabulary though; it's also the way we talk. Americans are much more direct, I think. When a Brit says 'We have a bit of a problem,' they don't actually mean it's a small problem at all. And when you ask them how they are, Brits will often say 'fine thanks', when really they're not OK at all! The worst misunderstanding though was when I didn't understand what had happened when they told me a colleague had been given the sack. I thought it was some kind of game, but he'd actually been fired, he'd lost his job!

Track 2.43

N = Nicky, S = Sean
N: So I hear you've been to the Diana Memorial?
S: That's right. It's in, um, Hyde Park in London actually.
N: Oh yeah.
S: And um I think it was opened in 2004, which was what, seven years after Diana died.
N: Oh yes, yes …
S: And um, I didn't realise it was actually a fountain, um, a fountain in an enormous ring shape and um, the water sort of flows from the top of the ring and flows very gently around the ring until it collects in this pool at the bottom. And it's really sort of a really modern untraditional fountain, I guess for a really modern, untraditional princess.
N: Yeah, that's a nice way of putting it. Were there lots of people there on the day that you went?
S: Loads of people, yeah, lots of families with young children sort of having a picnic and I think Diana would have really liked that, you know, she was – really liked children.
N: Um, yeah I agree.
S: Um.

Track 2.44

I have a very vivid memory of being a child and visiting a farm with my cousins. I was probably four at the time. There was a dark doorway up some steps into some sheds and I really wanted to go up there and I went to the doorway and it was very dark. You couldn't see anything.
And there was a very, very strong smell coming from the sheds and I could hear scuffling, hear noises at the end of the sheds. And my cousin told me there were monsters there. It was a very, very strong memory. I was terrified and I remembered it for many years. Later I realised they were probably cows at the end of the shed and they were completely harmless.
But for a long time I thought there were monsters there.

Track 2.45

M = Matt, C = Claire
M: So, what did you think about the column?
C: Well, I think there's a lot of truth in it, actually. I mean, I wish I had listened more to my grandfather's stories too. I just always felt too busy.
M: Yeah, I agree that we should probably listen more and talk less. I wish I was better at listening really.
C: And I think she's right about spending less time watching television and more actually getting out there and living. I'd like to travel a lot more than I do.
M: Yeah, I'm always talking about going to Australia, but there never seems to be a good time.
C: In fact, the only one I don't agree with. I don't wish I'd eaten more ice cream and less cottage cheese. I actually wish I'd eaten more healthily. I think it's important to look after yourself.
M: Well, I guess, but I think she means that life's too short not to treat yourself from time to time, and I'd agree with that. I wish I could lose some weight though, if I'm honest. I shouldn't have given up playing football.
C: Yes, exercise is important too, isn't it?

Track 2.46

1
Marie Sklodowska Curie was a brilliant scientist. She had a difficult start in life, however, as her family had lost all their money. Marie had to work as a governess to support her sister through medical school. She fell in love with Kazimierz Zorawski, the son of her employer, but he was not allowed to marry her because she was penniless. She moved to Paris where she studied physics, mathematics and chemistry, supporting herself by teaching in the evenings. In 1895 she married Pierre Curie and together they discovered radium. She won the Nobel prize in 1903 and 1911.

2
Baroness Tanni Grey Thompson was born with a disability and had to use a wheelchair from an early age. Her teachers remember her as a very determined little girl, who wanted to try lots of different sports. She first tried wheelchair-racing aged thirteen, and two years later won a national event. In 1988 she won her first Paralympic medal, but soon afterwards she had to stop racing because she needed surgery on her back. But four years later she entered the Paralympics again and this time she won four gold medals. She went on to win a further seven gold medals over her racing career.

3

In 1940, Edson Arantes do Nascimento, better known as Pelé, was born into a poor family in Minas Gerais, Brazil. He had his first job aged seven, as a shoe-shine boy, cleaning shoes for a few coins. Pelé used to play football in the streets, but he was so poor that he couldn't afford a proper ball and used to play with a grapefruit or an old sock stuffed with newspaper. Against the odds, Pelé went on to become one of the greatest footballers of all time.

4

Albert Einstein is widely considered to be a genius. However, his education did not start off so well. He didn't learn to speak fluently until six or seven and one of his teachers wrote on his school report, 'He will never amount to anything', meaning that he would never be successful. How wrong he was! Einstein is best known for his theories of relativity, but he published more than 300 other scientific works.

Track 2.47

Coco Chanel was born in France in 1883. Her father died when she was a child and her mother sent the children away to grow up with relatives. When she was a young woman Chanel met two rich men who helped her to start her business. She opened her first shop in 1913, where she sold perfume. Soon afterwards she opened a shop in Paris and began designing clothes. Her clothes and perfume business did very well until 1939, when she left France to go and live in Hollywood. In 1953 she returned to France. She dressed many famous film stars and she was still working when she died in 1971. She is considered one of the most influential designers of the twentieth century.

Track 2.50

1

So, thank you very much for coming, everybody. I hope you found the talks interesting and useful. If you want any more information, you can find it on our website. The address is in the programme, so do send us an email. Thank you and goodbye.

2

F = Father, D = Daughter
F: OK, you've got everything? Passport, ticket, money?
D: Yeah, I think so. Let me just ... .
F: Have you got the address where you're staying?
D: Yes.
F: Your mobile?
D: Yeah, it's right here.
F: So you'll give us a call when you arrive?
D: Yeah, it'll probably be late this evening.
F: OK, have a safe trip.
D: Thanks, Dad.
F: And we'll see you in a couple of weeks.
D: Two weeks. OK, bye.
F: Bye, darling.

3

M = Man, W = Woman
M: Right then, it's time I made a move.
W: Are you off?
M: Yes, sorry, I've got to dash.
W: Oh, OK. Have a nice weekend then.
M: You too.
W: Bye.
M: Bye.

4

M = Man, W = Woman
M: Thanks for everything. I really enjoyed it.
W: You're welcome. It's been great to catch up.
M: Yes, it's been a great evening.
W: Maybe see you next weekend. There's a party at Joe's.
M: Oh OK, yeah, sounds good. Alright then, thanks. See you.
W: Take care.

Track 2.51

A: Right, well I'd better be going.
B: Yes, me too, I've got loads to do.
A: Maybe see you next Wednesday then?
B: Yes, that sounds good. See you then.
A: Have a good weekend.
B: You too.
A: See you.
B: Yeah, bye.

Track 2.52

1   Ouch!
2   Yuck!
3   Shh!
4   Mmm!
5   Phoo!